The Management and Marketing of Services

BUSINESS SERIES

Series Editor: Professor Andrew Lock
Manchester Metropolitan University

The Contemporary Business Series is designed with the needs of business studies undergraduates and MBA students in mind, and each title is written in a straightforward, student friendly style. Though all of the books in the series reflect the individuality of their authors, you will find that you can count on certain key features in each text which maintain high standards of structure and approach:

- excellent coverage of core and option subject
- UK/international examples or case studies throughout
- full references and further reading suggestions
- written in direct, easily accessible style, for ease of use by full, part-time and self-study students

Books in the Contemporary Business Series

The Management and Marketing of Services

Peter Mudie and Angela Cottam

Butterworth-Heinemann Ltd
Linacre House, Jordan Hill, Oxford OX2 8DP

A member of the Reed Elsevier plc group

OXFORD   LONDON   BOSTON
MUNICH   NEW DELHI   SINGAPORE   SYDNEY
TOKYO   TORONTO   WELLINGTON

First published 1993
Reprinted 1993, 1994, 1995

British Library Cataloguing in Publication Data
Mudie, Peter
    The Management and Marketing of Services. –
    (Contemporary Business Series)
    I. Title   II. Cottam, Angela   III. Series
    658.8

ISBN 0 7506 0789 0

Set by Hope Services (Abingdon) Ltd
Printed and bound in Great Britain by Thomson Litho, East Kilbride

To Beatrice and Paul, my father Peter and
in memory of my mother, Janet.

P.M.

To Phoebe and Hector, Gervase and Rosemary,
and in memory of my father, Ian.

A.C.

Contents

Preface

We live in a service society. An increasing proportion of GNP comes from our consumption of services. An increasing number of the workforce are employed in this sector. The management literature and training, however, have continued to be dominated by product management and marketing techniques.

The distinctive characteristics of services merit their own management framework. Service management is more complex. Consumers buy something that is intangible. In most cases they are not entirely certain what they will receive in exchange for their money. The service provider is often none the wiser. The interactive roles played by the server and the served mean that service provision and consumption vary enormously.

This in turn changes the role of marketing. It must embrace functions traditionally regarded as the responsibility of operations or human resource management. For example, in services the traditional function of promotion must embrace such issues as the design of the physical environment and the motivation and appearance of personnel.

We believe that the best way to manage a service company is to develop a corporate culture, the management structures and the operations systems that recognize the sector's uniqueness.

In writing this book our aims were as follows:

- To provide a comprehensive treatment of the subject matter.
- To highlight the problems that service providers are likely to confront.
- To demonstrate a range of concepts and techniques for solving these problems.
- To present the solutions within a theoretical and practical framework to facilitate their application to a variety of service industries.

Peter Mudie
Angela Cottam

Acknowledgements

We are indebted to many people who gave unstintingly of their time in the rush to prepare the manuscript for publication. We would like to begin by acknowledging Jacquie Shanahan of Butterworth-Heinemann who encouraged us to write the book in the first place. Particular thanks are also due to Elma Farmer and Malcolm Jones of Napier University Library for their diligence and patience, and to Aileen Hunter, an author herself, for her help with the typing.

Invaluable contributions to the text were made by Les Mitchell of Edinburgh College of Art (Chapter 4 on the service setting), and by Paul Williams, Department of Mathematics, Napier University and Gervase Cottam (Chapter 8 on managing demand and supply).

Invaluable contributions were made to the presentation of the book by those organizations that kindly gave us permission to reproduce artwork or illustrations. In this context we would like to mention: Avis, British Airways, British Gas, Kwik-fit, Legal and General, Life Association of Scotland, Lucerne, Prudential, Reed Employment and Toys 'R' Us. We would also like to thank the *Guardian* for allowing us to reproduce Austin's cartoon and *Marketing Magazine* for allowing us to reproduce Peter Plant's cartoon.

For granting copyright clearance we are grateful to the following: Bowling Green State University for Figure 2 from R. Larsson and D. E. Bowen, 'Organisation and Customer: Managing Design and Coordination of Services', *Academy of Management Review*, vol. 14, no. 2, 1989, © Bowling Green State University 1989; Harvard Business School Press for Exhibit 1 from G. Lynn Shostack, 'Designing Services that Deliver', *Harvard Business Review*, Jan–Feb 1984, © President and Fellows of Harvard College, 1984; Sage Publications Inc for Figure 3 from M. Levine, 'Placement and Misplacement of You-are-here Maps', *Environment and Behaviour*, vol. 16, no. 2, 1984, © Sage Publications Inc 1984; *Cornell HRA Quarterly* for Exhibit 3 from W. B. Martin, 'Measuring and Improving Your Service Quality', *Cornell HRA Quarterly*, May 1986, © Cornell HRA Quarterly 1986; Gower Publishing Company Ltd for Figure 15.6 from T. Gillen, *Twenty Training Workshops for Customer Care*, 1990, © Gower Publishing Company 1990; Academic Press Inc (London) for Table 2 from G. H. Bower, J. B. Glack and T. J. Turner, *Scripts in Memory for Text, Cognitive Psychology II*, 1979, © Academic Press Inc (London) 1979; Pergamon Journals Ltd for Table 1 from S. D. Ball, K. Johnson and P. Slattery, 'Labour Productivity in Hotels: An Empirical Analysis', *International Journal of Hospitality Management*, vol. 5, no. 3, 1986, © Pergamon Journals Ltd 1986; The Marketing Journal and Publishing Company for Table 1 from G. H. G. McDougall and D. W. Snetsinger, 'Items, Products and Services, and Scenarios', *Journal of Services Marketing*, vol. 4, no. 4, Fall 1990, © The Marketing Journal and Publishing Company 1990; Chartered Institute of Marketing for Figure 5 from R. Brown, 'Marketing – a Function and a Philosophy', *The Quarterly Review of Marketing*, vol. 12, nos 3 and 4, 1987, © Chartered Institute of Marketing 1987; Cambridge University Press for part of Table 5.2 from M. Argyle, A. Furnham and J. A. Graham, *Social Situations*, 1981, © Cambridge University Press 1981; Peter Knight for extracts from 'Putting a Stamp on Progress', from the *Financial Times*, 17 October 1991, © Peter Knight 1991; MCB University Press Ltd for Figure 2 from G. L. Shostack, 'How to Design a Service', *European Journal of Marketing*, vol. 16, no. 1, 1982, © MCB University Press Ltd 1982; British Telecom for *Quality of Service Report*, April–September 1991; The American Marketing Association for Figure 1 from A. Parasuraman, V. A. Zeithaml and L. Berry, 'A Conceptual Model of Service Quality and its Implications for Future Research', *Journal of Marketing*, vol. 49, Fall 1985, © The American Marketing Association 1985; *The Financial Times* for excerpts from the pieces by D. Barchard, 'Services Grow on Branches', 18 February 1992, G. de Jonquieres, 'Retailers Plan for Last Minute Rush', 24 December 1991, R. Lapper, 'Fire Eaters and Contortionists', 6 January 1992, L. McLain, 'Hotels Nibble Away at the Fruits of Automation', 17 January 1990, A. Lane, 'Train Management Switches to the Screen', 12 January 1990, 'A Little Help for Nurses', 11 January 1990, M. Dickson, 'Bouquets and Barbed Ire', 3 February 1992, © *Financial Times*; MCB University Press Ltd for Table 1 from D. A. Tansik and W. L. Smith, 'Dimensions of Job Scripting in Service Operations', *International Journal of Service Industry Management*, vol. 2, no. 1 1991, © MCB University Press Ltd 1991.

Part One
Establishing a Framework for Service Creation and Delivery

1
Introducing services

1.1 Introduction

There are particular problems and challenges for those managing an organization whose major activity is providing some type of service. For the customer there may be little evidence, in advance, of what to expect. The service provider has often to produce the service under the watchful gaze of customers. Finally, both parties may fail to agree on what constitutes quality service.

To produce and deliver a service, management needs to recognize what that means in practice (see Figure 1.1 on page. 4). First an appropriate foundation must be laid through which the service will be channelled. If these 'bottom line' conditions of design, structure and setting are not properly thought out the prospect of providing a quality service is reduced.

The next stage involves the actual delivery of the service. People, materials and equipment must be deployed and managed to attract and serve customers in accordance with their needs and preferences. It is essentially a process in which customer and service interact in a variety of ways. Throughout that process the organization needs to demonstrate a commitment to service quality by setting appropriate standards and ensuring their implementation.

Finally, to test the success of that commitment, service performance must be monitored and evaluated. This must be an ongoing process that enables management to detect and rectify any deficiencies.

1.2 The goods–services continuum

In 1966 John Rathmell[1] observed that most marketers have some idea of the meaning of the term 'goods'; they are tangible economic products that are capable of being seen and touched and may or may not be tasted, heard, or smelled. As for services, Rathmell asserted that there was no clear understanding. He sought to change this by defining a good as a thing and a service as an act; the former being an object, an article, a device or a material and the latter a deed, a performance, or an effort.

Another distinction between a good and a service, according to Rathmell, lay in the nature of the product's utility. Does the utility for the consumer lie in the physical characteristics of the product, or in the nature of the action or performance. From such tests Rathmell concluded that there were very few pure products and pure services. Economic products were to be regarded as lying along a goods–services continuum with pure goods at one extreme and pure services at the other, but with most of them falling between these two extremes (see Figure 1.2 on page 5). Rathmell stated that some are primarily

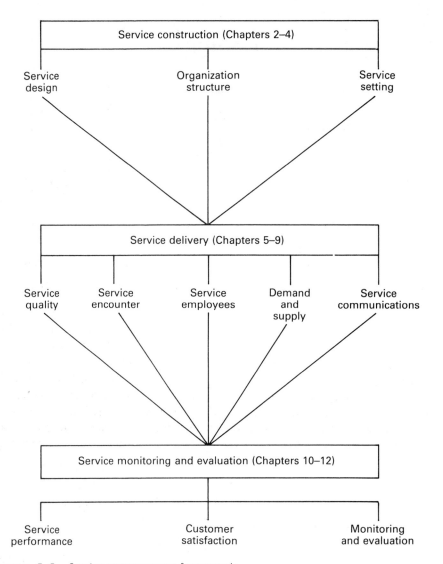

Figure 1.1 *Service management framework*

goods with service support, whereas others are primarily services with goods support. Most goods are a complex of goods and facilitating services; most services are a complex of services and facilitating goods. He applied the measuring rod of personal consumption to distinguish between goods and services. For the food and tobacco category, percentage personal consumption expenditure on the services was nil. For recreation it was 33 per cent and for religious and welfare activities, 100 per cent.

Sixteen years later Shostack[2] developed a refined version of the original continuum (Figure 1.3) and it remains a valuable perspective for understanding the nature of services. The essence of the continuum is that tangibility (ability to see, touch, smell, hear prior to purchase) decreases as one moves from left to right. Tangible entities are in evidence, such as the equipment used by the nurse but, in general, they cannot be owned or possessed like salt or dog food. Every organization on the continuum delivers some degree of service as part of

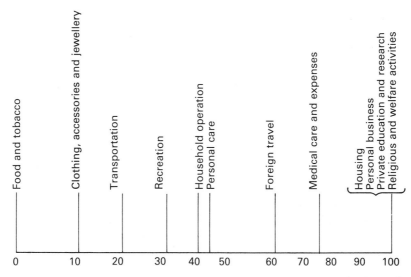

Figure 1.2 *Personal consumption expenditure related to services. Source: Rathmell, J. M. (1966)[1]*

its total offer. However, it is the organizations to the right which deliver most in the way of service and can therefore truly bear the hallmark 'service organizations'. It is important to make a distinction between those who deliver some service, (e.g. computer manufacturer, car dealer, fashion retailer), and those for whom service plays a major role, (e.g. hotels, banks, airlines, accountants, health), as the latter exhibit particular characteristics that merit attention.

In addition, there is another aspect that singles out services from other organizations. Marketing plans are usually structured around what is commonly

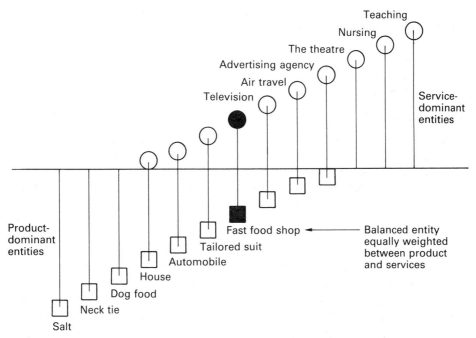

Figure 1.3 *A scale of elemental dominance. Source: Shostack, G. L. (1982)[2]*

5

known as the '4 Ps', namely product, price, promotion and place. But when it is service that is being marketed three more Ps – people, physical evidence and process must be added, making 7 Ps in all. As the additional three Ps figure prominently throughout this text, a brief description of each will suffice at this stage:

People: Service personnel and customers, e.g. appearance, attitudes, social skills etc.

Physical evidence: Everything from the appearance, design, layout of service setting to brochures, uniforms, cheque books etc.

Process: Just as raw materials are converted through a process into finished goods, services likewise go through a process, converting inputs to outputs. The process will involve, amongst other things, policies, procedures, mechanization, flow of activities, employee discretion, and customer involvement.

1.3   Employment in the service sector

One measure of the size of the service sector in the economy is the number of people employed relative to other sectors. Table 1.1 shows the number of employees in various industries in the UK. Since 1971 there has been a significant fall in the number of employees in manufacturing industries and a corresponding increase in the number of employees in service industries. Within the service sector, numbers employed in banking, finance and insurance have doubled since 1971.

In addition, the European Community, in common with most other industrialized parts of the world, has seen a long-term shift in the sectoral distribution of employment towards services and there is little sign of any slow down in the trend shift to employment in services. The ratio between full-time and part-time employment in services is on average 4:1 in Europe. This may come as a surprise to many. However when it comes to married women the split between full-time and part-time is much more easily balanced. (For further information see *The Eurostat Labour Force Survey and Employment in Europe* published by the European Commission.)

1.4   Characteristics of services

Services possess four key distinguishing characteristics. They are:

Intangibility
Inseparability
Variability
Perishability.

Table 1.1 Employees in employment: by sex and industry

United Kingdom	Standard Industrial Classification (1980)	1971	1979	1981	1983	1986	1989	1990 _(Thousands)_
All industries	0–9	22 139	23 173	21 892	21 067	21 387	22 661	22 855
of which								
Males		13 726	13 487	12 562	11 940	11 744	11 992	12 050
Females		8 413	9 686	9 331	9 127	9 644	10 668	10 806
Manufacturing	2–4	8 065	7 253	6 222	5 525	5 227	5 187	5 151
Services	6–9	11 627	13 580	13 468	13 501	14 297	15 627	15 868
Other	0, 1, 5	2 447	2 340	2 203	2 042	1 863	1 847	1 836
Employees in employment by SIC division								
Agriculture, forestry and fishing	0	450	380	363	350	329	300	298
Energy and water supply	1	798	722	710	648	545	465	451
Other minerals and ore extraction, etc	2	1 282	1 147	939	817	729	711	728
Metal goods, engineering and vehicles	3	3 709	3 374	2 923	2 548	2 372	2 351	2 316
Other manufacturing industries	4	3 074	2 732	2 360	2 159	2 126	2 125	2 106
Construction	5	1 198	1 239	1 130	1 044	989	1 082	1 087
Distribution, catering and repairs	6	3 686	4 257	4 172	4 118	4 298	4 730	4 824
Transport and communication	7	1 556	1 479	1 425	1 345	1 298	1 362	1 374
Banking, finance, insurance, etc	8	1 336	1 647	1 739	1 875	2 166	2 627	2 734
Other services	9	5 049	6 197	6 132	6 163	6 536	6 908	6 936

Source: _Social Trends_, **22**, 1992.

Intangibility

Services cannot generally be seen, tasted, felt, heard or smelled before being bought. The potential customer is unable to perceive the service before (and sometimes during and after) the service delivery. For many customers of car repair, for example the service is totally intangible – they often cannot see what is being done and many indeed are unable to evaluate what has been done. Rushton and Carson[3] asked a number of service organizations whether they consciously perceived a difference between the marketing of goods and services. Several respondents pointed to the intangibility of their products with comments such as:

> We haven't got anything to show to customers like a can of baked beans.

> It's more difficult trying to explain what they (the customers) get for their money.

Implications

Intangibility presents problems in that the consumer may experience difficulty in knowing and understanding what is on offer before, and even after, receipt of the service. The challenge for the service provider is to determine the extent of intangibility and the management action required to make the service more tangible. The first task implies resort to some form of measurement, and the second task involves the provision of tangible evidence, e.g. a brochure to help consumer understanding of the service.

Measurement

A system for measuring the relative tangibility of a service organization and its offerings has been proposed by McDougall and Snetsinger.[4] A number of products and services were selected together with nine statements designed to measure tangibility (Table 1.2). Their study concentrated on the mental aspects, namely the consumer's ability to picture or visualize the service prior to purchase. Their main conclusion was that services were arrayed toward the intangible end of the continuum and most products toward the tangible end. One interesting observation was that some services (e.g. movies, fast food) were rated as more tangible than some products, and some products (e.g. used car, a new compact car) more intangible than some services.

Evidence

The ability to picture a service may be assisted by the service organization providing something tangible. This may be in the form of tangible evidence, e.g. computerized representation of hairstyles or a tangible possession, e.g. a university prospectus. The aim would be to help the potential customer form expectations before using the service. Equally, tangible evidence and possessions could assist customer judgement of the service during and after usage (see Table 1.3).

Table 1.2 Items, products and services, and scenario

Items on the tangibility scale
1 I have a very clear image of this item.
2 The image is aroused immediately.
3 This is a very abstract item to picture.
4 This item is very tangible.
5 This is a complex item to think about.
6 This item would be easy to describe to another person.
7 This item evokes different images.
8 The item is difficult to picture.
9 I feel I have an accurate visualization of the item.

Products and services selected

Products	*Services*
• Carpet in bedroom	• Exercise club
• Box spring in mattress	• Television repair
• Mat for bathroom	• Lunch at fast-food restaurant
• New compact car	• Furnace overhauled
• Shampoo	• Movie
• Sweatshirt	• Accountant for income tax
• Toothbrush	• Life insurance
• Colour television	• Car oil change
• Used car	• Week's vacation in Caribbean

Example of scenario
Decision A: You have decided to buy a *new color television*. To what extent do you agree with *each* of the following statements. The nine items in the tangibility scale were then presented (see above).

Source: McDougall, G.H.G. and Snetsinger, D.W. (1990).[4]

Inseparability

There is a marked distinction between physical goods and services in terms of the sequence of production and consumption.

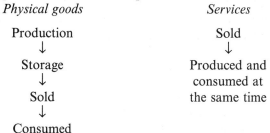

Whereas goods are first produced, then stored, and finally sold and consumed, services are first sold, then produced and consumed simultaneously. For the production of many services (e.g. counselling, museums, hairdressing, rail travel, hotels), the customer must be physically present. Some services may be produced and delivered in circumstances where the customer's presence is optional, e.g. carpet cleaning, plumbing. Other services may rely more on written communication, e.g. distance learning course, or on technology, e.g. home banking. Whatever the nature and extent of contact, the potential for inseparability of production and consumption remains.

Implications

The involvement of the customer in the production and delivery of the service means that the service provider must exercise care in what is being produced and how it is produced. The latter task will be of particular significance. How teachers, doctors, bank tellers, lawyers, car mechanics, hairdressers conduct themselves in the presence of the customer may determine the likelihood of repeat business. Therefore, proper selection and training of customer contact personnel are necessary to ensure the delivery of quality.

Variability

An unavoidable consequence of simultaneous production and consumption is variability in performance of a service. The quality of the service may vary depending on who provides it, as well as when and how it is provided. One hotel provides a fast efficient service and another a short distance away delivers a slow, inefficient service. Within a particular hotel, one employee is courteous and helpful while another is arrogant and obstructive. Even within one employee there can be variations in performance over the course of a day.

Implications

Reducing variability involves determining the causes. It may be due to unsuitable personality traits in an employee which are very difficult to detect at the selection stage. There is nothing much that can be done about this except hope that the employee decides to terminate his employment! However, there may be good sound reasons for variations in performance. For example, it could be due to poor training and supervision, lack of communication and information and generally a lack of regular support.

Some have argued for a replacement of labour with automation and a production line approach to service operations. This would mean a reduction in employee discretion and an increase in standardization of procedures. The operation of McDonald's restaurants is put forward as an ideal model of service industrialization.

The other source of variability is, of course, the customer, Peters and Waterman[5] in their bestseller, *In Search of Excellence* called for staying 'close to the customer'. Unfortunately according to one view[6] this is being 'steadily undermined by the zealots of increased productivity and back room operations. The customer is in danger of being controlled to the point where customer service is becoming just another stage in a systematic manufacturing process, McDonald's being the definitive example'.

Perishability

Services cannot be stored for later sales or use. Hotel rooms not occupied, air-line seats not purchased, and college places not filled cannot be reclaimed. As services are performances they cannot be stored. If demand far exceeds supply it cannot be met, as in manufacturing, by taking goods from a warehouse. Equally, if capacity far exceeds demand, the revenue and/or value of that service is lost.

Implications

Fluctuations in demand characterize service organizations and may pose problems where these fluctuations are unpredictable. Strategies need to be developed for producing a better match between supply and demand (see Chapter 8).

1.5   Classification

Classification is the act of dividing up phenomena and putting them into classes or categories.

In marketing there are many classifications e.g. consumer (socioeconomic groups); product (convenience shopping, speciality); market (industrial, consumer, international, service).

Why classify?

The major purposes are threefold:

1   To determine whether certain characteristics or behaviours are so important and distinct as to merit separate treatment.
2   To determine the extent to which certain characteristics or behaviours may apply across all categories.
3   To create better understanding.

If we take the example of socioeconomic groups in marketing; does a consumer in socioeconomic group B exhibit a pattern of consumption exclusive to that group and therefore, by definition, distinct from socioeconomic group C1? Furthermore, decision making is helped by knowing that consumption behaviour is explained by the existence of certain categories and membership within them.

1.6   Classifying services

The major question is whether we can classify services in a useful manner.Consider a short list of services selected at random and then ask yourself the questions cited below:

Services

- Hotels
- Airlines
- Social services
- Banks
- Colleges
- Computing services
- Recreation services
- Legal services
- Carpet cleaning
- Car repair

Questions

- Do they have anything in common?
- Should each be treated separately?
- Should each be allocated to one of a number of clearly distinct categories?

Historically each service has been treated separately but now the trend is towards identifying categories that possess characteristics distinct from each other and for services in each category to share similar problems and opportunities.

To achieve this requires a list of characteristics that will help in determining the categories and allocating the services accordingly.

One of the most valuable sets of classification frameworks has been developed by Lovelock.[7] The basic framework classifies services according to whom or what they are directed and whether they are tangible or intangible in nature.

Tangible actions directed at people's bodies:	Health care, passenger transportation, beauty salons, exercise clinics, restaurants, hairdressers
Tangible actions directed at goods and other physical possessions:	Freight transport, industrial equipment, repair and maintenance, janitorial services, laundry and dry cleaning, landscaping/lawncare, veterinary care
Intangible actions directed at people's minds:	Education, broadcasting, information services, theatres, museums
Intangible actions directed at intangible assets:	Banking, legal services, accounting, securities, insurance

The main appeal of this approach is threefold:

1 It highlights an important service characteristic, namely tangibility.
2 It focuses on whom or what the service is directed at.
3 It stresses the importance of a marketing perspective.
4 The categories are clearly distinct and collectively cover the entire services arena.

The above classification represents the foundation into which all services can be categorized. However, one may then proceed to build additional classification schemes (Lovelock developed four others) derived from a list of appropriate characteristics.

1.7   Customer involvement and uncertainty

What makes a service really a service, according to Teboul[8] is the interface: the front office, the dining room, and the actual difference between a service and a manufacturing facility is the size of the interface. Teboul correctly identifies the main characteristics of the interface:

- The customer is physically present
- The service and the delivery process are interdependent (simultaneous production and consumption)
- When the customer is in the interface he is visiting the factory – the place where the service is delivered. And the larger the interface the more visible the service is

The physical presence of the customer is an important issue as it raises the questions:

- How much physical presence of the customer is necessary for the delivery of the service to take place?
- What is the nature of the customer contact and the implications for service management?'

To say that a service cannot exist without simultaneous production and consumption is not strictly true. For example, a parcel delivery or data processing service is not consumed while it is being produced.

Finally, Teboul does not give an explanation of the 'size of the interface'. It could mean a number of things, e.g. physical space, amount of time, number of activities etc.

Teboul's view of service would seem to favour a counselling type situation where the production, delivery and consumption occur simultaneously and are visible to all concerned. This is a very important view of service but it cannot be regarded as an exclusive explanation of what is meant by service.

Many organizations do however fall into a category similar to that outlined above. They can be portrayed as visible operational processes in which the customer is directly involved in some way. Unlike the purchase of a packet of soap powder where it is fairly certain that it will do the job it is intended to, a stay in a hotel is potentially full of uncertainty in that so many things can go wrong.

Uncertainty about what the customer actually wants is a key factor for organizations whose major activity is providing a service. The uncertainty can occur before, during and after the service.

Before

The customer as a major input to the service production process is regarded as a major source of uncertainty.[9] The customer may bring with him his body, mind, goods or information to be serviced. The uncertainty for the service provider lies in not fully understanding these customer inputs, for example:

- Physical state of a body for a fitness clinic
- Mental state of mind for an education service
- State and complexity of a car for detecting faults during a service
- Capacity of clothing and carpet fabrics to withstand chemical treatment
- Amount and nature of customer information for a medical diagnosis

In the above situations the service provider is unsure about what to expect which in turn may affect his preparedness for creating and delivering an effective service.

During

Customers have been portrayed as posing problems for organizations by 'disrupting routines, ignoring offers of service, failing to comply with procedures and making exaggerated demands'.[10] The challenge for service organizations is the development of strategies to manage customer behaviour, hopefully in a way acceptable to both parties.

After

Intangibility of service means that the object of exchange is often an experience that can neither be touched nor possessed. Therefore, the customer may have difficulty understanding what has been obtained on receipt of a service. For

Table 1.3 Tangibility of the service at each stage of consumption

Usage stage	Tangible evidence	Tangible possession
Before usage	Insurance representative, computerized or photographed hair styles	Holiday brochure, college prospectus
During usage	Security firm guard dog, restaurant interior design, fellow customers	Library book, car from car hire
After usage	Advertising by organization	College diploma, report from second-hand car dealer or car repair business

example what does the customer purchase when buying insurance? The more intangibility there is in a service, the greater this problem becomes. This is known as performance ambiguity.[11] As intangibility increases, the customer has less evidence available to assess the service (Table 1.3).

1.8 The service package

With the purchase of the tangible item like a car or a washing machine it is a relatively straightforward matter as to what the customer has received and how it meets his needs. For a service it is not always quite so simple because after purchase and use the customer, in many cases, has nothing tangible in his possession. Whether or not there is anything of a tangible nature, service organizations need to recognize that its package is composed of a number of elements, tangible and intangible.

Tangible elements

- Items bought by the customer, e.g. restaurant meal
- Item whose status is altered by the service, e.g. car repair, health and fitness club
- Items that are peripheral rather than main parts of the package, e.g. bank cheque book, cinema admission ticket, hospital appointment card.
- Items without which the service would not exist, e.g. the bank branch, the aircraft, the car of a rental company.
- Items that form part of the process, e.g. technology (computers, automatic teller machines, vending machines etc.)

Intangible elements

- The personal contact with the service personnel
- The atmosphere generated by the service environment
- Emotions felt by the customer, e.g. peace of mind, enhanced self esteem

What the service organization must now do is decide its core and peripheral services.

Core service

As with tangible products, the core elements beg the question, 'What are consumers really buying?' It was the late Charles Revson of Revlon who said, 'In the factory we make cosmetics; in the store we sell hope'. In similar vein, a manufacturer of ball bearings is marketing antifriction devices. The message is clearly one of defining products or services in terms of customer benefits rather than emphasizing technical features. Otherwise another product or service may appear that will meet, more effectively, underlying customer needs. Many service organizations provide a range of packages rather than just one. Never-the-less attempts should be made to determine and communicate the benefits, e.g.:

British Rail – safe and reliable transportation
Tax consultant – peace of mind
Education course – career enhancement, self-actualization
Hotel – hospitality, rest and recuperation
Hairdresser – feel more attractive, confidence booster.

In some cases, different market segments will perceive different core benefits from the same service, e.g. a keep fit programme may be made up of people who wish to lose weight, get very fit or simply enjoy themselves.

Peripheral services

Comprise the following:

Facilitating services

These are a necessity as they make it possible for a customer to use the service, e.g. check-in services at an airline.

Supporting or augmented services

These are not necessarily required but they can differentiate an organization from the competition and give it a competitive advantage, although it has to be said that innovations in service can often be copied quickly and at little cost. An example of supporting services would be Virgin Airline's free head massages and aromatherapy kits to help overcome jet lag.

1.9 Expectations, perceptions and satisfaction

Expectations are formed prior to usage of the service and perceptions are the customer's evaluation of the service. After the service has been consumed customers compare the perceived service with the expected service and if the perceived service meets or exceeds the expected service, the customer is satisfied.

In this context it can be revealing for a service organization to ask the customer:

How do you feel about us?
How have we failed you?

Customers may respond:

You have not lived up to my expectations.
You have failed to take an interest in any of my problems.

If comments such as these are widespread and have any basis in fact they should be a matter of some concern for the management of service organizations. They need to recognize the importance of the first law of service which states:[12]

Satisfaction = Perception – Expectation

However, care must be exercised in the interpretation of the formula. For example, it is difficult to come to terms with the fact that if someone attends a hospital outpatient appointment expecting to wait needlessly for two or three hours along with other individuals who might well have been assigned an identical appointment time, then the customer is satisfied if indeed the duration is of two or three hours.[13] (See Chapter 11 for further discussion of the components of satisfaction.)

Expectations have two components: a probability of occurrence (e.g. the likelihood that a service employee will be available to wait on customers) and an evaluation of the occurrence (e.g. the degree to which the employee's attention is desirable or undesirable, good or bad). Both are necessary because it is not at all clear that some attributes (service employees in this example) are desired by all customers. When these components are properly combined, 'high' and 'low' expectations can be defined:[14]

Expectations	Customer's anticipation
High	Desirable events will occur. Undesirable events will not occur
Low	Desirable events will not occur. Undesirable events will occur

To obtain a measure of customer satisfaction (or dissatisfaction) a comparison must be made between customer expectations and the actual, or customer perception of, performance.

Where perceptions are found to be lower than expectations, the customer is said to be dissatisfied. An international study of UK and USA bank customers[15] uncovered gaps between perceptions and expectations, on both an intra and inter country basis. A number of service elements (e.g. physical features and facilities, contact staff, response to customers' needs and automated facilities) were researched and the overall findings suggested that although expectations were high, perceptions of the actual service quality delivered were equally high. Overall, customers were satisfied.

Another study of the banking industry[16] found that for the small business customer, the cosmetic elements, e.g. branch decor, appearance of staff, are not perceived as indicators of quality service. Indeed, as the authors state, many took the view that they were paying for such peripherals in the form of higher bank charges. In this case it is clear that perceptions did not match up to expectations. In addition, it could be said that what the bank perceived to be important failed to find the agreement of the customer.

Measuring the consumer's perceptions and expectations is vitally important. However, the following question must be asked of the service organization, 'What does it think of customer expectations and perceptions?' To arrive at an answer, two variants of the original perceptions/expectations formula must be used. The objective is to determine whether or not any gaps exist between the customers' view and the service organization's perception of the customers' view. The formulae are:

Customer expectations – service organization's perception of customer expectations

Customer experience – service organization's perception of customer experience

A study which examined doctor/patient relationships,[17] found that 'gaps can arise from inconsistent perceptions of expectations and experiences between patients and physicians'. This research was prefaced with a statement that should act as a continuing reminder for all service organizations:

> From a marketing perspective, the provider would design, develop, and deliver the service offering on the basis of his or her perceptions of client expectations. Likewise, modifications to the service offering would be affected by the provider's perceptions of client experiences. Whether these experiences exceed, match, or are below expectations can have a profound effect on future client/professional relationships.

To measure the three gaps, doctors and patients were required to indicate their agreement/disagreement with a long list of statements, e.g.

	Strongly agree	Strongly disagree

Perception–expectation:
In an emergency doctor is available
Customer expectation – service organization's perception of customer expectations:

	Strongly agree	Strongly disagree

I expect my doctor to talk clearly, using words that I understand
Customer experience – service organization's perception of customer experience:
My doctor spends enough time with me.

Not surprisingly, significant gaps were found. This is a profound problem for service organizations where the expectations/perceptions of one party are at odds with those of the other. There is no simple resolution to this problem. But unless greater effort is made to understand each other, the problem will remain.

1.10 Perceived risk

Buying any product or service involves risks. Consumers will consider what these risks will be, the likelihood of them arising and evaluate the possible consequences. The distinctive characteristics of services promote the feeling that greater risks are involved than for physical products.

Intangibility

Means that potential customers cannot, for example, see and touch many services prior to purchase or use. A typical thought might be, 'What's it going to be like?'

Variability

A machine usually performs to a consistent standard wherever and whenever it is used. Not so human beings. The car mechanic does a perfect job one day but, for a variety of reasons, a less than perfect job the following day. The car owner's apprehension might find expression in, 'My life is in your hands!'

Guarantees

Historically services have not enjoyed the protection of guarantees. You can return a faulty washing machine but not a bad haircut or a poorly taught course. However, progress is being made in this area. The difficulty is putting a monetary value on the consequences of a bad haircut or a poorly taught course (see Chapter 11).

Complexity

Services can be so technical and specialized that the consumer, through lack of experience, is unable to evaluate it properly. The unanswered question for the customer is often, 'How do I know he has done a good job?' The consumer puts his trust in the surgeon, car mechanic, financial advisor etc., but is it well founded?

Types of risk

Jacoby and Kaplan[18] proposed a typology of risks for the consumer:

1 Performance risks – how well will the product work?
2 Physical risk – will the product harm the consumer?
3 Financial risk – will the product be worth all the costs involved?
4 Psychological risks – how will purchase of the product affect the consumer's self-esteem or self-concept?

5 Social risks – how will the consumer's image, as seen by friends, peers etc., be affected after purchase?

A sixth type is often added:

6 Time loss – the waste in time, convenience and effort of getting a product adjusted, repaired or replaced.

The above types of perceived risk were written with products very much in mind and most of the research has concentrated on products. Very few studies have researched perceived risk for services. A recent study[19] found that consumers perceive services to be more risky than goods across several types of risk and more variable in nature.

Perceived risk will not only vary between goods and services but also according to the amount of consumer self-confidence (e.g. knowledge and experience), the degree of uncertainty felt and the importance and cost of the service.

Risk reduction

Again most of the methods of risk reduction were developed for products.[20] For services the following actions should be taken:

1 The service provider should determine the consumer's expectations prior to buying and using the service. The importance of this lies in the opportunity of adjusting expectations to perhaps more realistic levels and preparing the consumer for the outcome before the service is performed (see Chapter 11).
2 To avoid unrealistic consumer expectations developing, the provider should exercise care with promises made in any promotional literature. Such promises should only be communicated where the organization can confidently deliver.
3 As consumers may often experience difficulty in evaluating services, they should be assisted in terms of what to look for before, during and after service delivery.
4 Since services are characterized by a great deal of human interaction attention must be given to selection, training and supervision of customer–contact personnel.
5 Encourage trial of the service. This will not be possible for all types of services. For example a consumer could be encouraged by a carpet cleaner to try out the service on an older and less conspicuous piece of carpeting or a student could be given the opportunity of experiencing a subject for the first few weeks. However, customer trial would be difficult for services such as hairdressing and dentistry.
6 Customer anxiety over variability in service delivery could be reduced by ensuring standardization of much of the procedures. Also the provision of tangible pieces of evidence before, during and after service can reduce a feeling of variability.
7 Guarantees and money-back offers – despite the problems in this area, increasing interest is being shown by service organizations.

Service organizations need to give more attention to perceived risk.

1.11   Summary

Service as an activity has a very long history. However, it is only within the last thirty years that it has been marked out for special attention. More people than ever are employed in the service sector. All organizations offer service in some degree or other. However, a growing number can accurately be described as service organizations. For such organizations understanding the nature of service is fundamental.

Whether the organizations are public or private, large or small, the characteristics of intangibility, inseparability, variability and perishability need to be addressed and the implications managed. Classification systems can help in this regard.

Customer uncertainty and involvement will always be the subject of intense interest along with definitions of what the service actually offers in the form of the service package.

A key issue is that of expectations and perceptions and the gaps that seem to be present. Closing these gaps is an enormous challenge for many service organizations.

Whatever service organizations do managing their affairs there will always be an element of perceived risk in the consumption of services. Action can however be taken to minimize it.

Questions

1   A private health and fitness clinic wants to locate in a geographical area not renowned for active participation in such a venture. As part of a strategy to attract customers what advice would you give the clinic on the types of perceived risk it may encounter and how they may be reduced?

2   Is it your experience that the gaps in expectations and perceptions, mentioned in the chapter, between customer and service provider,
    (a)   exist
    (b)   are caused by the customer or service provider, or both
    (c)   could be avoided, and if so how.

3   How effectively can the four characteristics of services be managed?

4   What do you believe to be the core and peripheral services for the following:
    (a)   Packaged holiday
    (b)   Car hire
    (c)   Library
    (d)   Professional association/trade union.

References

1 Rathmell, J. M. (1966). What is meant by services. *Journal of Marketing*, **30** (October), 32–36.

2 Shostack, G. L. (1982). How to design a service. *European Journal of Marketing*, **16**(1), 49–64.

3 Rushton, A. M. and Carson, D. J. (1985). The marketing of services: managing the intangibles. *European Journal of Marketing*, **19**(3), 19–40.

4 McDougall, G. H. G. and Snetsinger, D. W. (1990) The intangibility of services: measurement and competitive perspectives. *Journal of Services Marketing*, **4**(4), 27–40.

5 Peters, T. J. and Waterman, R. H. (1982). *In Search of Excellence: Lessons from America's Best Run Companies*. Harper and Row, New York.

6 Wolstenholme, S. M. (1988). The consultant customer – a new use for the customer in service operations. *Proceedings of the Operations Management Association Annual International Conference,*University of Warwick (Johnson, R. ed.), pp. 195–203.

7 Lovelock, C. H. (1991). *Services Marketing*. Prentice Hall.

8 Teboul, J. (1988). De-industrialise service for quality. *Proceedings of the Operations Management Association Annual International Conference*. University of Warwick (Johnston, R. ed.), pp. 131–138.

9 Argote, L. (1982). Input uncertainty and organisational coordination in hospital units. *Administrative Science Quarterly*, **27**, 420–434.

10 Danet, B. (1981). Client–organisation relationships. Handbook of Organisation Design, **2**, 382–428.

11 Bowen, D. E. and Jones, G.R. (1986) Transaction cost analysis of service organisation – customer exchange. *Academy of Management Review*, **11**(2), 428–441.

12 Maister, D. H. (1985). *The Psychology of Waiting Lines. The Service Encounter*. (Czepiel, J. A., Solomon, M. R. and Suprenant, C. F., eds). Lexington Books, D. C. Heath and Company, Lexington, Mass, USA.

13 Moores, B. (1989). *Management of Service Quality. Management in Service Industries*. (Jones, P. ed). Pitman, London.

14 Oliver, R. L. (1981). Measurement and evaluation of satisfaction processes in retail settings. *Journal of Retailing*, **57**(3), 25–48.

15 Lewis, B. R. (1991). Service quality: an international comparison of bank customers' expectations and perceptions. *Journal of Marketing Management*, **7**(1), 47–62.

16 Smith, A. M. and Turnbull, P. W. (1990). Service characteristics and their implications for quality. *Proceedings of the Marketing Education Group Annual Conference*, **3**, Oxford Polytechnic, Oxford.

17 Brown, S. W. and Swartz, T. A. (1989). A gap analysis of professional service quality. *Journal of Marketing*, **53** (April), 92–98.

18 Jacoby, J. and Kaplan, L. B. (1972). The components of perceived risk. *Proceedings of the Third Annual Convention of the Association for Consumer Research* (Venkatesan, M. ed).

19 Murray, K. B. and Schlacter, J. L. (1990). The impact of service versus goods on consumers' assessment of perceived risk and variability. *Journal of the Academy of Marketing Service*, **18**(2), 51–65.
20 Roselius, T. (1971). Consumer rankings of risk reduction methods. *Journal of Marketing*, **35** (January), 56–61.

2
The organizational setting

2.1 Introduction

Services are not created and delivered in a vacuum. They are produced by organizations which vary in size, structure and culture. To explain service provision we need to examine the organization in detail.

This means we need to analyse the structure, unearth the dominant and prevailing values and beliefs with a view to arriving at some explanation for the character of the service. In all of this, there must be a determination to ascertain whether, and if so what, organizational factors lead to success or failure in providing a good service. Having established the factors, reasons should be suggested for the success, or actions required to overcome failure.

It is vital that employees at or near the point of customer contact should be given a voice in any appraisal of organization structures, systems and procedures. Their understanding of how and why the organization does or does not work in the service of its customers is often vastly underrated. Researching employees' perceptions of their role, their value and how they behave can help explain lots of things about 'organizational life' and suggest, whether or not, there is need for change.

2.2 The organization chart

The traditional organization chart is shown in Figure 2.1. It portrays a top down rigid hierarchy with heavy emphasis on narrowly defined functions and roles, deadening rules, procedures and controls. The appropriateness of this type of structure nowadays, and in particular for service organizations where the front-line employees' role is pivotal is the subject of much debate.

What the organizational chart does not reveal is:

- The informal organization structure
- The effectiveness of the prevailing communication channels
- The source and nature of power within an organization

In other words, there may be a contrast between how one envisages the organization in a formal sense on paper and how the organization operates in practice.

Arguments have been put forward in favour of turning the traditional organization chart upside down (Figure 2.2). In service organizations, the person at the point of contact is the most important person to the customer. What hap-

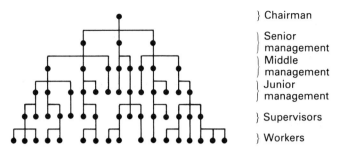

Figure 2.1   *Organization chart: top down rigid hierarchy*

pens at this encounter will demonstrate either the organization's commitment to, or disregard for, the customer. Inverting the organization means making all systems and support staff in the company 'work for' the front-line person to deliver the company's full capabilities at the moment of customer contact.[1] Support for this proposition grows from the technology factor whereby the front-line employee sits at a computer that enables him to handle a whole range of customer enquiries.

For a service organization the logic of this approach is appealing. However, the advocates of this approach fail to address the implications of their proposal. Certainly, the consumer would be much better served but only if, under their new status, the front-line employees are given the appropriate authority and responsibility. This is known as empowering front-line employees. Turning the chart upside down reverses all our thinking about status, power and authority. If front-line employees are to be given new and expanded roles, they should receive commensurate rewards. This part of the concept of empowerment is often found lacking.

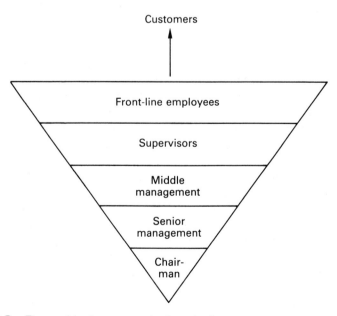

Figure 2.2   *The upside down organization chart*

Empowerment is regarded as the opposite of enslavement where one does what one is told. It is hailed as the answer to improved quality and productivity and the solution to the argument for reductions in middle management ranks. The front-line employees' authority and responsibility would be greatly enlarged. Bell and Zemke[2] regard empowerment as both exhilarating and awesome for managers with a healthy respect for Murphy's law to contemplate.

It is significant, however, that authority is omitted from the definition. Asking people to take authority and responsibility in the area of decision making may be met with resistance, but success in achieving it will result in a more profitable and effective business.

Flattening the pyramid

Instead of an inverted structure, there is an argument to be put for a flatter structure with fewer layers of management and consequently more effective responsiveness to customer needs (Figure 2.3). In a stable and predictable environment, mechanistic rigid structures may be appropriate, but in unpredictable, dynamic circumstances, organic, flexible structures are more appropriate. Organizations in the UK tend to cluster at the mechanistic end of the spectrum.[3]

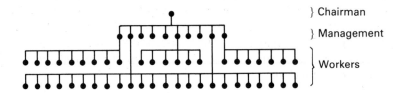

Figure 2.3 Flat organization structure

Whether the environment is stable or dynamic, the importance of structure led Peters[4] to observe that 'good intentions and brilliant proposals will be dead-ended, destroyed, sabotaged, massaged to death or revised beyond recognition or usefulness by the overlayered structures at most large and all too many small firms'.

Peter Drucker[5] recommended seven layers as the maximum necessary for any organization, while Tom Peters[4] more recently drew on the example of the Catholic Church in support of his maximum of five layers.

Federal Express, with 42,000 employees in more than 300 cities worldwide, has a maximum of only five layers between its non-management employees and its Chief Executive Officer. Direct writers in the insurance industry have flat management structures with three or, at the most, four layers of management compared with around ten in a typical insurance company. 'Infinitely flat' service organizations have been achieved by the creative implementation of technology in which there seems to be virtually no limit to the reporting span (the number of people reporting to one supervisor or centre)[1].

Jan Carlzon[6] of Scandinavian Airlines demonstrated how flattening the pyramid works with the following before and after scenario:

Let's say that you've pre-ordered a special vegetarian meal for your SAS flight from Stockholm to New York. Nervously, you approach the check-in counter to find out whether your meal has been delivered to the plan.

'I don't know', the agent sighs. 'I'm sorry but I'm too busy and I'm not familiar with the food service.'

'But what can I do?' you ask.

'You'll have to ask at the gate', she replied. 'They'll certainly be able to help you there.' The agent quickly moves on to help the next person in line. Given no alternative, you go to the gate and ask again.

The gate attendant is friendly, but he doesn't know where your meal is either.

'I wish I could help, but I don't have anything to do with food service. Just check with the stewardess when you get on board and things should certainly work out.'

Reluctantly you board the plane. When you ask the stewardess about your vegetarian meal, she is bewildered. She hasn't heard anything about special food orders, but the plane is about to take off and nothing can be done now.

'You should have contacted us earlier', she reprimands. 'There would have been no problem if only we had known in time.'

In this situation, the hierarchical organizational structure has caused the airline to run three 'moments of truth' (Carlzon's term for fleeting contacts with a customer). No-one the passenger encountered had the authority to handle the specific problem, and no-one dared step out of his normal role to solve it.

Let us now suppose that the organization has changed its structure by flattening the pyramid and putting a team of people in charge of the Stockholm–New York flight from start to finish. The team has fifteen members, two of whom, function as 'coaches', one indoors and one out by the plane. The indoor coach sits in on the flight crew's briefing and consults with them about preflight information such as the appropriate time to begin boarding, whether any infants or disabled people are on the passenger list, and whether anyone has ordered a special meal.

In the morning, the indoor team assembles at the check-in counters to solve passengers' ticketing problems, assign seats, hand fragile baggage and so forth. When a mother arrives with her baby, she is greeted with a smile and told that a suspended cradle has already been put on board and that the seat beside her will be kept free if at all possible.

When you arrive at check-in and ask about your vegetarian meal, you will not be hurriedly dismissed by the agent behind the counter. Thanks to the new team arrangement, your meal request becomes that agent's responsibility. She can confirm that it is already on board, or takes steps to make sure it is loaded by the time you step into the plane.

As more and more passengers check in, the SAS team gradually moves to the departure gate, where they nod to their passengers in recognition. They are well acquainted with the flight to New York and can answer all the usual questions: how to transfer from JFK to La Guardia, why there is a stopover in Oslo, the actual flight time and whether the captain will announce when they are flying over Greenland.

Problems are solved on the spot as soon as they arise. No frontline employee has to wait for a supervisor's permission. No passenger boards the plane while still worried or dissatisfied. Furthermore, by giving more responsibility to the front-line personnel, we are letting them provide the service that they had wanted to provide all along but could not because of an inflexible hierarchical structure.

Flattening the structure helps to eliminate the gap between customer expectations and management perceptions of customer expectations. It does so by:

- Increasing interaction between management and customers
- Improving upward communication from contact personnel to management
- Reducing the number of levels between contact personnel and management[7].

Management should ask itself:

'To what extent does the structure create opportunities to experience first hand what the customer wants?'

Customers should ask themselves:

'How easy is it to obtain access to a manager?'

Front-line employees should ask themselves:

'To what extent is upward communication encouraged? How often do they see management? How often are their suggestions put into practice?'

Front-line employees are often reticent about communicating up the organization ladder. Several reasons for this have been given:

- Fear of losing their job
- Potential to have their job loads increased
- Their suspicion of wrong usage or under-utilization of the information they would provide.

Management in service organizations need to take a far greater interest in upward communication. They need to take time to speak to employees and find out what is required to do the job efficiently and effectively.

For service organizations, ongoing operational decisions should be managed much lower down the organization, even to the point of the front-line employee. Clearly the greatest competitive weapon in many service industries is people and the way they are organized.[8] The organizational culture is critical for service organizations since so much of their activity involves human interactions. Operational decisions must still be guided by organizational policies, rules and procedures for no other reason than to facilitate smooth execution and maintain consistency.

However, service organizations need to demonstrate a willingness to depart from the 'rules' if by doing so it can be shown that customer satisfaction is achieved.

2.3   Organizational variables

According to Peters, Waterman and Phillips[9], diagnosing and solving organizational problems means looking not merely to structural reorganization for answers, but to a framework that includes structure and several related factors. Their research led to the view that any intelligent approach to organizing had to encompass, and treat as interdependent, at least seven variables:

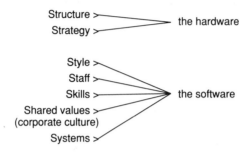

The objective was to get management to accept that the solution to understanding how organizations work lies as much in the software as it does in the hardware. For service organizations this is particularly appropriate as they are often people-intensive and the selection of particular procedures and commitment to certain values (corporate culture) play a prominent part in the final service delivered to the customer. As Peters, Waterman and Phillips[9] point out, if you want to understand how an organization really does (or does not) get things done, look at the systems (all the procedures, formal and informal, that make the organization go, day by day and year by year). How employees and customers feel they are treated is very much a reflection of organization design.

2.4   Corporate culture

Trying to understand and explain what happens in organizations can be a frustrating experience. The concept of corporate culture offers hope to the process of unravelling the mystique of organization life.

Numerous definitions of corporate culture have been proposed.[10] Here are a few:

*   Observed behavioural regulations when people interact, such as the language used and the rituals around deference and demeanour
*   The norms that evolve in working groups such as the particular norm of 'a fair day's work for a fair day's pay'
*   The dominant values espoused by an organization such as the delivery of quality
*   The philosophy that guides an organization's policy towards employees and/or customers

- The rules of the game for getting along in an organization, 'the ropes' that a newcomer must learn in order to become an accepted member
- The feeling or climate that is conveyed in an organization by the physical layout and the way in which members of the organization interact with customers or other outsiders.

All of these meanings reflect the organization's culture, but the essence of culture is reserved for the deeper level of basic assumptions and beliefs that are shared by members of an organization, that operate unconsciously, and that define in a basic, taken for granted fashion, an organization's view of itself and its environment.

In brief, the corporate culture framework stresses:

- Values and assumptions prescribing what is important
- Beliefs on how things work
- Norms defining appropriate and inappropriate behaviour

For the new recruit to an organization to be told, 'This is how we do things around here', captures the notion of corporate culture in everyday language.

Types of organization culture

Culture is the key to understanding service.[11] An organization's cultural orientation will have implications for every aspect of its operations and its internal and external relationships. Organizations will have certain attitudes and styles of service.

However, the effect of culture is a separate matter from whether the service is 'good' or 'bad'. Services will differ in 'taste' and 'feel' and the definition of 'good' and 'bad' service will differ from one culture to another.

The goodness of a service must not be confused with its style.[11] A service may be warm, friendly and relaxed but that does not necessarily make it 'better' than a service which is fast, efficient and impersonal. The style of a service is very much determined by the type of service. For example, customers would expect a warm, friendly, relaxed service in a guest house. On the other hand, customers in a post office expect fast, efficient, impersonal service. One particular style does not need to be exclusively adopted. There may be a mix of styles used. It is really a question of selecting a style which is appropriate for the nature of the service. This in itself is often not an easy task. In the case of some services, for example education, disagreement may exist over which style of service to adopt.

Organizations have been classified in terms of cultural types.[12–15] No organization fits exclusively into one type. The major benefit, however, is that it helps us understand organizations. The crucial question is whether the typologies address the particular characteristics of service organizations. It has to be remembered that service organizations have the additional problem of consumers participating directly in the 'manufacture' of the output.

Cultural typologies that could represent service organizations are:

Culture	Characteristics and examples
Role	• Large pyramid organizations • Authority based on place in hierarchy • Emphasis on roles and job titles • Fast, efficient systems designed to produce uniform and predictable outcomes • Rules and procedures predominate • Customers feel depersonalized • Uncaring, rigid, unresponsive, e.g. private and public utilities, government departments, banks.
Club	• Small organization (<20 employees) where the owner exerts a strong influence • Emphasis on personal interaction rather than memos and meetings • Personality and speed of response often critical • Service delivery can be erratic and range from excellent to poor • Demand can outstrip organization's capacity to cope, e.g. plumber, garage, hairdresser, guest house.
Task	• Organization is active and creative • Dedicated to excellence, innovation, professional integrity • Warm and friendly with little emphasis on hierarchy and procedure • Challenging and questioning environment • Staffed, usually, by young, clever energetic people, e.g. advertising agency, consulting firm.
Person	• Puts the individual rather than the organization first. Individual talent is all important • Do not think in terms of 'organization and management' • Employees can have considerable autonomy • Can be chaotic, e.g. solicitor, accountant, university professor.
Support	• Compassionate, caring, responsive, receptive • Listening to customers/clients, empathizing, responding to their concerns • The essence of the support culture is 'what can we do for you?' e.g. the caring services like social work.

The nature of the service operation can therefore pigeonhole an organization, e.g. British Rail is a role culture and bureaucracy. The health service however is an interesting example of the clash of two cultures – the caring professionals and the business efficiency of the administrators.

The personal culture of the professionals like lawyers is giving way to more organizational disciplines. The support culture has historically been associated with the social services but any service organization or individuals within it can adopt the values of caring, responsiveness, receptivity and a sense of belonging.

Overall, what is clear is that regardless of the type of service there is a growing emphasis on areas such as organization, management, efficiency, budgets and performance measurement. Whether this means 'progress' toward a 'business culture' remains to be seen.

2.5   Role

In any organization people are required to undertake a role, e.g. supervisor, marketing manager, office secretary. The role represents the set of behaviours and activities to be performed by the person occupying that position. In service situations role behaviour is of added importance because:

• The customer is frequently in direct (face to face) or indirect (telephone) contact with organization employees
• The image of the organization is largely determined by how customers (actual or potential) are treated when, for example, making an enquiry or registering a complaint.

Much of the everyday activity of a service organization involves people. The role of the front-line team is crucial but so, equally, is that of the background personnel who are meant to provide support. Uncertainty about what one is expected to do and how one is expected to behave can be a problem for service organizations.

Consider the following expressions of feelings from service employees:[7]

> You feel like management doesn't know what you are doing. We need more support and regulation.

> They should give more recognition to people who are really performing. So many times you are judged by your immediate supervisor. That person may not like you. I wish other managers higher up, would know how people are performing.

If comments such as these are in any way typical, it is hardly surprising if employees take a cavalier, couldn't care less attitude to what their role should be.

The role set

The way in which a role is (or should be) performed is communicated through what is known as the role set (Figure 2.4). In trying to satisfy the various expectations and cope with the pressures and demands of the job, the catering

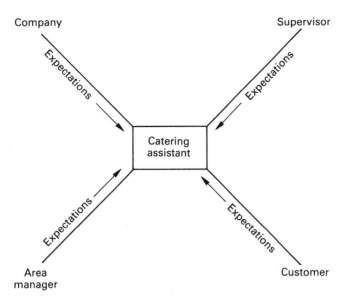

Figure 2.4   Role set for a catering assistant

assistant may experience role ambiguity and role conflict. Willingness and capacity to perform at an acceptable level may be reduced.

Role ambiguity

This refers to a condition where an individual e.g. the catering assistant or supervisor (see Figure 2.4) is uncertain about several matters relating to how to do a specific task, the scope of authority and responsibility, expectations of members of the role set and how performance is to be evaluated and rewarded. The reduction or avoidance of ambiguity lies in providing proper training, keeping people well informed and giving feedback on performance and what is expected.

Role conflict

This refers to where an individual, in this case the catering assistant, experiences conflicting expectations from two or more members of the role set as to how the job should be performed (see Figure 2.4).

An individual may also experience conflict of another kind. A common example is when a friendship develops between the supervisor and the catering assistant. What the supervisor may be expected to do as a boss (e.g. be tough) may conflict with the behaviours expected as a friend (e.g. be sympathetic). In this case the supervisor is playing two roles and it may be difficult to fulfil the demands of both roles simultaneously.

Measurement of role ambiguity and role conflict

A more effective service can be provided for customers if role ambiguity and conflict are reduced. As a first step the organization must determine the magnitude of the problem.

Table 2.1 Role ambiguity measurement

Item	*I am certain/uncertain*

1 About how I should perform my job in order to satisfy my supervisor
2 About how much authority I have
3 How my performance will be evaluated
4 About what activities in my job are most important to my manager
5 About what is expected of me
6 How much time I should spend socializing with customers
7 About company rules and regulations
8 How I should perform my job in order to satisfy my customers

Score of 1 means 'absolutely certain' and 7 means 'absolutely uncertain'

    Items that exceed a score of 4 on the scale of 1 to 7 may warrant further investigation to establish the reasons for the ambiguity.

    For role conflict the formats listed in Tables 2.2 and 2.3 may be used.

    Comparison of the scores of the employee and supervisor in Table 2.2 will determine the degree of conflict that exists between them.

    A second format (Table 2.3) considers the extent to which front-line employees perceive any conflict between for example the supervisor and customers on how they (the front-line employees) should perform their role.

Table 2.2 Role conflict measurement

My supervisor expects Me:	Employee					Supervisor				
	SA	*A*	*N*	*DA*	*SDA*	*SA*	*A*	*N*	*DA*	*SDA*
1 To enforce rules and regulations always										
2 To be completely honest with customers										
3 To have the knowledge to answer customers' questions										
4 To accept orders without question										
5 To think up better ways to do my job										

Scale: strongly agree (SA), agree (A), neutral (N), disagree (DA), strongly disagree (SDA)

Table 2.3 Role conflict measurement

Expectation	Perceived conflict				
	SA	*A*	*N*	*D*	*SD*
Be completely honest with customers					
Deal with complaints concerning my work performance					
Develop close relationships with customers					

Scale: strongly agree (SA), agree (A), neutral (N), disagree (D), strongly dis-agree (SD). The front-line employee, for example, is required to indicate whether he agrees/disagrees that the expectations of his role partners are in conflct.

For each statement employees would be asked to indicate their strength of agreement/disagreement on whether they perceive conflict between the supervisor and customers.

The above frameworks for measuring role ambiguity and conflict are simply illustrative. What is important is a willingness to investigate and act on the findings.

Role overload and underload

In addition to feelings of role ambiguity and conflict service personnel suffer from overload and underload.

Overload

Employees are required to do more work than they feel they can handle either in terms of the time allocated or the necessary skills and abilities to perform the job.

Underload

Employees spend part of their time doing nothing and the job is not felt to be mentally stimulating or challenging. (See Chapter 6 for further discussion of role.)

2.6 Defensive behaviour in organizations

Political and power-seeking behaviour is present in many organizations. For service organizations characterized by a great deal of human involvement and inter-action, defensive, as distinct from offensive, behaviour is much in evidence. Understanding the reasons for defensive behaviour is not straightforward, but being aware of its existence may help explain why there is low efficiency, lack of customer loyalty and a poor image.

Customers and employees of service organizations should recognize many of the following defensive behaviours.[16]

Avoiding action

Over conforming

Action is often avoided by resorting to a strict interpretation of one's responsibility, e.g. 'The rules clearly say . . .' and citing supportive precedents, e.g. 'It's always been done this way'. Rigid adherence to rules can be potentially explosive in a service like social security. The situation may be defused by distancing oneself from the rules, e.g. 'I didn't make the rules', or 'Listen, if it were up to me . . .'.

Passing the buck

Responsibility for doing something is passed to someone else, e.g. 'I'm too busy' or 'That's not my job'.

Playing dumb

Avoiding an unwanted task by falsely pleading ignorance or inability, e.g. 'I don't know anything about that . . .' or 'X is better able to handle that . . .'.

Depersonalizing

Avoiding unwanted demands from clients or subordinates by treating them as objects or numbers rather than people, e.g. a doctor referring to hospital patients not by name but by their illness, talking about them in the third person, using medical terminology incomprehensible to patients, avoiding eye contact, and providing curt and patronizing answers to patients' questions.

Stretching

Prolonging a task so that one appears occupied or performing trivial tasks during slack periods in order to appear busy.

Smoothing

Masking fluctuations in effort or output to create the impression of steady productivity. Employees agree to work within specified minimum and maximum levels of output.

Stalling

Appearing more or less supportive publicly while doing nothing privately, e.g. a service situation where long queues are allowed to form to discourage use of the service.

Avoiding blame

Buffing

This term was coined to describe the practice of rigorously documenting activity or fabricating documents to project an image of competence and thoroughness. It is widely referred to as 'covering your ass'.

Playing safe

Avoiding situations that may reflect unfavourably on a person.

Justifying

Minimizing responsibility for a certain event by acknowledging partial responsibility and including some expression of remorse.

Scapegoating

Deflecting blame.

Misrepresenting

Avoiding blame by manipulating information.

Escalating commitment

Individuals responsible for a failing course of action often 'throw good money after bad' – the white elephant.

Avoiding change

People like to protect their own turf through actions like stalling, playing safe, over-conforming etc.

Explanation for defensive behaviour

There may be organizational and individual factors causing defensive behaviour[16]. Of particular relevance for service organizations are the following.

Individual factors

Factors which may be of interest, though not exclusively to service organizations are insecurity and anxiety, emotional exhaustion and work alienation.

Employment in service organizations can be stressful due to the nature and amount of personal contact with customers. The full range of emotions must be held in check at least for front-line employees. Smiling and generally being nice is the rule.

Work alienation stems from a lack of job involvement and identification with the organization. Many service occupations are simple 'dead-end jobs'. Service organizations, characterized by uncertainty and intensity of demand, are more of a pressure chamber than their manufacturing counterparts where a more orderly and less hectic routine is in evidence.

Organizational factors

- The specialization of tasks and formalization of rules and procedures in a bureaucracy encourage defensive type behaviour. For example, specialization means people feel responsible for a specific, not the whole task, creating a tendency to pass the buck, play dumb, over-conform and depersonalize. Formalization of rules and procedures tells people what they can and cannot do which again may promote over-conforming, passing the buck, playing dumb and stalling.
- Defensive behaviour may also be a means of coping with a work environment in which there is uncertainty felt over areas of responsibility and the interpretation and application of rules and procedures. People may feel that the demands of the work environment are just too great and a feeling of powerlessness only makes the capacity to cope even worse.

2.7   Organizations of the future

Charles Handy[17] sets forth his radical vision of organizations of the future. According to Handy, 'life in the core of more and more organizations is going to resemble that of consultancy firms, advertising agencies and professional partnerships. The organizations are flat, seldom with more than four layers of rank, the top one being the assembly of partners, professors or directors'. Handy envisages organizations becoming more like the shamrock. The first leaf represents the core workers made up of qualified professionals, technicians and managers who are essential to the organization. The second leaf is the contractual fringe which performs work not usual to the organization. They are paid for results not for time, in fees not wages. For example, an organization may arrange for a contractor to do much of their clerical work. The third leaf of the shamrock is the flexible labour force, all those part-time workers and temporary workers who are the fastest growing part of the employment scene. This is of particular interest for service organizations. They are not, in Handy's view, concerned about careers and job satisfaction. They will, however, require training, in some cases leading to a qualification, along with decent pay and conditions. A fourth leaf, proposed by Handy, should be of special interest to service organizations. Although not part of the formal organization structure, the practice of getting customers to do the work is growing fast. Many service organizations are now requiring customers to play a more prominent part in producing the service. Handy, perhaps optimistically, believes that all organizations will soon be shamrock organizations.

2.8 Summary

To obtain a picture of an organization the first thing we usually refer to is the organization chart. Although it is an obvious starting point, we need to 'dig much deeper' if we wish to increase our understanding of how organizations work.

For services the development of an appropriate culture is important given the numerous and direct interactions with customers. The 'way we do things around here' requires explanation and justification if we are to encourage debate about 'creating a customer-centred culture in service organizations'.

Questions

1   'Using industrial models to manage service-based corporations makes as little sense as using farm models to run factories' Stanley Davis, *New Management*, Spring (1983). How much do you agree/disagree with this statement and why?
2   The following statements are often made about organizations:

(a) There is a great deal of criticism in this organization.
(b) The pay is poor.
(c) Specific standards are laid down for most tasks in this organization.
(d) The organization really cares about its employees.
(e) You must 'watch your back' in this organization
(f) Promotion in this organization does not seem to be based on merit.
(g) Employees are given a great deal of responsibility but not much authority.
(h) Everything seems to be governed by rules and regulations.
(i) Employees are involved in determining how their job should be done.

For each statement, consider the following:

 •   What does it say about the culture of the organization?
 •   Consider the likely effect on delivery of service to the customer.
3   Are there any service situations or occupations where there is a great deal of role conflict and/or role ambiguity? If so, why do you think this is the case?
4   The following extract from the *Idea of Neighbourhoods* by J. Seabrook (1984) recounts the experience of a member of the public:

'. . . I rang the environmental health department. 'There's rats in Goscote. Could you give us some advice?'
'Oh, you speak to the Public Works.' So I ring Public Works.
'Where are the rats?'
'Goscote.'
'Now, are they above ground or below ground? If they're below ground they're our responsibility. If they're above you'll have to ring the environmental health.'
'You're kidding me.'
'No,' they said, 'that's the way it works.'
I said, 'Whose responsibility is it if they're in the bloody roof – the RAF?'

How typical, in your experience, is the above in dealing with service organizations?
What are the organizational implications?

References

1 Quinn, J. B. and Paquette, P. C. (1990). *Technology in Services: Creating Organisational Revolutions. Sloan Management Review*, Winter, pp. 67–87.
2 Bell, C. R. and Zemke, R. (1988). Do service procedures tie employees' hands? *Personnel Journal*, September, pp. 77–83.
3 Burnes, B. (1991). Barriers to organisational change: the role of culture. *Management Research News*, **14**(1/2), 24–29.
4 Peters, T. J. (1987). *Thriving on Chaos*. Knopf, New York.
5 Drucker, P. (1954). The practice of management. Harper & Row, New York.
6 Carlzon, J. (1987). *Moments of Truth*. Ballinger Publishing Company.
7 Zeithaml, V. A., Parasuraman, A. and Berry, L. L. (1990). *Delivering Quality Service*. The Free Press, Macmillan Inc.
8 Heskett, J. L., Sasser, W. E. and Hart, C. W. L. (1990). *Service Breakthroughs*. The Free Press, Macmillan Inc.
9 Peters, T. J., Waterman, R. H. and Phillips, J. R. (1980). Structure is not organisation. *Business Horizons* (June).
10 Schein, E. H. (1985). *Organisational Culture and Leadership*. Jossey Bass.
11 Harrison, R. (1990). *Organisation Culture and Quality of Service: A Strategy for Releasing Love in the Workplace*. Association for Management Education and Development, London.
12 Mills, P. K. and Marguilies, N. (1980). Toward a core typology of service organisations. *Academy of Management Review*, **5**(2), 255–265.
13 Handy, C. B. (1978). *Understanding Organisations*. Penguin, London.
14 Harrison, R. (1972). Understanding organisation's character. *Harvard Business Review*, **5**(3), 119–128.

15 Mintzberg, H. (1991). The effective organisation: forces and forms. *Sloan Management Review*, Winter, pp. 54–67.

16 Ashforth, B. E. and Lee, R. T. (1990). Defensive behaviour in organisations: a preliminary model. *Human Relations*, **43**(7), 621–648.

17 Handy, C. B. (1991). *The Age of Unreason*. Business Books Ltd.

3
Service design

3.1 Introduction

Services require an operating and delivery system in order to function. That system should be designed in such a way as to offer effective customer service through an efficiently operated process. Needless to say the drive to achieve efficiency and effectiveness can become unstuck to the detriment of provider and/or customer. Whatever the service, the basic design question will always be, 'How should it be operated and delivered to the customer?'. Design formats can, of course, vary with the type of service and even within a particular service there may be different approaches to what constitutes the best design. Whatever is decided, the design in effect is the service.

3.2 The customer mix

However, before the design of the service can take place, the marketer must decide which customers he will serve. Which segment of the population is he aiming to satisfy? The selection of a target market is perhaps the most critical decision that he makes in the design of a service.

The process that should be adopted for customer group selection depends on the current market situation. If there is no similar service already available then there is more scope for choice. The brand map lies empty. The organization proposing to launch the service will attempt to match the skills and capacity of the company with the needs of a group of consumers. The choice of customer group will, for the majority of companies, be driven by the profit motive.

This may mean servicing one niche with a highly differentiated service. In most cases the value added by the uniqueness enables the service provider to earn large margins. This compensates for the smaller pool of customers. For companies with a large capacity or fixed costs it can often mean serving several niches simultaneously with differentiated service offerings as in the case of the Storehouse Group which owns the Conran Shop and Heals – both household furniture retailers serving different niches.

In consumer services a mass market approach is often taken, e.g. high street banks and fast food shops. In these instances the company has decided that it can function most profitably by offering a relatively undifferentiated service to a wide target market.

There is an opportunity to adopt this targeting strategy in many consumer markets. The target market may vary significantly in terms of demographics or psychographics. However, many of these differences evaporate when it comes to the variables that are key to the selection of a brand in that particular market. A supermarket may hope to attract most of the population living or working near the store. The key variable here is that of convenience, regardless of the individual's age or lifestyle.

Note that we have said in mass markets the company will offer a *relatively* undifferentiated offering. The volume of consumer demand can support a number of service companies. However, in order to survive each individual company needs to achieve a competitive advantage. The way in which each company strives for this will often affect the type of customer that it attracts. To take the example of food retailing, offering quality produce will often have a price implication (Marks and Spencer). While their concept will still have broad appeal it is probably most attractive to affluent consumers or those to whom convenience is very important.

Therefore, even in mass markets, there is generally some degree of segmentation. The competing companies will occupy different spaces on any brand map. So what makes a company select a particular group of customers? There are two key factors. First, the company believes that it can deliver what the customer wants. And second, from its understanding of the market there is a gap to be filled. For many services the opportunities presented allow the company to serve a mix of customers. British Rail offers all its customers the same core-benefit travel. It makes the most efficient use of its resources by segmenting the travelling public and tailoring its service offering to meet their needs more precisely, e.g. pensioners and businessmen will have differing needs. (For a further discussion of target market selection see Chapters 8 and 12.)

3.3 Design elements

In designing any service, eleven key factors should be taken into account.

Customer contact

- How much contact will the customer have with the service and what will the nature of that contact be?

Service mix

- What service will be provided in terms of breadth and depth? Breadth equals the number of items in each line; for example, a local authority sports and leisure service may offer the following service lines (breadth): outdoor sports, indoor sports, adventure sports and leisure activities. Within the last mentioned might be art galleries, theatres, museums and parks (depth).

Location of service consumption

- Will the customer come to a service facility (single or multi-site) or will the service come to the customer (at home or mobile)?

Design of service facility and accessories

- What should the layout, furnishing, colours etc. of the facility be?
- What design discussions need to be made in respect of staff (uniforms), vehicles (colour, logo), and non-personal communication (letter headings, signs, brochures etc.)?

Technology

- What will be the balance between technology and people, e.g. how will it apply to the employee's work and the customer's usage of the service?
- Will the technology be predominantly hard, e.g. automation or soft, e.g. pre-planned systems – pre-packaged tours?

Employees

- How many will be required?
- What will the ratio be between full-time and part-time?
- What will be the ratio between back office employees and front-office employees?
- How many supervisors will be required to control front-line employees?
- What skills will be needed and how will they be acquired?
- How flexible will employees need to be?

Organization structure

- How many layers in the organization are desirable?
- How should the finance, operations, personnel and marketing functions be organized?

Information

- What information is desirable for running the organization and how easily will it be acquired?
- How will it be stored?
- How accessible will it be and who will have access?

Demand and supply management

* How much knowledge is there about demand patterns and levels?
* What strategies are known for influencing demand?
* How flexible is capacity for meeting demand fluctuations, e.g. work schedules, sub-contracting, reservation systems, stock control?

Procedures

* Will the service be mainly standardized or customized?
* How complex will the service be?

Control

* What systems will be in place and what techniques will be available for ensuring the smooth running of the operation and the provision of quality output, e.g. critical path analysis, forecasting methods, flow charts, queueing theory application?

The above listing is by no means exhaustive. Its main purpose is to signal areas that need to be addressed. Larger organizations generally adopt a more strategic approach to the area of design. The design of smaller companies' operating systems will bear the stamp of the owner's personality.

3.4 Operating systems classification

The design elements must be combined to deliver outputs required by customers. How they are combined has given rise to a particular classification of service organizations. A possible drawback is that the classification has drawn heavily on types of manufacturing organizations. For example, services can be classified depending on the extent of client contact and customization, and the degree of labour intensity. Service operating systems are said to exhibit the characteristics of a factory, mass production and a job shop. The actual terms used are service factory, mass service, service shop and professional service. The classification is as follows:[1,2]

Service factory – low in personal interaction and customization and labour intensity, e.g. airlines, hotels, resorts and recreation.
Mass service – low in personal interaction and customization and high in labour intensity, e.g. retailing, schools, retail banking.
Service shop – high in personal interaction and customization and low in labour intensity, e.g. restaurants, hospitals, car and other repair services.
Professional service – high in personal interaction and customization and high in labour intensity, e.g. doctors, lawyers, accountants.

Such a classification provides a useful basis for discussing design options in operational systems. However, problems remain:

1 It is not particularly enlightening to draw a distinction between a factory and a mass service. They are not mutually exclusive. A factory is a place where various forms of production can take place, e.g. flow production, batch production and including mass production of service. One is simply a place where various processes may occur and the other is one example of the possible processes.

2 There is no breakdown of the different processes and how relevant they may be for services. For example, flow processing systems are more characteristic of patients going through various departments of a hospital or students going through various stages in a college course. Batch processing on the other hand occurs in certain services in which availability and operation occur only when a given number or minimum number of customers are available, e.g. some entertainment services and guided bus tours.

3 The service shop is derived from its manufacturing equivalent, the job shop, where small individual orders are processed from a variety of customers. Jobs are meant to be ordered in priority and resources scheduled accordingly. However, there is no uniformity of operation across all the services that could fall into this category. Consider the contrast in operational characteristics of two services, car repair and restaurant, regarded as examples of service shops (Table 3.1). There is a greater likelihood of the garage experiencing difficulties in designing a system that will operate and deliver a service efficiently and effectively.

Table 3.1 Two 'service shops': a contrast in operational characteristics

Characteristics	Garage (car repair)	Restaurant
Customer access to 'production area' creating disruption	√	
Unpredictability surrounding customer appearance and service requirements	√	
Loyal customers can 'jump the queue'	√	
Difficulties in allocating and scheduling capacity and employee skills	√	

√ = greater likelihood of occurring

4 Even within the existing classification there will be argument over the examples; not only about where they are allocated but also the assumption that each service type is homogeneous, i.e. all hotels are alike, all restaurants are alike. Within any particular service, say hotels, one needs to consider:

- The design options in terms of operating and delivery systems
- Should service design be broadly similar across all hotels or is there scope for different structures (see Chapter 10 for design options in hotels).

5 Labour intensity is calculated as a cost of capital to cost of labour ratio. According to this method services like hospitals, which are thought to be very labour intensive, are in fact relatively low in labour intensity due to the very expensive equipment involved. The basis for calculating the ratio, namely cost, is not however an ideal way of revealing the respective roles of equipment and personnel in delivering the service. It is an economist's or accountant's approach that lends itself to measurement. More effort needs to be directed towards examining the contribution that equipment and personnel make to delivering customer satisfaction. The capital-ratio should not be regarded solely as a financial equation. It could act as a basis for deciding the proper balance of resources in achieving efficiency and meeting customer needs.

In terms of the measure of interaction and customization, care must be exercised in assuming that they always go together. In some services like insurance underwriting at Lloyds considerable customization is coupled with a low degree of client interaction.[2]

3.5   The front and back office

Whatever decision is made in respect of a design classification, service organizations must address the issue of front and back office allocations.

The front office – that part of the system directly experienced and visible to the customer. This is where the service is performed and is thereby open to customer scrutiny, e.g. the hotel diningroom.

The back office – that part of the system from which the customer is excluded, e.g. the hotel kitchen. It is often referred to as the manufacturing side of the service, not seen by the customer. However there are instances, e.g. banks, building societies, where the back office is visible to the customer.

This means that often the technical core of an organization (commonly referred to as the production process) is sealed off from any uncertainties that may occur in other parts of the organization. This is known as 'decoupling'.[3] The back office becomes separated from the front office and is allowed to work without hindrance or interference. The main objective is to enable efficiency to be maximized in the 'production processes'.

Striking the right balance between front and back office responsibilities can be a difficult exercise and one that many service organizations fail to achieve. As Wostenholme[4] argues, 'There is a "back office" mentality currently permeating service operations thinking. The front office is seen as a complex interactive process where the customer is variable and unpredictable. The back office, on the other hand, is controllable and affords labour cost savings by restricting the number of customer contact personnel. Further, the degree and type of customer contact is progressively moving towards the "hard" forms of contact as witnessed by the introduction of ATM's and mechanical ticket machines'. The precarious future for the front office is reflected in his comment that, 'There is undoubtedly a clearly definable trend towards the distancing of the service organisation from the source of its wealth – the customer'.

What all this means is that in the drive for operational efficiency and control (back office supremacy), service organizations run the risk of neglecting customer expectations of what constitutes a satisfactory experience (front office impoverishment).

A key factor in the debate over front versus back office dominance is customer contact. Chase[5] asserts that, 'The potential efficiency of a service system is a function of the degree of customer contact entailed in the creation of the service product'. He proposes a formula which states that:

$$\begin{array}{l}\text{Potential}\\\text{facility}\\\text{efficiency}\end{array} = f\left(1 - \frac{\text{Customer contact time}}{\text{Service creation time}}\right)$$

If we apply the formula hypothetically in two contrasting service situations, hotels (high customer contact) and the social security office (low customer contact), the efficiency measure might be,

for hotels: $1 - \dfrac{2 \text{ hours}}{4 \text{ hours}} = 50\%$ efficiency

for social security office: $1 - \dfrac{0.25 \text{ hours}}{2 \text{ hours}} = 87.5\%$ efficiency

The ratio of customer contact time relative to service creation time is obviously much greater in the case of hotels but does that mean that they are that much less efficient? Furthermore, if the hotel was to take an 'inefficient 8 hours' to create the service, the resulting efficiency index would be 75 per cent! The nature, as well as the amount, of customer contact merits attention. Customer input to the hotel facility could be defined as rather passive, whereas a relatively low contact organization like a social security office may experience a significant degree of uncertainty in the form of customer disruption.

Whatever its deficiencies the customer contact model does represent an important advance in the thinking about service design. The extent of customer contact (whether passive or active) can have an effect on shaping the design elements listed above. In addition, it encourages development of strategies for improving and/or reducing customer contact. For example a number of widely used, common-sense heuristics have been suggested.[6]

Contact improvement

- 'Take a number' systems
- Assign contact workers who are people-oriented and knowledgeable about service system processes and policies

- Maintain consistent work hours
- Partition back office from the public service counter; do not permit work breaks in front of the customer
- Provide queueing, patterns and signs to indicate standardized and customized service channels.

Contact reduction

- Handle only exceptions on a face-to-face basis; all other transactions by phone, or better still by mail
- Use reservations or appointments-only systems
- Decentralize using kiosks with one person for information handling (this takes pressure off the main facility)
- Use drop-off points such as automatic teller machines
- Bring service to customer through postal rounds or mobile offices
- Use a roving greeter or signs outside the facility to act as buffers and information providers

As already mentioned, the Chase approach has been criticized for concentrating on the amount of customer contact. Furthermore, there is a suggestion that it offers little guidance on how to coordinate back and front office operations, and fails to consider customer input in the design of service work. These issues have been addressed by examining how varying forms of co-production by employees and customers affect the design and coordination of service systems. The service design options are determined by the existence and combinations of the following concepts:[7]

- Input uncertainty – refers to the service organization's incomplete knowledge of what the customer is going to bring to the service and how he is likely to behave during the service encounter.
- Customer willingness to participate – refers to how far customers wish to play an active part in the service. Customers' capacity to become involved can be limited by lack of knowledge, skills and understanding their role.
- Diversity of demands – refers to the uniqueness of customers' demands. Are they to be met in a customized or standardized way?
- Interdependencies – refers to different patterns with respect to division of service work (between front and back office and customer) and customization versus standardization of service actions and interdependencies.

Four service design options can now be constructed (Figure 3.1). A brief explanation of each follows:

- Sequential standardized service design – a customer-dominated design in which they serve themselves after service employees have provided the goods and facilities needed for self-service. It is a standardized service in which the front and back office can be decoupled to allow for efficient delivery of service.

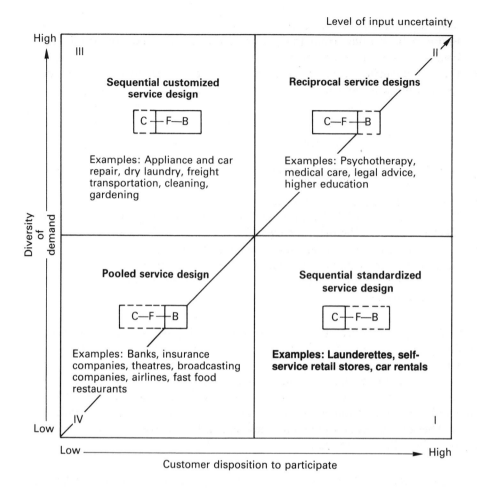

Figure 3.1 *A typology of service interdependence patterns matching input uncertainty. C = customers; F= front office employee(s); B = back office employee(s);* ☐ *= main locus of interdependence;* [¯] *= supporting interdependencies.*
Source: Larsson, R. and Bowen, D. E. (1989)[7]

- Reciprocal service design – joint participation of the parties 'in which the output of each becomes the input for the others'.[3] The service is produced largely on the basis of significant interactions between front-office employees and customers.
- Sequential customized service design – the bulk of the work here is performed by the service employees in a system of strong interdependence between back and front office.
- Pooled service design – most of the work done by an efficient back office, largely decoupled from front-office disturbances. Customers do not interact extensively with service employees but engage in the sharing of resources that makes mass service possible.

The examples given in Figure 3.1 are only examples of services that typically apply the service design illustrated. For example, it could be argued that banks, particularly at branch level, exhibit some of the characteristics of quadrant III. Equally there is sometimes a tendency for some services not to comply with what is deemed an appropriate design, e.g. customers in quadrant II might suggest that the back office plays a much greater role in reality. Recent suggestions to make social security offices open plan can be regarded as a radical departure from established approaches to service design.

3.6 Service blueprint

A service blueprint is basically a flowchart of the service process. It is a map in which all the elements or activities, their sequencing and interaction, can be visualized. There are a number of essential steps in blueprinting a service:[8]

- Draw, in diagrammatic form, all the components and processes (Figure 3.2). The service in this case is simple and clear cut and the map is straightforward. More complex services may require large, complicated diagrams.

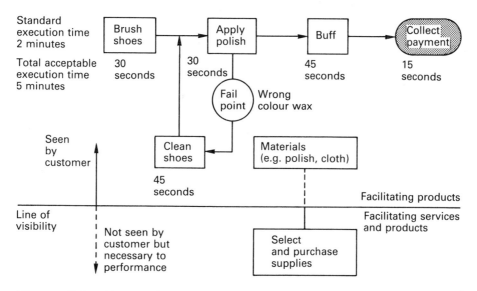

Figure 3.2 Blueprint for a corner shoeshine. Source: Shostack, G. L. (1984).[8] Reproduced by permission of Harvard Business Review, © 1984 by the President and fellows of Harvard College. All rights reserved

- Identify the fail points – where might things go wrong? In Figure 3.2 the shoeshiner may pick up the wrong wax.
- Set executional standards – these are tolerances (band or range) set around each function and regarded as acceptable from a customer and cost viewpoint. Time is a good example. In Figure 3.2 the standard execution time is

two minutes, and research showed that the customer would tolerate up to five minutes before lowering his assessment of quality.
- Identify all of the evidence (see Chapter 4) that is available to the customer. Each item represents an encounter point.
- Analyse profitability – delays in service execution through errors or working too slowly affects profit. The shoeshiner estimates the cost of delay; anything greater than four minutes execution time and he loses money.

Consider the application and value of blueprinting for a car repair service. The perspective is that of a customer using it for the first time (Figure 3.3). Prior to making the initial contact with the garage (phoning for appointment and arrival at the garage) the customer will have formed some expectations from, for example, word-of-mouth and advertising. The telephone call and particularly arrival at the garage will go some way towards confirming or contradicting the customer's expectations, and are in fact more powerful tools once he has made contact. The customer will use various pieces of evidence (telephone response time and manner, attitudes and appearance of proprietor/employees, equipment and layout etc) as clues to the likely quality of service. Making assumptions about service quality from the type of evidence mentioned above is understandable but has the potential to mislead. The seemingly chaotic, untidy garage manned by employees covered in oil and possessing little by way of modern equipment may be perceived as likely to render a poor service. Yet the opposite may be nearer the truth.

The diagnosis represents an encounter point where the customer may, for example, describe symptoms to assist in determining the problem. It is critical in the sense that promises made to the customer and the resource implications of the job are determined on the basis of the diagnosis. If the diagnosis is subsequently found to be incorrect, relationships with the customer may be impaired. After the initial diagnosis the customer will depart, without ever seeing the repair section.

Where the organization draws the line of visibility, distinguishing the front office from the back office, is of some significance for service organizations. The nature of the service and how it is delivered offers guidance on where to draw the line, e.g. a hairdresser's operation will be predominantly front office, while a credit card company operates a very large percentage of its service in the back office. Other services like a restaurant may feel ambivalent about where to draw the line separating the front and back office.

In making the distinction a service organization needs to address the following questions:

- How much of the service does the customer need to witness/experience?
- Will greater involvement lead to more understanding and favourable impressions, i.e. improved effectiveness.
- What effect will there be on efficiency if the customer is allowed greater access to the service process?

As already mentioned earlier in the chapter, a delicate balance may have to be struck between the need for efficiency and the desirability of customer involvement. In the case of the car repair business, allowing the customer to experience the service may create minimum disruption in terms of efficiency but maximum reward in terms of customer education and understanding.

Service design

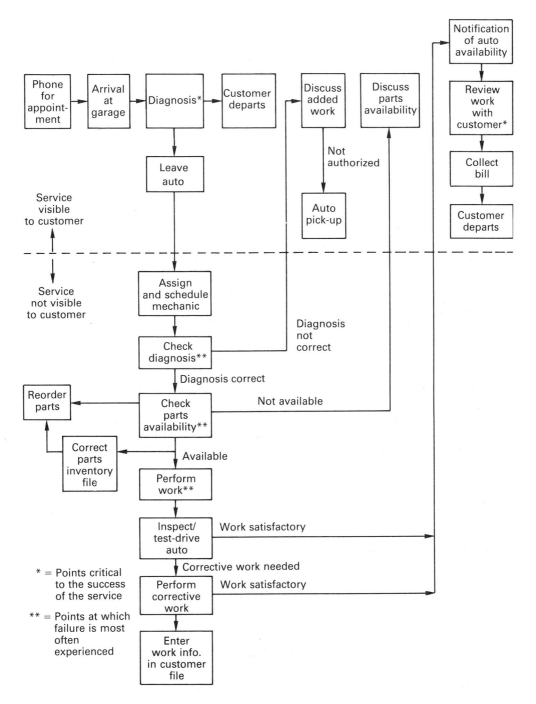

Figure 3.3 A process flow diagram for the auto repair business. Source: Heskett, J. L., Sasser, W. E. and Hart, C. W. L. (1990)[10]

53

The repair process in Figure 3.3 is sealed off from the customer but the objective must be to schedule work, deploy the necessary skills and arrange the timely availability of parts in order that promises made to the customer can be achieved.

On paper this is a good example of the construction of a service blueprint. Undertaking such an exercise provides an opportunity for the service provider to take a fresh look at the service and how it works. Stephen H. Baum, vice president of Booz, Allen and Hamilton Inc, New York, believes three factors are critical to making a pay off:[9]

> The value delivered: what customers perceive they have actually received. The service mix: the features and levels of service the customers really care about. Plans and budgets: signals they send employees that are consistent or inconsistent with what management is trying to do.

He cites the example of a fast food business intent on cost savings in the kitchen which was convinced that automation would result in cost reduction. 'But they were wrong', Baum said. The issue, according to Baum was not automation, but labour and time management. His analysis led him to the conclusion that, 'Employees spend a lot of time waiting, walking, and doing other things that customers did not perceive as adding value. Much of the problem was caused by equipment choices, process sequences, and layout – not by employee performance'. Baum was able to show, through blueprinting, that automation would actually increase idle time and that by focusing on value-added time major reductions of in-store labour could be effected.

Blueprinting, then, can be regarded as a valuable and versatile tool in systems design. Its deployment can range from the simple design of a hotel bathroom through to monitoring the process flow of an important and confidential company document.[10] In developing a service blueprint it is worthwhile considering, 'Who does what, to/with whom, how often, and under what conditions'.[11] Whatever the process under scrutiny the aim must always be improvements in service operation that will both deliver customer satisfaction and utilize organizations' resources efficiently. Improving the capacity, ability and willingness to serve must always be the expressed goal of any service organization. It will not be an easy task as the process moves away from the standardized design of a fast food restaurant where time is the major design element. Clearly, performance standards, in terms of response time, are easier to set than, for example, degree of care and attention required by employees in other service situations. Of equal importance is the establishment of critical or pressure points and fail points. In many cases these are the 'moments of truth' for the customer and any vulnerability to breakdown must of necessity be minimized.

From an organizational culture perspective the blueprint allows all the employees to see their role in the process. Such an approach may bring to the surface previously unspoken tensions, but at the same time it can give, particularly the front-line employees, a voice in how the service should be delivered. Far too often the customer contact employees are simply left to 'carry out orders'. It may well be, as a result of a blueprinting exercise that the way these orders are carried out requires drastic overhauling. Management can be criticized, sometimes, for thinking they know best. Mapping out the process is as much a test of the validity and endorsement of management's belief as to how things do or should work.

A process cannot be improved until there is a clear understanding of how it works. There may well be different viewpoints as to how a process should be performed and monitored. It is advisable, therefore, that the views of management, employees and even customers should be solicited. Several types of information must be gathered and in so doing a distinction drawn between peoples' perceptions of the existing processes and their suggestions for improvement. The areas for investigation should be:

- Process activities
- Information required to perform the process
- Products generated by the process, e.g. documents, services etc
- People and equipment required to perform the process
- Documents that direct how the process is to be accomplished.

3.7   Service design strategy

In the future, choice, if that is the correct word in the context of service design options will be between technology and people. As far back as 1972, Levitt[12] was berating the service sector for thinking in humanistic rather than technocratic terms. He argued that companies need to 'stop thinking of service as servitude and personal ministration if they are to effect drastic improvements in quality and efficiency'. The example of McDonald's is used to stress the benefits of an industrial mode of thinking. In effect, 'the systematic substitution of equipment for people, combined with the carefully planned use and positioning of technology, enables McDonald's to attract and hold patronage in proportions no predecessor or imitator has managed to duplicate'. The discretion and availability of service are replaced by standardization, predictability and control. Some may view the application of the McDonald's model as inapplicable at best and frightening at worst. It is, nevertheless, a constant reminder for service organizations that efficiency improvements may only be secured at the cost of the personal touch. Whether or not there is a commensurate increase in effectiveness is somewhat more problematic and one to which Levitt does not pay sufficient attention.

Technology, whether hard or soft, is being increasingly adopted by service organizations and without a doubt it does bring advantages. However, there should always be a place for the 'personal ministration' so ridiculed by Levitt.

Another 'choice' for service organizations is between greater customer or service provider input in the production process. Designing service in such a way that the customer is given a greater role can lead to benefits in terms of costs, speed and convenience. The technology that Levitt talked about is enabling this to happen (see Chapter 8). The ultimate expression of customer involvement is self-service in which the customer undertakes most of the tasks required to produce the service.

Finally, a strategic change on the part of a service organization will necessitate some adjustments to the operating system. For example a fast-food restaurant broadening its product mix may require staff training, changes in layout and revision in stock control. A garage wishing to improve the quality of its engine tuning service may involve the purchase of expensive equipment. The ambulance service has, over the years, made strategic changes in the service it offers the public and this has meant, for example, the purchase of mobile cardiac units and the development of paramedic skills. This last example raises another important point; design issues arise regardless of whether the customer comes to the service organization, the organization goes to the customer, or the service is delivered at arm's length. In fact one could argue that these are by definition design options. Refer back to service design elements and think about just how many design options there may be, not only for each element but combinations of the various elements. Service design can range from the simple and straightforward where the process is pre-packaged and standardized to the complex and variable where the process is subject to variety and customization. The options may apply to services as a whole or different parts within a particular service.

Although the design alternatives appear to be limitless, there will often be a trade-off between efficiency maximization and customer need satisfaction. Design options will also be increasingly influenced by developments in information technology. This, along with the degree and nature of customer involvement, will be the service design issues of the future.

3.8 Summary

Selecting a system is a subject of design and to arrive at a choice a range of elements must be considered. There have been, for a long time, several systems in operation. They have been developed in the manufacturing sector and attempts to apply them in services has been difficult. The problem is essentially one of finding the correct variables or characteristics that will allow service systems to be classified in design terms.

One feature that is particularly helpful in design is the idea of a front and back office. Service providers are often confronted with the dilemma of where to draw the line between operational efficiency and customer contact, the latter being a key consideration in any design decision.

The service blueprint is a valuable tool for specifying the precise details of a service. It enables the provider to determine critical/fail points the existence of which can often be attributed to a design fault.

The future for service design strategy will be between technology and people and whether services adopt a more production line approach.

Questions

1 Is it possible for a service organization to substitute technology for people or use a self-serve design and still keep a high customer focus (put the customer first)? Explain and support your answer with examples.

2 The four operating systems (service factory, mass service, service shop and professional service) face different challenges and problems. Explain and discuss what you think they are.

3 Identify the high and low contact operations of the following services:

   (a) an airline
   (b) an accounting firm
   (c) a college
   (d) car repair business
   (e) a dentist's surgery

4 Develop a blueprint for a service of your own choice. On completion consider:

   (a) whether all steps are really necessary
   (b) the extent to which standardization is possible, and advisable, throughout the process
   (c) the location of critical or pressure points and points where failure is likely to occur
   (d) measures of performance at each step.

References

1 Maister, D. H. and Lovelock, C. H. (1982). Managing facilitator services. *Sloan Management Review*, (Summer) pp. 19–31.

2 Schmenner, R. W. (1986). How can service businesses survive and prosper? *Sloan Management Review*, (Spring) pp. 21–32.

3 Thompson, J. D. (19670. *Organisations in Action*. McGraw Hill, New York.

4 Wolstenholme, S. M. (1988). The consultant customer – a new use for the customer in service operations. *Proceedings of the Operations Management Association Annual International Conference*, University of Warwick, pp. 192–203.

5 Chase R. B. and Tansik, D. A. (1983). The customer contact model for organisation design. *Management Science*, **29**(9) September, 1037–1050.

6 Chase, R. B. (1981). The customer contact approach to services: theoretical bases and practical extensions. *Operations Research* **29**(4), 698–705.

7 Larsson, R. and Bowen, D. E. (1989). Organisation and customer managing design and coordination of services. *Academy of Management Review*, **14**(2), 213–233.

8 Shostack, G. L. (1984). Designing services that deliver. *Harvard Business Review*, January–February, 133–139.

9 Quoted in Coleman, L. G. (1989). Blueprint gets foundation for better service and customer satisfaction. *Marketing News*, **23**(26) (December 18) 24.

10 Heskett, J. L., Sasser, W. and Hart, C. W. L. (1990). *Service Breakthroughs*. The Free Press, Macmillan Inc.

11 Kingmann-Brundage, J. (1989). Blueprinting for the bottom line. *Proceedings of AMA Annual Services Marketing Conference*.

12 Levitt, T. (1972). Production-line approach to service. *Harvard Business Review*, September–October, 41–52.

4
The service setting

4.1 Introduction

The setting and surroundings in which a service is delivered can be vital. It shapes expectations since it is the first tangible clue that the consumer is given about potential service delivery.

The control by the designer of corporate elements that form interior spaces can impact on the success of that delivery in a variety of ways. It can influence the client's or customer's perception of the particular service sector and can enhance the function, appropriateness and ambience of the activity.

It is important to regard design in terms of the possibilities it has to offer marketing. Every situation is unique and a 'painting by numbers' approach to design is inappropriate.

4.2 The service setting framework

On viewing and subsequently entering a bank, hotel, restaurant, or solicitor's office, customers will have reflected consciously or subconsciously on some or all of the following:

- What does the exterior say about what is on offer inside?
- Does it communicate, clearly, anything about the nature of the service?
- What does the interior communicate in terms of atmosphere?
- What mood/feeling is evoked?
- How is one expected to behave?

Many service providers have not given elaborate consideration to how the design of the service setting may affect consumer feelings and responses. Unfortunately, there are no ten commandments which would determine how a service setting should or should not be designed. From the customers' viewpoint it is still very much a matter of taste coupled with perceptions of what is appropriate. Nevertheless, just as companies want to know how and why customers respond to packaging, price, product, advertising, service organizations should develop understanding of customer responses to layout, furnishings, colour, light etc. Research should focus on overall impressions and feelings (Table 4.1) followed by an investigation of specific environmental ones.

The atmospheres displayed in Table 4.1 generate an expected response. The wider questions are:

- Does the environmental design always bring about the appropriate response?

Table 4.1 Atmosphere and feelings

Environmental atmosphere generated	Reaction in terms of customer feelings
Elegance	Status
Professionalism	Trust, security
Welcoming	Happiness, enjoyment
Sombre	Depressed, gloomy
Forbidding	Anxious
Warmth	Comfort
Lively	Inviting

- What is meant by 'elegance, professionalism, welcoming etc'?
- What aspects of the environment convey such atmospheres?
- How should a solicitor's office, hairdresser, hospital, advertising agency, social security office appear?
- Are there limits (in a cultural rather than physical sense) on design options for particular services?
- If there are limits, how severe should they be?

Specific environmental cues should be subjected to user evaluation. Research must reveal:

- What is important/unimportant
- What is liked/disliked
- How various aspects are rated on a scale of excellent through to poor.

Users' attitudes and perceptions can be gathered by open-ended discussion and/or measurement of scales. The following list is a sample of the kind of topics that could be covered:

- How adequate is the space? Does it lead to overcrowding and is this desirable or stressful?
- What is the effect of the layout on safety?
- How appropriate is the layout for the activity involved?
- Is the temperature comfortable or uncomfortable?
- Is the noise unobtrusive or uncomfortable?
- Is the lighting adequate?

The primary objective would be the determination of relationships between environmental conditions and behavioural outcomes.

Drawing on developments in decision-making in which customers were responding to more than simply the tangible product or service, Kotler[1] proposed that atmospheres be regarded as an important marketing tool. He suggests that, 'In many areas of marketing in the future, marketing planners will use spatial aesthetics as consciously and skilfully as they now use price, advertising, personal selling, public relations and other tools of marketing'. He maintains the atmosphere of a place affects purchase behaviour in three ways:

1 As an attention-creating medium – use of colours, noise etc to make it stand out.
2 As a message-creating medium – communicating with the intended audience, level of concern for customers etc.
3 As an affect-creating medium – use of colours, sounds etc to create or heighten an appetite for certain goods, services or experiences.

Kotler concludes with an example of antique retailing. It would seem that there is more to atmospherics than meets the eye!

> Many antique dealers also make use of 'organizational chaos' as an atmospheric principle for selling their wares. The buyer enters the store and sees a few nice pieces and a considerable amount of junk. The nice pieces are randomly scattered in different parts of the store. The dealer gives the impression, through his prices and his talk, that he doesn't really know values. The buyer therefore browses quite systematically, hoping to spot an undiscovered Old Master hidden among the dusty canvasses of third rate artists. He ends up buying something that he regards as a value. Little does he know that the whole atmosphere has been arranged to create a sense of hidden treasures.

Supermarkets, of course, have known for some time, that consumption behaviour can be manipulated by the judicious use of lighting, space etc.

What this means is that when planning the design of a service setting, service providers should have in mind a framework that will assist debate over the impact of the physical surroundings.[2] They should consider this design in terms of the three headings in Figure 4.1.

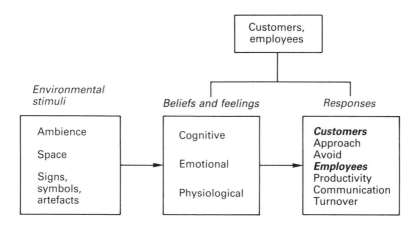

Figure 4.1 A service setting framework for understanding behaviour and relationships. Adapted from Bitner, J. (1992)[2]

Environmental stimuli

- ambience – temperature, air quality, noise, music, odour
- space – layout, equipment, furnishings
- signs, symbols, artefacts – e.g. style of decor, personal objects displayed.

Beliefs and feelings

- Cognitive – beliefs
- Emotional – mood, likes/dislikes, attitudes
- Physiological – pain, comfort, ease of movement

Responses

- Approach – willingness to stay, explore, interact and subsequently return
- Avoid – avoid interactions, a wish to get out and not return.

It may be that users of a service are largely indifferent to the physical surroundings – 'it's just what we expected'. It is the times when expectations are not met that require attention. Consumers may see the setting as an extravagance reflected in an 'inflated' price. Alternatively, it may be seen as so impoverished as to cast doubt on the quality of service. Even the credibility and competence of the employees may be called into question. Such matters as these should not be left unanswered as customers and employees need to feel comfortable and secure in the knowledge that the physical surroundings are appropriate for the service on offer.

4.3 Elements of the service setting

Spatial considerations/planning

Most design training centres around historical precedent and ideas sourcing from either nature and/or mathematics. Precedent has meant that the most common source of creativity has come from a vast visual dictionary that has evolved from concepts being tested and re-tested until principles are established. Symmetry, proportion, rhythm, texture, colour, and other fundamentals can be considered, combined and developed to present the viewer or user with an intellectual, emotional response that is perceived as visual quality. This quality can be manipulated or controlled by the designer to create environments that elicit desired responses from the subject (in our case the service user/client or customer).

Space planning

In an ideal world, the interior designer works alongside the architect from the initial planning concept stage – by doing so, coordination of the arrangement of all of the interior elements with the architectural features is assured. A large proportion of the sites that the interior designer finds himself faced with however do not offer this luxury – most jobs are concerned with refurbishment of spaces and buildings originally designed for other purposes. Certain 'rules' do make up the fundamental approach to the planning process.

Generally speaking, the planning exercise with most interiors falls into five categories:

1 The identification of the problem (the brief)
2 The synthesis of the solution
3 The design development
4 The solution
5 The testing of the efficiency of the solution.

The identification of the problem will fall into several sub-sections. For example:

- What are the functional requirements?
- How will the users circulate?
- What does the client wish to feel like?
- What does he wish to see?
- What does he want others to see?
- What is going on in adjoining spaces?
- What are the safety and legislative requirements?
- Are exterior spaces involved?
- What kind of lighting, heating and other services are required?
- What is the desired 'mood' or character of the space(s)?
- What is the likely budget?
- How long must the scheme last before refurbishment?
- Are future developments, growth or flexibility prerequisites?

The synthesis or sketch designs of the planning process can take several forms. The most common is to formulate a graphic or schematic model which enables the designer to rank the requirements. Usually this process begins without regard to the physical constraints of the particular site and the designer can indicate space relationships and traffic throughput on a purely functional level and can test his ideas against the model formed in the brief.

The development phase occurs when the designer transcribes his findings from this schematic visual into the constraints of the actual space. The fitting of furniture and equipment into the space, establishing correct circulation routes, working out all the complex requirements to enable the drafting of a floor plan and associated working drawings and details.

The solution begins to take shape when all of the other phases are in place. It lasts from the time of client approval to the opening ceremony of the successfully completed building.

The final phase is the testing and modifying of the solution when the user or client can be interrogated and suggestions for improvement taken on board. This is as important a phase as any of the other four described. A list of priorities can be formulated without being dogmatic in terms of 'generalized rules'.

Circulation is of primary importance – traffic levels and direction of the user – but also of allowing sufficient space around objects, equipment and furniture to enable them to be used efficiently and safely. Unobstructed approaches to doorways, corridors, and escape routes are obvious considerations. The designer above all hopes to create interest and a particular ambience to the space which is appropriate to its function. A sense of scale, balance of proportion and interaction between adjoining space is important. Simplicity in planning is invariably successful and can lay the foundation for all of the other elements which make up the service setting.

Furniture/equipment/furnishings

Furniture can host people, or it can form a barrier between people. Furniture can host equipment such as computers, cables and cash registers. Furniture can protect precious or delicate objects. It can project or display. Furniture can be welcoming or austere and can have a great deal to say about the status of the owner or user.

Places, tools, furniture and decoration are interdependent elements of our lives. They contribute to our quality of life by dint of functionality and aesthetic enrichment. They can be designed, controlled, and become tools to further the designer's intentions.

Furniture and equipment become of architectural proportions when one considers the cost of subdividing rented space. Often modern refurbishments have a 'designed-in' longevity – two years, five years, ten years. The cost of partitioning and its accompanying rigidity soon provides good reasons for considering the functions of walls and doors being replaced with free-standing furniture elements. Most of the established thinking to do with the subdivision of space is fast becoming outdated with the proliferation of office and business automation. Wide, open spaces are no longer required. The need to keep people in proximity is redundant as office information now flows down cables. In a modern building with a life expectancy of say thirty to forty years, the initial capital cost is only 10 per cent of the complete cost. Ninety per cent will be devoted to staff costs associated with maintaining a working environment and the machines and technology necessary for the purpose.

In general terms there is incredible freedom of choice available to the occupier of a commercial interior – artificial environmental qualities (light, ventilation, heating etc) are controllable. Heights and inclinations of chairs and worktops are variable, furniture and equipment can be 'high tec' or soft and domestic in nature. The only reason for producing ranges in different materials or colours is to allow for personal or corporate choice – a marketing strategy!

Technological development has wrought overwhelming change to the service setting; the office-based service industry means that the office can now be a club, it can be a factory, a series of cosy meeting places, a street-scape or a market place. This choice will, hopefully, reflect some of the functions of the particular service. Other changes wrought by the shrinking of class differentials are the loss of importance of status – a bank is now a money shop and one expects to meet a bank manager on equal terms: not so 15 years ago! Financial whiz kids are more dependent on the micro chips and cell phone than the old school tie!

Perceptions of equipment are also changing. The typewriter keyboard was invented in the 1860s – this meant the standardization of letters – obvious but nonetheless staggering. The mechanical keyboard is now electronic and pressure requirements are now infinitesimal in comparison to the earlier typewriters but operator posture and ergonomics have changed to accommodate the new requirements. Operators rarely view paper, displays are on VDUs. Five or ten years ago an operator in the service sector would probably search for documents in a filing system, make notes, write letters and memos, use the telephone, exchange words with colleagues and be constantly on the move. Now as a link in the technology-based environment, eye contact might only be between customer/client or VDU and the service operator. The office now is still a 'shelter' to its occupants but is also a 'display window' to the clients and customers of that particular service sector. The demonstration of the efficiency of the now visible 'working parts' of the organization is a tangible sales promotion tool. The idea of 'front office' as the only area visible to the client is long gone. The customer has also experienced the impact of technological change. Most people have drawn money from a 'hole in the wall', spoken to an answerphone or received a computer print-out on some occasion.

Lighting

This is often a key element in the design of the service setting.

The design and specification of lighting schemes is a specialized activity and is developed by a process similar to that described in the previous section on furniture.

When considering lighting design for a service setting the following factors must be taken into account: daylighting, colour, the nature of the activity to be performed in the space/s, the service provider's perception of the task, levels of vision, and finally ambience, the desired mood.

1 Daylighting and the way in which it is controlled influence heat, glare, penetration, visibility, and the perception of colour – most schemes take account of the orientation of the building to the sun, its changes daily and seasonally, as well as poor daylighting conditions and darkness.
2 The direction and strength of daylight affect the perception of colour.
3 The particular activities to be undertaken in the space under consideration must be clearly defined; accuracy, speed, safety, recognition etc.
4 What does the organization really want from the space? Is it to sell visual satisfaction or is it to sell hamburgers? Is it to indicate the conservative solidity of the world of financial services or is it to reassure people about to board an aeroplane?

5   The level of vision required can depend upon the nature of the task. It can also depend upon the age of the client or customer. If the task requires detailed work from the customer or service provider then strong light is required. If the background setting is well lit then even greater intensity of light will be required for the detailed work as the eyes become accustomed to the relative lessening of the contrast.
6   In many situations the achievement of the desired mood or ambience of the space is paramount. A church or library would generally exude a peaceful calm whereas a fast-food diner or modern music store would wish to create a youthful, exciting, gregarious atmosphere.

On a scientific level, the perception of colour and lighting is governed by a vast array of data such as the depth of penetration of daylight, glare or the reflectance value of the surface that light is falling on and the psychology of colour contrasts. Other constraints on the design of lighting systems have to do with variables such as energy conservation, heat gain and ease of maintenance programmes.

On the designer's level, there is the additional burden of wanting to create magic. The creative use of light can bring an interior to life – the interaction of light and shadow can sculpt, can expand scale, can highlight, can wall wash, can silhouette, can attract the curious, can sparkle and can move merchandise.

Colour

Colour has a language of its own. Much like music, it can evoke moods and emotions – excitement, happiness, serenity, sadness. We daily refer to 'feeling blue', 'seeing red', 'being green with envy', 'in the pink' etc.

The symbolic nature of colour has for centuries fulfilled a role in religion, magic, heraldry, communication, and ritual, as well as being a major player in creative processes.

The 'fashion' element of colour use is a subject in its own right but suffice to say that as with most fashions, its use can be traced in cycles. Ancient classical architecture of the Greek and Italian Empires used brilliant, bold colours. This was followed by muted, earth colours. Renaissance Italy revived boldness and we can compare the affluent 1960s in the West with the sombreness of the 1980s.

Colour composes three elements:

1   Hue – the name of the colour, e.g. red, blue, yellow.
2   Value – the lightness or darkness of a colour.
3   Chroma – the intensity of strength or purity of colour.

There are numerous theories about the way in which colour works. It is not sufficient, however, to consider colour without an understanding of the effects of light, the discrimination of relative colours – that is to say the different appearance of one colour or hue which is in the proximity of another hue, the spatial and the emotional effects of colour.

It is always dangerous to pragmatize when discussing a notion such as colour and any statements that might appear as 'rules' should only be read as examples in the context of suggestions for the particular service settings discussed.

The effect of light

If lighting values in an interior have not been well thought out, any creative application of colour will be in vain. Well designed lighting, however, enhances the choice of colour. Low lighting levels with warm colours provide a friendly, intimate environment that evokes an atmosphere of relaxation and rest. Soft lighting with warm colours enhances and flatters the complexion. Warm colours (pinks, oranges, reds and yellows) generally 'work' with low levels of illumination. The converse is true in that blues and greens generally 'don't work' in low lighting situations and complexions appear pallid and unflattering. These same colours applied under high levels of illumination, however, can create good working environments and under 'white light' make for a more natural appearance. Consider fruit and vegetable displays in supermarkets – strong, white light against 'artificial grass'.

The colour white, like its opposite, black can be one of hundreds with different chroma values but the same white sample viewed in bright sunshine will appear as grey if taken into a dimly lit environment.

Colour in relation to other colours

Colour can only be measured in relation to other colours and while an adult with normal vision can distinguish probably two thousand colours, this experience is, at best, highly subjective. Colour can never be isolated and the resultant experience modifies the perception. Look at a strong red sample for about a minute and then focus on a white surface – the resultant green vision is the after-image of a colour's opposite or complement. A colour always has to be considered in relation to its neighbour in any successful lighting design. In simplistic terms one can say that colour schemes that are largely monochromatic (different values of the same hue) are the safest solution. Next best in terms of little risk are schemes which rely on using colours that are adjacent in the spectrum and therefore have one hue in common. The riskiest and therefore sometimes the most rewarding or interesting schemes are those based on complementary colours or those of high contrast. This almost elementary appeal perhaps stems from experiences and memories we had as children. Nature of course employs exotic schemes in the plant world and colours of courtship or warning in animals, fish, birds and insects.

A further problem in relation to controlling colour in the service setting is that the units are required to be balanced so that adjacent rooms have some relationship or harmony. Generally speaking, large spaces are better balanced by using a scheme of soft, low intensity colour with strong, vibrant hues reserved for accent or highlight value. Again as a general rule, background colours are selected and developed first for the large planar areas (floor/ceiling/walls) with 'accessories' (equipment, furniture, curtains, pictures) figuring as stress or accent points.

Optical and emotional values of colour

Warmth and coolness are easily distinguished by colour choice so that red, orange, yellow and their family are warm; green, blue, violet and their family are cool. A finer division can occur at junctions in the spectrum so that red-violet and yellow-green can occupy both camps or form a bridge between warm-cool.

Red indicates danger, excitement, stop etc. – the pulse rate and blood pressure of a viewer increase when shown the colour. Conversely, green indicates peacefulness, safety, go etc., likewise for blue. Perceived sizes of areas of colour vary with the selection of hue – warm colours appear to advance towards the viewer, cool colours to retract or recede. Colour choice can therefore be used to modify the perceived size and shape of areas.

It will come as no surprise to the reader to learn that these colour theories can be, and are, used as a functional tool in the design of interiors. Colour is utilized to improve efficiency in the workplace, colour can help people to relax, colour can help lower accident rates, aid convalescence, help market merchandise or create an appetite where food is served. Specifics will be discussed under the five colours selected.

In their book based on the television series *The Colour Eye*, Cumming and Porter[3] give some valuable insights into colour psychology. For example:

Red – the colour of fire and passion, suggesting activity, energy, joy. It is used by interior designers to increase comfort levels in unheated spaces and is also regarded (along with pink) as good for restaurants, especially the fast-food variety. One study showed that red-stimulated diners tend to eat more quickly and move on for the next person.
Orange – although researchers have claimed that an orange environment improves social behaviour, cheers the spirit and lessens hostility and irritability, it is seldom used by professional designers.
Yellow – conflicting evidence here which on the one hand suggests its ideal stimulative effect where concentration is required. However, if used too strongly those in its environment are likely to get 'stressed up'.
Green – symbolizes the natural world and is widely believed to be a calming hue. Ideal for areas where relaxation is required and along with blue is found to enhance our appetite; thus good for dining areas.
Blue – symbolizes authority and implies truth, prudence and wisdom – ideal for banks and building societies. It is considered as having a calming effect which makes it ideally suited for hospital cardiac units.
Purple – regarded as disturbing and psychologically 'difficult'. In a Swedish study it was the most disliked colour in terms of environmental settings.

Signage

Graphically transmitted messages or signage are fundamental to communication in all areas of the service sector. The visual appearance, the placing, the

physical construction, the colour, lighting and choice of typeface are all important and interdependent.

'Letters are signs for sounds' is a well known quote and serves as an apt definition of what signs are about. A good sign is one which imparts information as simply and directly as possible. As with colour and spatial considerations, letter forms can evoke visual and emotional responses.

Signs, unlike print, are read quickly and therefore the choice of weight of the letter form is paramount. It should seek to provide maximum clarity and contrast from the sign's surroundings.

Signs can be of some importance in many service settings. The 'you are here' map (YAH) is designed to answer the questions, 'Where am I?' and 'How do I get from here to there?'. The trouble with many of these maps apart from not being particularly well designed is that they are not always aligned with the territory. The difficulty seems to be with the fact that YAH maps are usually placed vertically on a wall. 'If', as stated by Levine, Marchon and Hanley,[4] 'the direction which is in front of you is up, on the vertical map, the map and the terrain are aligned and the map will be relatively easy to use. If, on the other hand, the direction in front of you is down on the map, they are contraligned, the map will be relatively difficult to use'. Contralignment and alignment can be demonstrated quite simply (Figure 4.2).

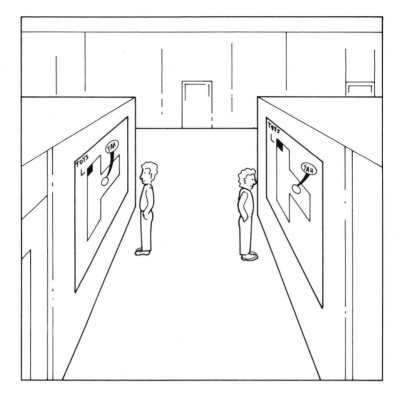

Figure 4.2 *Placement and misplacement of YAH maps. Source: Levine, M., Marchon, I. and Hanley, G. (1984)[4]*

4.4   Three service settings

Financial services

The public interface with financial services especially in banking and other high street institutions has undergone radical change in the last generation.

We have witnessed the metamorphosis from elegant, dark, expensive and foreboding interiors to the 'fun money shop' era of the past decade to the current trend of serious design, professional service and interaction between people.

During the 1980s, the yuppie mentality was all – High Street banks and building societies resembled retail establishments and nightclubs in contrast to the Victorian approach of previous decades. Neon light, distressed surface finishes and dreamy uplighting housed high-tech machines that obviated the need for personal contact. Banks and the like became 'take-away' or 'fast money' outlets resembling the franchised fast-food chains that proliferate in every shopping mall or provincial high street. There is no doubt that the money business itself has undergone radical change.

Building societies initiated the change by offering attractive interiors. The banks have had to follow to continue to compete successfully.

In general terms, layouts tend not to vary and follow a common design. Entrances have become lobbies that house self-service cash dispensers (and other routine transactions – deposits, statement provision etc). These are often fitted in fairly sturdy surroundings that recognize the out-of-banking-hours activities and the need for anti-theft, anti-vandal and in some cases anti-weather protection. The reception area is found behind this area and this first point of customer–staff interface is afforded adventurous front-line reception desking that is generally modern and colourful. The transition for the customer is marked by a change in floor covering from marble or tile or hard surface to soft surface such as carpeting of a warm hue. Wall surfaces likewise will blend from a stone cladding or laminate surface to a textile base or wallpaper and lighting will change from security conscious task lighting to uplit pools that are warmer and more 'domestic' in context. Beyond the reception point is the area design for financial consultations where bandit-proof glass screening and counter tops are being replaced with informal, low-level, comfortable and discrete consulting areas. The customer will feel that he is being afforded status and personal attention. Much of the brutality of design approach has disappeared to be superseded by a thoughtful more gentle approach where the customer is allowed to feel less threatened.

Interestingly, one area of comparison with the fast-food industry remains. Behind the area designated for personal consultations, the working area of the institution often remains as open-plan and clearly visible personnel movements reflect the exposed working kitchen seen in Mcdonald's and Burger King establishments.

The financial service sector is also responding to the rapidity of change by generally reviewing interior design policy every five years or thereabouts and recognizes that the 'service setting' is an increasingly important asset to its marketing strategy.

Fast-food restaurants

Born in the USA out of the hot-dog stand or lunch-wagon genre, the fast-food chains and franchises have spread throughout the world.

Previously the menu revolved around 'burgers and fries'. The quick service restaurant industry has changed out of all recognition since the early part of the 1980s. The 'yuppy youth' culture demanded healthy food, salads, baked potatoes, pulses and pastas, fresh fruit and vegetables.

The menu says it all. The interior design reflects the menu and what it says is 'quick turnover'.

The successful design is the one which attracts the customers in to the restaurant, organizes their traffic flow, creates just enough (and no more) comfort, arranges seating configurations that are economic and then hustles the customer out!

Fast-food outlets have produced a lot of innovative designs. Successful schemes (financially rewarding *and* aesthetically pleasing) invariably combine slick and lively ambience with often whimsical, youthful, colourful surroundings enhanced with a good portion of pop music or musak.

Wall and floor surfaces are invariably hard – usually tile or laminate for durability, ease of maintenance and cleaning. Soft base colours always serve to contrast with a dramatic slash of colour red or green. All interior materials are simple and appear inexpensive. Seats are just too short and just too close to the next table to encourage customers not to linger. An emphasis is often on serve yourself and dispose of the debris yourself in self-consciously sign-posted receptacles.

The kitchen is the focal point, always busy, clean in appearance and in some instances forming a stage or 'altar' in the case of pizza ovens.

Lighting is brutally harsh and no attempt is made to pool light over individual tables as this would create an intimate ambience and invite the diners to dally too long. Graphics are over-sized, unmistakable and again centre around blown-up versions of the menu.

In this industry, success or failure may depend on the ability of the service setting to stimulate a speedy throughput of customers.

Hotels

Hotels have also undergone a tumultuous change in recent periods.

The total design package employed in the creation of a hotel is awe-inspiring. The architect and designer today must be capable of creating a village within four walls. Landscaping, construction and fitting of offices, lobbies, themed restaurants, coffee shops, guest rooms, suites, conference centres, gymnasiums, swimming pools, casinos, lifts, foyers, rest rooms, shopping malls, bars, bathrooms and all associated services must present a cohesive theme that identifies the corporate strategy of the operator or franchisee.

The entrance to a hotel must invite the client in. It should appear and feel gracious and extravagant yet afford some weather protection. Resort hotels that double as conference centres are different to urban hotels that are one-night stops for business people or vacationers. Whatever the location, the space must be designed with flexibility to cater for a multitude of users.

First impressions last! The reception area which greets the guest is in itself a multifunctional space – lobby, reception/welcoming/check-in/out facilities, baggage handling, and lift entrances. Staircases all have to be blended to welcome rather than overwhelm the guest. If too sumptuous the guest may baulk at what he thinks the room rates might be.

Signposting is important, making it easy for the guest to find the entrance from the car park and then the check-in. Graphics can help but nothing works as well as careful attention to the detailed arrangement of the functions listed. Sculpting a huge space that is multifunctional can be useful. Generally conceived as atrium spaces, the lobby has to double as 'my club' to the guest, a place to meet friends, colleagues or business associates, somewhere to read the financial papers, somewhere to hail a taxi from etc. This space is the key which indicates the status and standing of the particular hotel or group. It signifies what is happening behind the front of house facade.

Spatial excitement is important, sparkling lighting, judicious use of planting and water, large vistas broken down into intimate club-like private spaces. Comfortable 'classic' armchairs and sofas, rich materials like stone, leather and glass all bound together in muted autumnal colour groupings. People respond to small spaces they can commandeer – no one will sit on a large sofa that is isolated in the middle of an area.

Lifts and their foyer areas are important in the marketing strategy. People have to congregate and wait. The designer has to recognize that people will fidget, lean on walls, smoke, deposit luggage etc and the surface qualities and their maintenance will reflect this wear. Mirrors work well in this instance. People generally are not bored if they can contemplate their own reflections. They also provide the opportunity to observe fellow travellers with discretion.

Coffee shops differ from fast-food type outlets in that they offer a different pace and can usually be operated by a skeleton staff (often 24 hours). It is likely that floor surfaces will be in a soft fibre which can be easily cleaned. Lighting will be very controllable to enable staff to ring the changes reflecting time of day or night. Unlike the main restaurants, however, the ambience cannot be too elegant or sumptuous but will rather reflect its purpose and offer a feeling of cleanliness and purposefulness. Bright colours and sharp forms help, and the treatment of graphics, menu, dishes and table settings reinforces a strong visual identity.

Guest rooms form the very raison d'etre of the hotel and take on a domestic scale in contrast to the public areas of the hotel. Sizes are determined by economics. Lighting can be employed to pool discrete areas of the room or wash uncluttered walls. The use of vertical furniture as opposed to our usual norm of horizontal can make good use of limited space.

Some hotels group rooms on colour themes so that individual preferences can be catered for – this can present problems if for example the guest wants a blue room and they have all been let. If however there is only one scheme repeated through the hotel, the guest is rarely disappointed since he has no choice. A single palette of colour reduces costs and facilitates easy refurbishment or replacement. A hotel is always a transitory place and strong or bold schemes rarely achieve success since the guest usually wants to relax or feel at home as soon as possible and does not want to spend (even unconscious) time adapting to foreign surroundings.

Hotels are invariably filled with corridors. The design must aim to make the guest feel more at home; foreshorten the vista, break up the long, narrow spaces by changes in ceiling form or height, texture or colour of floorcoverings, and lighting intensity. The designer can treat the corridor as a gallery and position stimulating pictures or other graphics at strategic points.

The designs reconcile all of the varied guests' expectations, function, glamour, excitement, comfort and service.

4.5 Summary

Where a service takes place is now receiving the attention it deserves. Designers are being called upon by organizations to create an environment that will support and reflect the service being offered.

Atmospheres must be engendered that will stimulate appropriate customer feelings and reactions. To achieve this the designer applies his knowledge and skills in respect of space idealization, lighting, colour and so on.

There are no ten commandments which state that different service activities should be designed in particular ways. It will be for the customer, in the final analysis, to decide whether the design has any meaning and impact on what is being received.

The three 'case studies' emphasize the point that there is no exclusive design for a certain service. However, there will be clues from the selection of colours, lighting and the layout of space etc as to the nature of the activity in operation.

Questions

1 Can you think of a service setting that, in your opinion, represented an affront to your senses; a design you regarded as particularly inappropriate and not at all what you expected?

2 Using the framework in Figure 4.1 conduct a limited survey, say 50, designed to elicit the views of customers and/or employees about a particular service setting. Give some thought to how the information should be collected and after completion reflect on the value of what has been obtained.

3 Select a particular service and consider 'the message' you think it wishes to promote through its choice of colour, layout, graphics, furniture, lighting etc.

4 What do you feel should be the key considerations in the design of service settings of the future?

References

1 Kotler, P. (1973). Atmospherics as a marketing tool. *Journal of Retailing*, **49**(4), 48–64.

2 Bitner, M. J. (1992). Servicescapes: the impact of physical surroundings on customers and employees. *Journal of Marketing*, **56** (April), 57–71.

3 Cumming, R. and Porter, T. (1990). *The Colour Eye*. BBC Books, London.

4 Levine, M., Marchon, I. and Hanley, G. (1984). The placement and misplacement of you-are-here maps. *Environment and Behaviour*, **16**(2) 139–157.

Part Two
Managing Customer and Service Interaction

5
Service quality

5.1 Introduction

It is widely acknowledged that efforts to define and measure the quality of tangible products, as distinct from services, have proved more successful. The characteristics of services have made the determination of what constitutes quality that much more difficult and thereby its measurement less than complete. To increase our understanding and to enable practical steps to be taken two things need to be present:

- Specification of the determinants of service quality
- Measurable quality standards set.

Achievement in these two areas will vary depending on whether the focus is:

- A low contact or a high contact service, e.g. a fast-food outlet versus an education course
- Process or output.

Determining the process and output quality of a fast-food restaurant is arguably more straightforward than an education course.

Whatever the service, it is useful to bear in mind the following questions when it comes to quality:

- What is the service supposed to do?
- What does the service actually do?

Quality then refers to the extent to which a service is what it claims to be and does what it claims to do. It must not be confused with grade. For example the quality of a library cannot be judged in an abstract way by, say, counting the number of Shakespeare volumes possessed and subtracting the number of light romances. Instead the prime aspect of quality is whether the library provides people with what they want – it is a good library if it does and a bad library if it does not.[1]

In recent research conducted into the management of the UK service sector, companies were asked to explain what the word 'quality' meant to them. Only a minority actually mentioned the customer, i.e. quality had an external focus. Responses included satisfied customers, repeat business, exceeding customer expectations and no complaints. The majority of respondents mentioned factors that are undoubtedly there to help achieve satisfied customers, e.g. polite competent staff, well resourced service, product knowledge and responsiveness.[2]

5.2   The impact of service quality

Quality needs to be understood and managed throughout a service organization. Four areas in particular may serve as an arena within which the question of quality can be addressed (Figure 5.1).

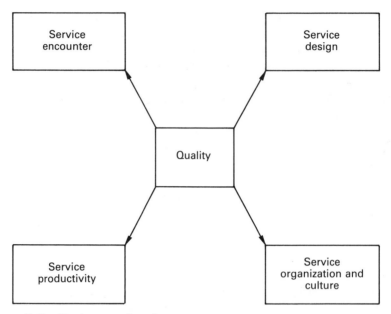

Figure 5.1   *The impact of quality*

Service encounter _ the customer interacts with animate (the service employees) and inanimate objects (the physical evidence, e.g. an information sign).

*   How knowledgeable and courteous is the service employee?
*   How effective is the sign in terms of visibility, information provided, positioning?
*   How can the customer contribute to the quality of the encounter?
*   What contribution do script theory and role theory make?

Service design – the customer goes through a process to obtain a service.

*   How well designed is the process?
*   Is there a blueprint/flowchart of the process?
*   To what extent is there flexibility in the system?
*   Does the process require customization or standardization?

Service productivity – there is a relationship between the quantity and quality of goods or services produced and the quality of resources used to produce them.

- What are the possible relationships between changes in quality and changes in quantity? i.e. if quantity increases (number of patients seen by a general practitioner), what effect could that have on the quality of service?
- What role should the customer play in the productivity equation?

Service organization and culture – the culture of an organization and the way it is organized can affect the quality of service.

- How do the various organizational cultures (power, role, achievement and support) act as a key to understanding the kind of service produced?
- What characteristics/features of an organization enable it to respond positively to customer needs and deliver a quality service?

Another way to consider quality and its impact throughout an organization is to put the customer at the centre of the process and highlight the number of encounters, or 'moments of truth' he or she may have with the organization. Consider the case of a student in an educational institution (Figure 5.2). Expectations of both the educational institution and potential student can be determined at the beginning. We can then compare these expectations with the perceptions of students and staff during and at the end of the course.

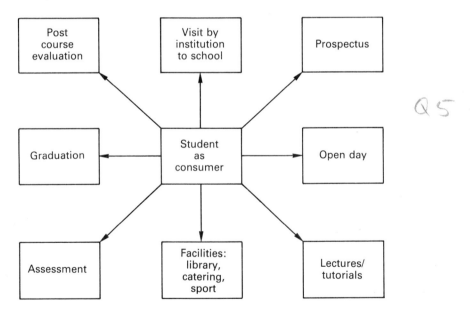

Figure 5.2 Student contact with service

This kind of exercise can be undertaken with any service organization. The benefit of doing so is that it disciplines the service provider to think of how all aspects of the organization contribute to service quality. The customer can be asked how important each part of the service is and how well the organization performs on each aspect.

5.3 A model of service quality

To enhance knowledge of service quality and encourage investigation of the key issues, a model has been developed[3] (Figure 5.3).

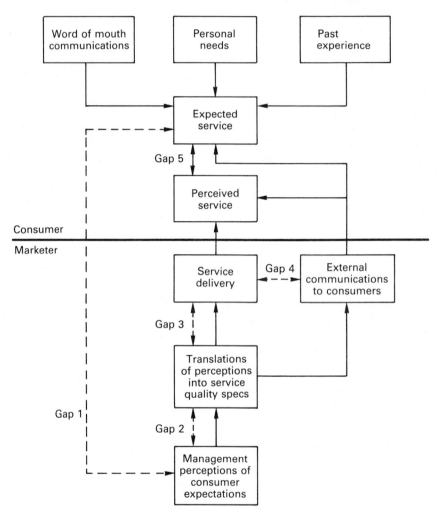

Figure 5.3 *Service quality model. Source: Parasuraman, A., Zeithaml, V. A. and Berry, L. L. (1985)*[3]

Its key features are:

1 The identification of key attributes of service quality from a management and consumer perspective.
2 Highlighting the gaps between consumers and service providers with particular reference to perceptions and expectations.
3 Understanding the implications for service management of closing the gaps.

The service quality model was developed from research undertaken by the authors. The most important insight obtained was that:

A set of key discrepancies or gaps exists regarding executive perceptions of service quality and the tasks associated with service delivery to consumers. These gaps can be major hurdles in attempting to deliver a service which consumers would perceive as being of high quality.

The following is a brief account of the gaps:

Gap 1 – this is the overall gap between service provider and consumer. It states that many organizations just do not understand what consumers expect in a service.

Gap 2 – service organizations often experience great difficulty in even meeting far less exceeding consumer expectations. This is invariably attributed to a number of factors but the authors cite three in particular – absence of total management commitment to service quality, lack of resources, and excessive demand.

Gap 3 – even when formal standards or specifications for maintaining service quality are in existence, the delivery of a quality service is by no means certain. The main reason given is that the performance of customer contact personnel can be so variable.

Gap 4 – advertising and other forms of communication by a service organization can affect consumer expectations. The danger is that promises made are not kept. Many service organizations use the brochure or prospectus (some very glossy) for communicating with potential customers. It should be a statement of what the customer will receive, not an attractive set of promises that cannot be delivered.

Gap 5 – this gap represents the key challenge, to ensure good service quality the provider must meet or exceed customer expectations. Perceived service quality is the result of the consumer's comparison of expected service with perceived service delivery.

5.4 Causes of service quality problems

Several reasons have been put forward as explanations of poor service quality:[4]

Inseparability of production and consumption and labour intensity

The provision of service, as distinct from the manufacture of goods, occurs in the presence of customers. Inevitably as with any human encounter, problems do arise. The service employee may exhibit poor presentational skills, conduct himself improperly and dress inappropriately. All of these and others may influence the customer's perception of service quality. The intensive involvement of humans in service delivery will always have the potential to pose problems for quality.

Inadequate services to intermediate or internal customers

The front-line employee is by definition at the 'sharp-end' of the service delivery system. To execute the service effectively, the employee requires proper support from further back in the organization (Figure 5.4).

Figure 5.4 *Importance of employee support in the execution of effective service*

The support will emanate from the main management functions (operations, marketing and human resource) and involve:

1 equipment e.g. tools, materials, uniforms
2 skills training
3 information e.g. of a new service launch's operating procedures.

Communication gaps

Good communication is the life-blood of a healthy organization, and its contacts with customers. However, it is a problem of some magnitude and manifests itself in the following ways:

1 Failure to deliver promises made
2 Failure to keep a customer informed
3 Failure to communicate in a manner the customer can understand
4 Failure to listen.

Viewing customers as statistics

For a service organization there are often compelling reasons for offering a standardized service, not least of which are the efficiencies to be gained from treating a large number of customers in a standardized manner. For the customer, this approach to service delivery is often welcomed. By contrast, customization of the service seeks to recognize the particular needs of individual customers. Service organizations should be sensitive to how their customers feel about how they are treated. A remark made by a student perhaps exemplifies the issue. He said, 'In my two years at college, not once did a lecturer recognize me by name'.

Short-run view of the business

Organizations in general, and particularly in the UK, take a short run view of the business when it comes to performance evaluation. Management are frequently required to meet targets on a yearly basis. The obsession inevitably becomes one of cost reduction and productivity increases to meet a profit target. This is understandable but detrimental to building a quality service in the longer term.

5.5 How to improve service quality

Improving service quality is certainly not a simple, straightforward exercise. It will have implications for the whole culture of the organization. Some ideas put forward are worthy of consideration:[4]

Identifying primary quality determinants

Knowing what determines quality is, of course, crucial. However, consumers and producers of services do not necessarily perceive service quality on common dimensions and even when they do hold common dimensions, they evaluate them differently.

Managing customer expectations

To attract custom, organizations are often tempted to raise customer expectations. Companies make promises to consumers on aspects of their business that they think the customer will value in order to give the organization a competitive advantage. However care must be exercised in making promises to customers. For example, consider the following sample taken from the Yellow Pages Directory:

'Nobody does it better'
'The very best of care'
'Immediate delivery from stock'
'On time – every time'
'You can't beat our service'

They are both difficult to measure and raise consumer expectations unrealistically. As a rule it is better to exceed customer expectations than to let the customer down.

Managing evidence

The 'evidence' from the viewpoint of a service organization includes many things and consumers look to these as an indicator of what the service might be like (pre-service expectation) and what, in fact, the service was like after using it (post-service evaluation).

Physical and human evidence play a significant part in image formation. Retailers are interested in several aspects relating to architecture and design for promoting an image. Similarly, atmosphere influences image. The term 'atmospherics' has been coined to define the conscious design of space to influence buyers. The atmosphere influences the buyers' expectations and perceptions of the service. For example lawyers' offices and banks are designed to communicate confidence.

Various factors such as colours, music, furnishing, space etc. can evoke a variety of feelings about the service organization, e.g. friendliness, austerity, sobriety, authority, rationality, stability, flexibility. One author stresses that it will be the physical aspects of a service that will allow us to make sense of it and we expect the physical signs to be in tune with the nature of the service. Incongruity can make us uncertain and uncomfortable.

Educating consumers about the service

Helping the customer to understand the service would appear to be a *sine qua non* for dispensing a quality service. However, for many services, e.g. garage repair business, professional services, the challenge can be a daunting one and one that perhaps they are not willing to confront. Equally, the willingness of the customer 'to be educated' requires evaluation along with their capacity to assimilate the nature of the service being delivered.

Developing a quality culture

Quality is not delivered in a vacuum but through an organization with all its imperfections. Commitment to quality must pervade the whole organization. A number of institutional factors can either help or hinder the provision of quality service. They are:[5]

1 Human – job descriptions, selection, training, rewards, career path.
2 Organization/structure – integration/coordination of functions and reporting structure
3 Measurement – complaint and customer satisfaction tracking and performance evaluation.
4 Systems support – technical, computers, databases.
5 Services – value added, range and quality, standards of performance, satisfying needs and expectations.
6 Programmes – complaint management, sales/promotional tools, management tools.

7 Communication (internal) – policies and procedures, feedback within the organization.
8 Communication (external) – consumer education, creation of expectations, image.

A useful tool for identifying the causes of poor service quality is the fishbone diagram (Figure 5.5).

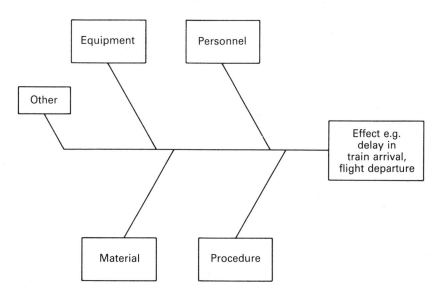

Figure 5.5 *Fishbone diagram: cause and effect analysis. (Identify the effect and then attribute causes in the five major categories, e.g. personnel – late arrival of crew; equipment – mechanical failures; other – weather conditions; material – late fuel; procedures – delayed check-in.)*

All that is required is the identification of a poor output and then work backwards in order to attribute the cause(s). It is versatile in that it can be applied to a range of situations. When several such analyses are conducted, a distribution of the causes can be plotted on a Pareto histogram (Figure 5.6).

Automating quality

The variability in quality service emanating from human inadequacy can be avoided through automation. Before such a decision is made, research needs to establish which parts of the service require the human touch and which require automation. The danger is that automation takes over for reasons other than automation.

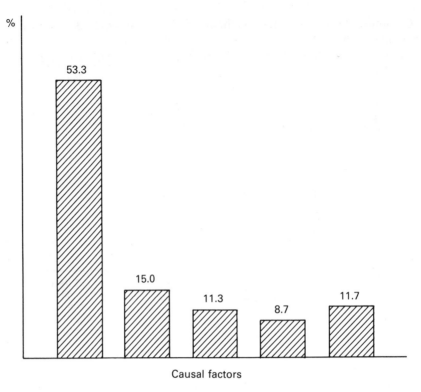

Figure 5.6 Pareto histogram

Following up the service

Organizations need to continuously monitor their performance by contacting customers to determine their view of the service delivered.

More recently, organizations have been asked to consider five imperatives for improving service quality:[6]

1 Define a clear service role and standard for service employees and communicate and reinforce these standards.
2 Compete for talent – allocate people to jobs according to ability and aptitude and give them more flexibility and control to do the job. The problem with this is that many service jobs are by nature narrow in scope and perceived as 'dead end'.
3 Emphasize service teams – getting people to work as a team is an attractive proposition and potentially very effective for delivering quality. However, entrenched attitudes (negative) to work and strong personalities can quite easily prevent the development of a team spirit. The action (or inaction) of management is crucial here. Good employees need to see management doing something about the members of the team who are simply not pulling their weight.
4 Go for reliability – at the heart of excellent service is reliability and it is argued that nothing less than 100 per cent reliability is acceptable:

Think for a moment about what it would mean in our daily lives if people got things right only 99 per cent of the time: at least 200,000 wrong prescriptions would be processed every year; there would be nine misspelled words on every page of a magazine; we'd all have unsafe drinking water; there would be no telephone service for fifteen minutes every day.[6]

Reliability has been defined as the 'ability to perform the promised service dependably and accurately'.[7]

- When an organization says it will call you back within fifteen minutes, does it do so?
- Is your bank statement free of errors? Is your plumbing repaired correctly the first time?

Service organizations should strive towards achieving 100 per cent reliability. However, the existence of certain conditions often impede the service organization in pursuit of that goal, e.g. lack of resources, unpredictable swings in demand levels. Furthermore, is it necessary for all services to achieve 100 per cent reliability? It is in the case of prescriptions because of the obvious consequences that may befall patients. But how many readers of a magazine would find it unacceptable, or even notice, that nine words are misspelt on every page? Perhaps they would and that only two or three misspellings would be tolerated. For British Rail it is impossible to ensure that every train runs and arrives on time. What commuters would more readily accept is 95 to 98 per cent of trains arriving within say five minutes of the scheduled time. Such 'unreliability', unlike the prescriptions, is simply of no great consequence.

5 Be great at problem resolution – service organizations cannot avoid things going wrong for a customer but it is their reaction to this that is critical. Their response can make things better or very much worse. Customers need to feel that actions are being taken to try to resolve the problem. For large service organizations client dissatisfaction of attempts at problem resolution is a real issue.

Customers are categorized and treated by the application of general, abstract rules, without regard for individual needs and situations. The depersonalized behaviour is considered functional because it prevents emotional involvement with the customers' problems and tends to promote consistency in behaviour throughout the organization. Also, the careful and thorough establishment of rules by the organization makes it possible to delegate substantial authority to people far down in the organization structure. In effect, complex problems can be routinely handled by a person with relatively little training or commonplace ability.

5.6 Monitoring and measuring service quality

Galileo Galilei is reputed to have said, 'Count what is countable, measure what is measurable and what is not measurable, make measurable.' In order to control and evaluate (and therefore improve) service quality there needs to be some form of measurement, whether it is qualitative or quantitative. Unlike product quality, however, the measurement of service quality is more difficult.

What to measure

The first step in any quality assessment programme is the determination of what to measure. Clearly the question of what to measure will vary from one service organization to another, but a list of criteria by which consumers judge quality has been developed. It is arguably general enough to apply to most service organizations. The criteria are:[7]

Tangibles – appearance of physical facilities, equipment and communication materials
Reliability – the ability to perform the promised service dependably and accurately
Responsiveness – the willingness to help customers and provide prompt service
Assurance – knowledge and courtesy of employees and their ability to convey trust and confidence
Empathy – caring, individualised attention the firm provides its customers.

To apply these factors to a particular service organization will require definition in specific and behavioural terms. For example, what does reliability mean in Service A as distinct from Service B? How does an organization show responsiveness? How does assurance differ between Service A and Service B? What can an organization do specifically to demonstrate empathy?

Measuring quality means evaluating performance against a previously agreed set of standards. The following examples illustrate the easily quantifiable side of service quality:

British Telecom (Quality of Service Report April 1991–September 1991) (Figure 5.7).
British Rail Passenger's Charter 1992 – Quality is equated predominantly with punctuality and reliability e.g., Inter-City standards:

Punctuality – 90 per cent of trains to arrive within *ten minutes* of scheduled time
Reliability – 99 per cent of services to run

For rail and other services like fire brigade, police etc, a quality control chart can be devised for monitoring service levels (Figure 5.8). The punctuality of trains or response times of fire and police can be plotted over a period of time and performance evaluated against the standard set.

For the five determinants of service quality already mentioned (tangibles, reliability, responsiveness, competence, courtesy) a multiple-item scale called SERVQUAL has been developed.[8] It aims to measure customer expectations and perceptions and the gaps as described in the service quality model.

April 1991 – September 1991

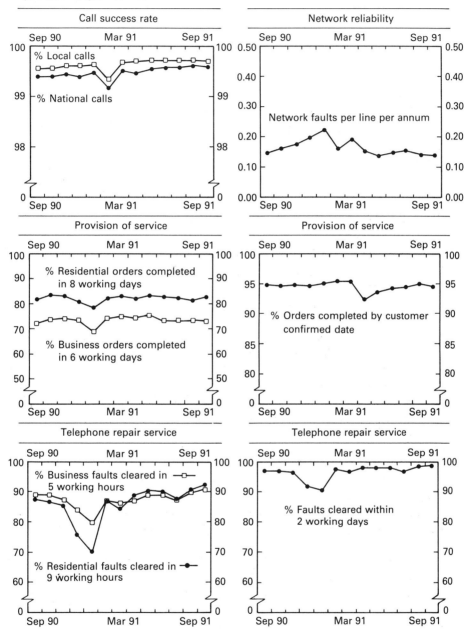

Figure 5.7 BT Quality of Service Report (April–Sept. 1991)

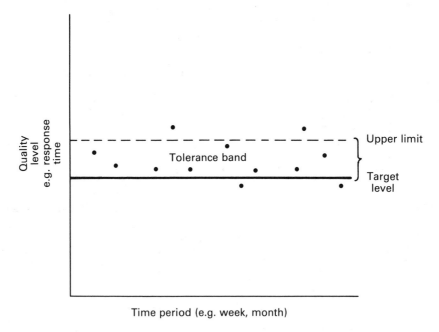

Figure 5.8 *Quality control chart – the dots represent actual responses*

Measurement is done through a Likert scale in which respondents are required to indicate their strength of agreement/disagreement to statements about the delivery of service quality.

A service audit of quality

The financial health of companies has long been measured and reported according to generally accepted accounting principles (GAAP). It has been argued that service organizations would benefit from a similar approach. Generally accepted service principles (GASP)[9] would provide service organizations with explanations of upward and downward trends in quality, just as companies explain good and bad trends in terms of sales and profits. It would be an index of customer satisfaction, measuring all the activities and attributes that affect customer satisfaction (see Chapter 12).

The findings of a service quality audit[10] may be portrayed as in Figure 5.9 and it might prove quite revealing to ask your customers, 'of the four, which one best reflects your perception of us?'

5.7 Total quality management

An approach, now much in vogue, to delivering quality is total quality management (TQM). It can be defined as managing the entire organization so that

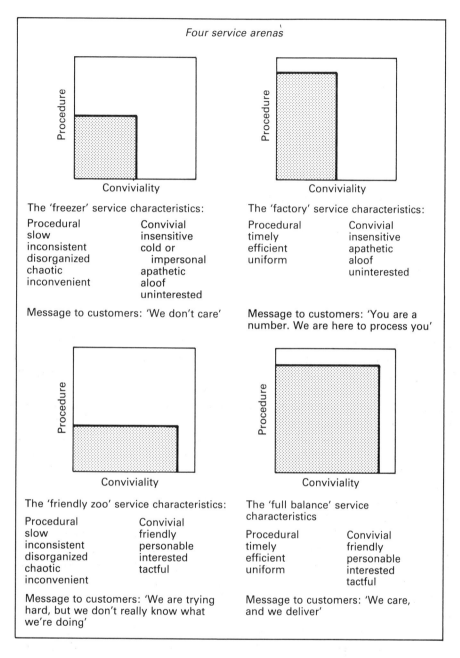

Figure 5.9 Four arenas of service quality. Source: Martin, W. B. (1986)[10]

it excels in all dimensions of products and services that are important to the customer. Attention to quality must extend throughout the organization and the customer will be the ultimate judge of what constitutes quality. Its essential elements are:

- Customer-driven quality standards
- Customers are internal (organization employees) as well as external
- Prevention rather than cure
- Commitment at the highest echelons
- Each employee is a quality inspector
- Two way communication
- Continuous improvement
- Measurement – using pareto analysis, process flow charts, cause and effect diagrams, scatter diagrams etc.

5.8   Quality awards

In recognition of the importance of quality a number of awards have appeared in the past few years.

The Baldridge award

The origins of the Baldridge award lie in a simple American emotion: fear of the Japanese industrial machine and a desire to emulate it.[11] The Japanese had instituted their own quality prize as far back as the 1950s and named it after W. Edwards Deming, the foremost of American advisers. The US finally followed suit in 1987 with the Baldridge Award, named after a US Commerce Secretary who died in a rodeo accident. It is run by an offshoot of the Commerce Department, the National Institute of Standards and Technology, and gives up to two awards a year in each of three categories – manufacturing, service and small business.

Companies nominate themselves and have to submit a lengthy application form describing their quality practices and performance. Those which score well are visited by a team of examiners for a detailed look at their operations.

What are the Baldridge judges looking for? Primarily, adherence to the underlying principles of the quality movement. These include a belief that the customer is the most important judge of a company's quality. It is also deemed important for the company's top management to create clear quality values, that the workforce be fully involved, and the whole enterprise aim for continuous long-term improvement.

The judges examine a business under seven categories awarding points in each area (Table 5.1). Applicants must obtain between 875 and 1000 points to receive the award.

The debate over the award will find some echo in Europe which has copied the idea. In Autumn 1992 the Dutch based European Foundation for Quality Management handed out its first award for total quality management.

The Baldridge award has not been without its critics. They point to the fact that it has been won by subsidiaries of several large US companies which are hardly examples of financially successful American business – IBM, Westinghouse Electric and General Motors. The latter won it for their Cadillac division at a time when surveys showed American consumers did not rate its

Table 5.1   Scoring the 1991 Baldridge award.

1.0   Leadership (100 points)
1.1   Senior executive leadership (40)
1.2   Quality values (15)
1.3   Management for quality (25)
1.4   Public responsibility (20)
2.0   Information and analysis (70 points)
2.1   Scope and management of quality data and information (20)
2.2   Competitive comparisons and benchmarks (30)
2.3   Analysis of quality data and information (20)
3.0   Strategic Quality Planning (60 points)
3.1   Strategic quality planning process (35)
3.2   Quality goals and plans (25)
4.0   Human resource utilization (150 points)
4.1   Human resource management (20)
4.2   Employee involvement (40)
4.3   Quality education and training (40)
4.4   Employee recognition and performance measurement (25)
4.5   Employee well-being and morale (25)
5.0   Quality assurance of products and services (140 points)
5.1   Design and introduction of quality products and services (35)
5.2   Process quality control (20)
5.3   Continuous improvement of processes (20)
5.4   Quality assessment (15)
5.5   Documentation (10)
5.6   Business process and support service quality (20)
5.7   Supplier quality (20)
6.0   Quality results (180 points)
6.1   Product and service quality results (90)
6.2   Business process, operational and support service quality results (50)
6.3   Supplier quality results (40)
7.0   Customer satisfaction (300 points)
7.1   Determining customer requirements and expectations (30)
7.2   Customer relationship management (50)
7.3   Customer service standards (20)
7.4   Commitment to customers (150)
7.5   Complaint resolution for quality improvement (25)
7.6   Determining customer satisfaction (20)
7.7   Customer satisfaction results (70)
7.8   Customer satisfaction comparison (70)
1000 Total Points

Source: National Institute for Standards and Technology. US Department of Commerce.

cars very highly. They also argue that it lays down a list of broad quality criteria without specifying how a company should go about achieving them. Finally, it is criticized on the grounds that it rewards process rather than market place results. This is a strange observation in that one would expect there to be a linkage between process and output.

Supporters of the award point, in the first instance, to the fact that it has had a significant effect on waking up American managers to the need for total quality management. The award was not meant to be a blue ribbon for the highest market share or profits. Instead the idea was to make US industry aware of how essential quality is in global competition and to provide a blueprint that might work.

A former member of the Baldridge's board of overseers has claimed that criticisms of the award represented deep misunderstandings. In a lengthy article,[12] he argues that, 'the best way to understand the Baldridge criteria is as an audit framework, an encompassing set of categories that tells companies where, and in what way, they must demonstrate proficiency – but not how to proceed'. He goes on to say that 'the award was never designed to reward product or service excellence. The bulk of the award focuses on management systems and processes'. He does however recognize one flaw – the award is a competition with a limited number of winners, rather than a qualification prize which any number can achieve.

The Charter initiatives

Recently in the UK there has been a host of initiatives (Appendix 5.1) aimed primarily at service in the public sector.

The key objective of these charters is to find better ways of using public funds for better public services. Raising standards, whether in the health service, schools or the railways, will be the agenda for all concerned. The proposed Charter Mark will recognize and reward excellence in the delivery of public services. The winners will be the organizations that have delivered services to the highest standard at present available. It is open to public sector organizations and the privatized utilities (Water, Gas, British Telecom and their main competitors) which service the public directly.

Individual hospitals and schools that have their own budget can apply for the Charter Mark. So too can individual units within organizations, such as local authority departments, provided they have sufficient managerial and financial independence to justify the individual application.

Organizations that serve citizens as individual businessmen or women, for example the VAT operations of Customs and Excise and Next Step Agencies can also apply.

Organizations are free to make their own case in their own way using graphics and other supporting material (e.g. a short video of no more than five minutes) if they wish. Achievements must be set out clearly against the six Charter standard principles. Written material, which should not exceed ten pages, should be crisp and factual.

The Citizen's Charter White Paper set out six key principles for a charter standard:

- Publication of standards of service and performance
- Customer consultation
- Clear information about services
- Courteous and efficient customer service
- Complaints procedures
- Independent validation of performance and a commitment to value for money

Organizations must support the application with evidence of their performance against these six principles.

Achievement of the Charter Mark will provide public recognition of the quality of an organization's work. It will provide incentive for management and staff to adopt best practices in order to improve the services they provide and increase value for money to the tax-payer. And it will encourage organizations to maintain high standards of service in order to retain the Charter Mark. The award will normally remain valid for three years and organizations will be free to display them as they see fit throughout this period. Organizations will be able to advertise widely the fact that they have qualified for the award. They may do so in a variety of ways, e.g. on stationery, on vehicles, in advertisements and on promotional material. A Citizen's Charter Advisory Panel and cabinet ministerial responsibility is an attempt to ensure that the award only goes to those organizations that genuinely deserve them.

There have been criticisms of the charter initiatives from 'it's all a con trick' to 'quality is as much dependent on the level of resources as efficiencies in the management of them'. The Patient's Charter, for example, states that 'everyone must be seen immediately and their needs assessed'. The reality, under present resources, is that this is unachievable. The Job Seeker's Charter may provide better surroundings and shorter waits but is largely irrelevant when it comes to finding people jobs. Similar observations could be made in respect of the other charters. Alongside the implementation difficulties will be the danger that consumer expectations will rise markedly. As Fred Emery pointed out in a Panorama programme, '. . . will the Charter be able to contain them let alone satisfy them'?[13]

BS 5750

The British Standards Institution (BSI) is an independent body which works closely with industry and government and produces technical documents which lay down specifications for particular goods and services. BS 5750 was initiated in 1979 with the expressed aim of raising quality in manufacturing. It sets out the organizational and procedural mechanisms necessary for quality assurance. Companies are basically asked to reassess the way they process their service. Detailing the nature of the work to be undertaken, when it will be done and at what cost is laid out in the manual. Standards will be set and must be followed. After a company has been successfully assessed and registered to BS 5750 it will be entitled to use the BSI Registered Firm logo.

Although the standard was originally written with manufacturing companies in mind, service organizations have shown increasing interest. In fact a number have already achieved registration to the standard, e.g. solicitors, hotel and catering, colleges, executive recruitment consultancies, local authority departments. BSI makes the claim that BS 5750 is appropriate to any organization because it is a framework in which you can write your own standards. It is interesting to note however, particularly for services, that the standard does not directly assess the quality of the end product. In the case of a solicitor, certification does not guarantee the quality of advice. It is not covered in assuring clients that they will receive a quality service. Furthermore, non-measurable quality indicators such as taste, texture and colour in catering will have to rely on staff expertise.

There has been criticism of the standard. Mr Allen, managing director of contract caterer, COMPASS, has criticized BS 5750 as expensive and inapplicable to the industry because it failed to pay enough attention to customers' needs.[14] He believes that, 'it is in principle a good idea but it is very much a trick in the box approach'. He goes on to explain that 'the hospitality industry needs to look at it differently. All the bits could be right but at the end of the day the product could be wrong. In the manufacturing industry it is 110% certain to give customers what they want. But in our industry it's different – there are a lot of intangibles'. COMPASS dropped working on BS 5750 after nine months and decided to develop its own quality assurance programme. Others in that industry do not share this view and the Hotel Catering and Institutional Management Association believes COMPASS will fall back into line once it faces competition from accredited companies. It is felt that recognition obtained through accreditation is a great selling point of BS 5750.

SGS Yarsley, the third largest UK certification organization, recently surveyed 500 companies (manufacturing and service) on their attitudes to BS 5750.[15] They point out that despite great interest only 15,000 companies (2 per cent of the UK total) have achieved certification. The reasons, evidently, for this low take up are a natural reluctance to accept a new standard and the stringency of a system which requires proof of a company's quality system working in practice.

As far as services are concerned the study reveals that it is the business to business sector that is applying for registration. Of course, many services such as employment agencies, High Street photocopying, travel agencies etc. perform a dual role (customer and business), but it is the business arm which has been the driving force in gaining recognition.

Although services represented a minority of respondents, it is still of interest to reflect on some of the findings. As for reasons for wanting to achieve registration, 52 per cent said it was because of pressure from large customers and 21 per cent to improve efficiency. As to the recovery of costs related to registration, 90 per cent of respondents recovered them within 3 years and 10 per cent in less than 2 years. The major areas of cost savings are highlighted in Table 5.2.

It may be no more than a coincidence but as Yarsley point out, 'companies registered to BS 5750 saw a significantly lower rate of failures (0.2%) than UK companies as a whole (7.14%). Respondents to the survey cited stricter controls, improved efficiency and the marketing advantage of registration as the major reasons for their better performance'.

Clearly there is a long way to go for services in respect of BS 5750 registration. What is of interest will be the type of service applying and how much of that service it will cover.

Table 5.2 Major areas of cost savings from BS 5750 registration

Description	%
Fewer rejects	27
Reduced administration	20
Increased productivity	20
Removal of unnecessary procedures	18
Savings in overtime payments	15

Source: Attitudes to BS 5750, Executive Summary, SGS Yarsley, May 1992.

5.9 Summary

Customers desire a quality service but few can agree on a definition. It expresses itself in the service encounter, service design, service productivity and throughout the organization and culture. A model of service quality has been developed to increase our understanding. It states that gaps exist between the service provider and the customer over expectations and perceptions of quality. The message for management is one of managing customer expectations as well as ensuring that what is promised in respect of quality is actually delivered.

Apart from the contribution of the model, a good place to start is isolating the causes of poor quality. This will then serve as a basis for taking action to improve it. Improvements will be more detectable if steps are taken to set standards and measure performance against these standards.

The importance attached to the delivery of quality in all kinds of organizations and activities has given rise to a number of awards. Organizations in receipt of such recognition will inevitably be subjected to the test of whether the award is justified or not.

Questions

1 (a) For the following list of service organizations decide which element of the service that they offer would be described as process quality and those which would make up output quality:

   Airline service
   Dating agency
   Citizens' Advice Bureau
   Dentist
   NHS
   British Rail
   Refuse collection
   Nursery school

    (b) Using the same organizations suggest methods that would enable the quality of the service to be monitored.

2 A pizza parlour is experiencing problems with its home delivery service. A study done for the parlour revealed possible causes of failure and their contribution in not meeting target response times.

Causes	% Contribution to failure in meeting target response times
a giving orders to kitchen	3
b shortage of drivers	8
c slowness in preparation of pizzas	3
d drivers unfamiliar with fastest route	30
e breakdowns in delivery vehicles	15
f traffic congestion	25
g weather conditions	6
h slowness in boxing cooked pizzas	3
i extent of catchment area	7
	100

What would be an appropriate method of displaying the above data? What advice would you give the pizza parlour?

3 Awards for service quality focus on systems and procedures rather than outputs. Yet quality in the process does not necessarily lead to quality of service. Why do you think this is the case?

4 It has been said that 'quality is ballet, not hockey' and 'quality is in the eye of the beholder'. But to provide quality we need to be much more specific and that will involve setting standards. Thinking about various services, how do you think standards are arrived at and how do we know they are 'correct'?

References

1 *Measuring Up* (1986). Public Libraries Paper 3. National Consumer Council, London.
2 Cottam, A. M. and Mudie, P. M. (1992). Working Paper. Napier University, Edinburgh.
3 Parasuraman, A., Zeithaml, V. A. and Berry, L. L. (1985). A conceptual model of service quality and its implications for future research. *Journal of Marketing* **49** (Fall) 41–50.
4 Berry, L. L., Zeithaml, V. A. and Parasuraman, A. (1985). Quality counts in services, too. *Business Horizons*, May–June, 44–52.
5 Goodman, J. A., Malech, A. R., Bargatze, G. F. and Ledbetter, C. (1988). Converting a desire for quality service into actions with measurable impact. *Journal of Retail Banking*, **X**(4), 14–22.
6 Berry, L. L., Zeithaml, V. A. and Parasuraman, A. (1990). Five imperatives for improving service quality. *Sloan Management Review*, Summer, 29–38.
7 Zeithaml, V. A., Parasuraman, A. and Berry, L. L. (1990). *Delivering Service Quality*. The Free Press, Macmillan Inc.
8 Parasuraman, A., Zeithaml, V. A. and Berry, L. L. (1988). SERVQUAL: a multiple itemscale for measuring consumer perceptions of service quality. *Journal of Retailing*, **64**(1), Spring, 13–37.
9 Liswood, L. (1989) *Serving Them Right*. Harper and Row.
10 Martin, W. B. (1986). Defining what quality service is for you. *The Cornell HRA Quarterly*, February, 32–38.
11 Dickson, M. (1992) Bouquets and Barbed Ire. *Financial Times*, February 3.
12 Garvin, D. A. (1991). How the Baldridge award really works. *Harvard Business Review*, November–December, 80–93.
13 Emery, F. (1992). Citizen Major's Charter. *Panorama*, May 18.
14 Allen, (1991) quoted in Standard attack. *Caterer and Hotelkeeper*, November.
15 Attitudes to BS 5750: a Survey of 500 Registered Companies (1992) May 4. SGS Quality Assured Firms Limited.

Appendix 5.1

Charters published by April 1992

Charter	Date most new standards come into effect
Benefits Agency Customer Charter (Benefits Agency)	January 92
British Rail Passenger's Charter (British Rail)	May 92

Charter	Date most new standards come into effect
Contributor's Charter (DSS/Contributions Agency)	August 91
Jobseeker's Charter (Employment Service)	December 91
Northern Ireland Charter (Northern Ireland Office)	February 92
Northern Ireland: A Charter for Patients and Clients (Northern Ireland Office)	April 92
Parent's Charter (Department of Education & Science)	September 92
Patient's Charter (Department of Health)	April 92
Scottish Office Justice Charter (Scottish Office)	April 92
Scottish Office Parent's Charter (Scottish Office)	September 92
Scottish Office Patient's Charter (Scottish Office)	April 92
Scottish Office Tenant's Charter (Scottish Office)	December 91
Taxpayer's Charter (Customs & Excise)	August 91
Taxpayer's Charter (Inland Revenue)	August 91
Tenant's Charter (Department of Environment)	January 92
Traveller's Charter (Customs and Excise)	January 92
Welsh Office Parent's Charter (Welsh Office)	September 92
Welsh Office Patient's Charter (Welsh Office)	April 92

6

The service encounter

6.1 Introduction

Interaction between customer and organization lies at the heart of service delivery. The interaction may take many forms, from a brief encounter with a directions sign to a protracted encounter with a service employee. Whatever the nature and type of contact, each represents a moment of truth for the customer. According to Shostack,[1] 'Controlling and enhancing the encounter is a critically important task that no service organisation can afford to leave to chance'.

6.2 Types of encounters

Shostack describes three types of service encounters:

1 The remote encounter – where customers interact with a service, or part of it, through the mail e.g. financial services, mail order. The remote encounter may also occur via a machine, e.g. the ATM. Leaflets, brochures and forms sent by mail need to be designed with the consumer in mind. Machines need to function and be user friendly. This type of encounter should be the easiest to control as it is based on some form of physical object, be it printed material or a computer terminal. Quality should be assured as they can be tested, modified and made uniform.

2 The indirect personal encounter – where customers interact with a service by telephone. There is potentially more scope for variability entering the service delivery. This can be avoided by requiring the employee to work to a script, but problems may still arise if the customer's enquiry/complaint requires reference to other parts of the organization only to find their support is not forthcoming.

3 The direct personal encounter – where customers interact face-to-face with the service provider. Customers now have the opportunity of visualizing the providers of the service. Judgements about service quality may be made from the appearance and demeanour of the service provider. The increasing use of uniforms, now referred to as corporate clothing, and the development of interpersonal skills training are recognition of the impact direct personal encounters may have on customer satisfaction.

In addition to these three types of encounter, there is a host of other encounter points that may influence the customer's view of the service. For example:

- The front entrance to an organization
- The car park
- The organization's vehicles
- The interior of a building – type of furnishings, plants (real or plastic)
- Signs
- Brochures/leaflets

The above list is simply illustrative but indicates that service organizations contain a wealth of encounter points (not only human). It is at these points that impressions are formed which are subsequently converted into feelings, beliefs and perhaps lasting images.

In certain service situations (some observers may say the numbers are increasing) the customer has a choice between a personal and impersonal encounter. Langeard *et al.*[2] sought to measure customers' willingness to participate in the process of producing a service. By developing scenarios for a range of services (bank, petrol station, hotel, airport, restaurant, outlet selling travellers cheques) respondents were asked to indicate which type of encounter they preferred. An example of a scenario used is given below.

The bank scenario

It is 10.00 am and you wish to withdraw £50 from your account. You have a card which would enable you to use an automatic teller machine or you could go to a human teller with your cheque book. So your choices are:

Either use the automatic teller *or* use the human teller

There are equally short lines of people waiting to use the machine and at the teller window.

Respondents varied widely in their willingness to use the more participative of the two service alternatives presented in each scenario. Willingness to participate varied according to demographic characteristics and a number of influencing factors:

- Total amount of time required
- Customer control of the situation
- Amount of effort required by customer
- Customer need to depend on others
- Efficiency of doing it
- Amount of human contact involved
- Risk of something going wrong

This study would seem to raise the following issues:

- Greater participation by the customer in producing the service can lead to gains in productivity.
- Service organization reaction to an increasing desire by consumers to becoming involved in production and delivery?

• The extent of consumer involvement across service types and activities?

6.3 The human service encounter: an overview

Of all types of encounters, direct personal contact is the one that characterizes many service situations at some point in time.

A number of factors will play a part in determining the nature of the interaction and the final outcome (Figure 6.1).

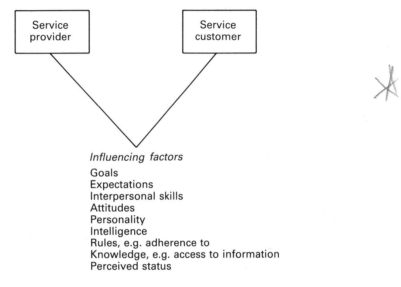

Figure 6.1 *Factors influencing interpersonal service encounters*

Explanations need to be sought for good or poor encounters. The factors listed in Figure 6.1 have an impact on the service encounter. Some, like personality, attitudes and adherence to rules are unpredictable and unstable. Exercising control over them may prove difficult. On the other hand, for the provider, effective interpersonal skills training and being well informed affords the opportunity of greater control and the likelihood of a positive outcome.

The question of perceived status enters the encounter relationship. A distinction is drawn between absolute status which derives from income, occupation and skill level, and relative status which derives from the differential absolute rankings of the participants in the encounter. Hospital patients, for example, are expected to follow nurses' orders no matter who they are in the general community. On the other hand the British Rail guards' absolute and relative status may be perceived as inferior by many passengers. Just what this means for the guard/passenger encounter is a subject for analysis. On the one hand there remains a sense of dependency on the guard. On the other perhaps a feeling of frustration borne out of a perception that status considerations renders the guard powerless. It is a paradoxical situation but one, nevertheless, not unfamiliar to many customers in service encounters.

'The rules of the game'

In service encounters people come together to obtain certain goals. To achieve these goals and coordinate the behaviour of the participants, rules must be developed. Rules specify the behaviour which is regarded as appropriate in a given situation.

Rules should be distinguished from norms and conventions. Norms refer to modal behaviour, i.e. what most people do; sometimes most people break the rules. Conventions refer to arbitrary customs, e.g. hats for nurses. Conventions can vary without affecting performance or attainment of goals. An experiment was conducted[3] to find out whether people could distinguish between conventions, rules and norms (basic to all social situations). The hypothesis was that deviation from conventions would be rated as the least disturbing, difficult to deal with etc., followed by rule breaking, followed by universal rules (Table 6.1).

Table 6.1 Job interview

You are interviewing for a job, and the applicant behaves in one of the following ways:
1 He puts his feet on the desk
2 He asks you questions all the time, but doesn't want to answer your questions
3 He repeatedly speaks while you are speaking
4 He wears clothes that are too dirty and informal for the occasion
5 He smokes uninvited
6 He tells what are obviously lies or gross exaggerations
7 He treats the interview as a friendly chat, and does not give serious replies to questions
8 He wants to discuss his sexual or other personal problems
9 He is clearly not at all interested in the job

Source: Argyle, M., Furnham, A. and Graham, J. A. (1981)[3]

Subjects were asked to rate each statement along five rating scales (Table 6.2).

In terms of results, disruptiveness was found to be a major dimension of rule-breaking. Allied to the above situation, the least disruptive (conventions) was dirty clothes and smokes uninvited; the most disruptive (rules) was asks question, speaks while you are speaking and tells lies.

Many readers may regard the study as rather academic and obvious in terms of answers. Nevertheless, it is a framework that service organizations could use in managing the service encounter. The behaviours and actions may be more subtle. Whatever the customer is portrayed as doing however, the value lies in specifying strategies of organizational response, with the help of scales similar to those in Table 6.2.

Table 6.2 Rating scales

Does not disrupt the situation	-----------	Totally disrupts the situation
Easy to deal with	-----------	Very difficult to deal with
Can be left or dealt with later	-----------	Needs to be dealt with first
Not annoying	-----------	Extremely annoying
Acceptable under some conditions	-----------	Never acceptable

Source: Argyle, M., Furnham, A. and Graham, J. A. (1981)[3]

There is a great deal of scope for creating added value by investigating customer behaviour, their effect on the situation and how they should be handled. There is a need to understand why customer experiences of service provision can range from excellent to 'vows never to return'.[4]

6.4 Service encounter as theatre

The writings of Erving Goffman, particularly *The Presentation Of Self In Everyday Life*,[5] have prompted service encounters to be portrayed as performances as in the theatre. Customers and service personnel are cast in the role of actors where every line, gesture etc, is rigidly specified in the sacred script. In playing a role the genuine identity of the actors is never revealed, hidden behind a mask donned to hide real feelings. The theatre analogy is not totally apt (e.g. masks slip, scripts get abandoned) but it does assist understanding of the service encounter.

Of fundamental importance in delivering a credible performance is the issue of impression management. To convey the right impression use is made of certain expressive equipment collectively termed the front. It comprises two aspects:

Personal front – insignia of office or rank, clothing, sex, age and racial characteristics, size and looks, posture, speech patterns, facial expressions, bodily gestures.
The setting – furniture, decor, physical layout and other background items which supply the scenery and stage props.

How appropriate then are the fronts used in conveying a particular service? What do they say about the particular service? For example, care must be exercised in deciding whether a pin striped suit is simply a statement of how a businessman should look or a fundamental projection of an air of competence. Is the service encounter and perception of quality enhanced if the car mechanic is covered in oil? The fronts then may convey impressions, rather than any revelations, about abilities, skills, attitudes and demeanours. What is important during the service encounter is maintenance of expressive control by service personnel. Unmeant gestures, indiscretion, faux pas, creating a scene, may jeopardize performance credibility. There should be consistency between the fronts. The appearance of the props, what people look like, say and do must combine to form a package of what the service aims to be. Otherwise, during the encounter, customers may feel confused by contrasting signals. The lawyer sitting in a pink boiler suit in his elegant office would be an extreme but nevertheless vivid reminder of the need to achieve consistency.

Role

Consistent with the theatre metaphor, employees and customers are role-players in the service encounter. Each participant is expected to act and behave in a way that is appropriate for the particular service. Situations can, of course vary, from one of mindlessness[6] to engrossment[7] extending all the way to ecstasy and bewitchment that might characterize situations where a consumer becomes totally engrossed in a service.[8] What this essentially means is that role behaviour will take its cue depending on where the situation lies on a service encounter continuum:

Role enactment will, therefore, vary from the exchange of a few pleasantries (i.e. a smile, friendly greeting with a bank teller, waiter) to one of deep, personal and emotional involvement.

The latter is more difficult to specify as most service encounters, it is argued, rest on the left-side of the continuum. Service encounters may be classified by the degree of psychological involvement and mechanisms required for creating the appropriate level of involvement. Psychological involvement is defined as 'the degree of psychological closeness, with the service provider, as experienced by the customer during the service delivery process. It can range from a customer experiencing the service employee as polite but essentially indifferent towards him/her as a person (resulting in a low degree of psychological closeness), to medium levels of involvement in which customers experience the service employee as sympathetic, to high levels of involvement in which customers experience service employees as concerned, caring and sympathetic towards them'.[9] Organization-designed 'rites of integration' are mechanisms for achieving the appropriate degree of involvement. By applying these rites in various ways (language, gestures, ritualized behaviour, physical setting, symbols, displayed emotion) the service encounter is clarified in terms of role behaviour.

There is an assumption however, that different levels of psychological involvement are associated with certain types of encounters. Many professional services are proposed as high in involvement. However, much as the customer may wish high psychological involvement, (say with a doctor, lawyer, lecturer), his experience may be the opposite. Therefore, a distinction must be drawn between what should be and what is, for those services high in psychological involvement.

Equally, some have argued that treating customers as individuals will not be well received and will probably not pay. There is no evidence to support this proposition. Encounters with bank tellers, waiters, barmen, taxi-drivers, hotel porters etc. will, in the main, be low in psychological involvement but concerned, caring sympathetic employee behaviour cannot be excluded, particularly when things go wrong.

Power and commitment are important factors in role relationships. Power is defined in terms of how much the consumer perceives he possesses relative to the service provider. Therefore, a relationship is categorized as 'low power' when the consumer believes he has less of it than the provider. Commitment involves intentions with regard to continuing or maintaining a relationship and identification with the role defined by the relationship. Combining the amount of power and commitment, has produced the following classification:[10]

High power, high commitment – hair stylists, health club, neighbourhood grocery and pharmacy services.
High power, low commitment – airline cabin service, individual bank tellers, waiters, hotel clerks, bus drivers.
Low power, high commitment – university education, religion, counselling services, lawyers retained for a trial.
Low power, low commitment – police services, funeral directors, professional tax preparers, lawyers engaged for brief consultation.

Although one could argue over the examples, every service encounter will have a mix of power and commitment. Depending on where an organization perceives itself to be, appropriate communication strategies can be devised to encourage and retain consumer loyalty, together with procedures for handling complaints. On commitment, the implication for role behaviour is one of willingness to cooperate and participate. On power, consumers may either exercise it to complain or feel frustrated by the lack of it. Although sources of power should enter the discussion one can derive some insight into how consumer power may be reduced or enhanced. For example, military style uniforms may be an attempt at reduction of consumer power and police officers stopping to chat as they walk the beat, an exercise in enhancement of consumer power.[10]

Whatever the strategies and views on role in the service encounter, organizations should develop some kind of framework within which the issue of role can be discussed and understood. Figure 6.2 is simply an illustration of how one may proceed.

The customer has been defined as a 'partial employee'[11] in the service delivery process. This means that services must determine whether customers or employees are the principal performers. For many services, customers will act as 'co-producers' with employees. In some cases, namely the automatic teller machine, the customer becomes the sole producer.

Allocation of production and delivery between customer and employee will be reflected in responsibility for technical and interpersonal skills. They can be summarized as follows:

Expectations

Technical skills
(the 'what')

Interpersonal
skills
(the 'how')

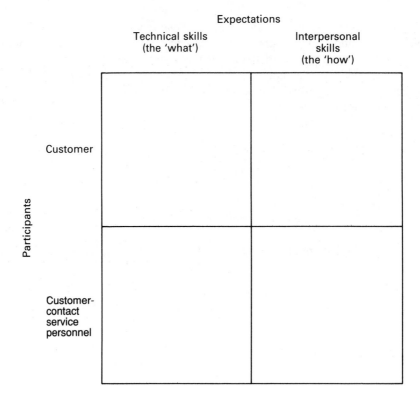

Customer

Participants

Customer-
contact
service
personnel

Figure 6.2 *Role framework in service encounter*

Employee technical skills – application of knowledge and equipment in providing solutions.
Customer technical skills – provision of information and labour.
Interpersonal skills – for employee and customer it means how they are going to behave, e.g. caring, assertive, domineering.

Effective performance will depend on how well the participants acquire and put into practice the appropriate skills. In addition, it is important to remember that delivering a quality service may require role undertakings before and after the actual encounter as well as during it. Education is a good example of this. Preparation before a lecture together with how the participants manage what they have learnt after it can contribute enormously to effectiveness in role performances during delivery.

Basically, the organization must ask itself:?

• What are the customers and employees expected to do, and
• How are they expected to do it?

Answers to these questions form the essence of role determination.

Script

A script is regarded as 'a predetermined, stereotyped sequence of actions that defines a well-known situation'.[12] People experience hundreds of stereotypic situations with routine activities, e.g. riding a bus, visiting a dentist, eating in a restaurant. Script theory has been proposed as evidence of how we use specific knowledge to interpret and participate in events we have been through many times. Scripts basically tell the customer what his role should be, the sequence of events and what other people are likely to do. Customer satisfaction will largely depend on whether the service received conforms to the script. Parts of a script are illustrated in Table 6.3.

The restaurant script is one to which most people can relate. It is perceived as a giant causal chain in which each action results in conditions that enable the next to occur. Any script will consist of a set of activities that has conventional roles, props, event-sequences, standard entering conditions and standard outcomes. The script approach is highly relevant as it depicts service delivery as a process. For each step in the process performance can be monitored and set against organization specifications and customer expectations.

Script generation

The importance of customer scripts is that they represent customer's knowledge of what to do for effective participation in the service production. People can be asked to describe what goes on in detail during a variety of service situations. From these descriptions an understanding of the level of agreement there is between consumer and organization on the nature of the characters, props, actions, the order in which they occur can be obtained.

As part of an investigation of cognitive process, a group of undergraduates were asked to write scripts about common activities[13] (Table 6.4). They were given the following instructions (the lecture script will serve as an example):

> Write a list of actions describing what people generally do when they go to a lecture in a course. We are interested in the common actions of a routine lecture stereotype. Start the list with arriving at the lecture and end it with leaving after the lecture. Include about 20 actions or events and put them in order in which they would occur.

Not surprisingly there was a large measure of agreement in the actions mentioned and the order in which they occur. This was because the situations were largely routine and familiar. Nevertheless, for the proper conduct and management of the service encounter, people (i.e. customers and service employees) need to agree on the essentials of the script.

Description of scripts may be less predictable and result in less agreement if the following qualifications are added:

- Inputs vary – a service situation as experienced by different customer types e.g. socioeconomic groups.

Table 6.3 Theoretical restaurant script (adapted from Schank and Abelson, 1977)[12]

Name:	Restaurant		
Props:	Tables	Roles:	Customer
	Menu		Waitress
	Food		Cook
	Bill		Cashier
	Money		Owner
	Tip		
Entry Conditions:	Customer has money	Results:	Customer has less money Owner has more money Customer is not hungry Customer is satisfied/dissatisfied
Scene 1:	Entering Customer enters restaurant Customer looks for table Customer decides where to sit Customer goes to table Customer sits down		
Scene 2:	Ordering Customer picks up menu Customer looks at menu Customer decides on food Customer signals waitress Waitress comes to table Customer orders food Waitress goes to cook Waitress gives food order to cook Cook prepares food		
Scene 3:	Eating Cook gives food to waitress Waitress brings food to customer Customer eats food		
Scene 4:	Exiting Waitress writes bill Waitress goes over to customer Waitress gives bill to customer Customer gives tip to waitress Customer goes to cashier Customer gives money to cashier Customer leaves restaurant		

- Processes vary – from simple to complex, standardized to customized.
- What should happen versus what does happen.

A couple of examples will illustrate part of this expanded view. Owners starting up small businesses could be asked to generate scripts following an application for a bank loan. Two scenarios would be researched. For example, start with 'Decide to apply to a bank loan' and end with either 'being granted a loan' or 'not being granted a loan'. This would provide an interesting contrast between the actions and events that lead to success and those that end in failure. Or, people could be asked to describe a visit to the doctor. In this case a distinction could be drawn between a patient experiencing a degree of discomfort, the origin of which is not very clear (at least to the patient and perhaps even to the doctor), versus a straightforward ailment. Comparisons could be made between what patients expected to happen in the course of the consultation and what actually did happen.

Opportunities are therefore available to extend script generation and establish the extent of agreement on the part of respondents.

Scripts for service jobs – job description.

Due to the very nature of their job, customer contact personnel in the service sector are subject to a great deal of attention and scrutiny. To achieve efficiency and effectiveness in employee performance, management must devote time and effort to developing proper job descriptions. Scripting is an important aspect of specifying how the job should be done. Tansik and Smith[14] proposed a model that specifies the dimensions of scripts and how these may be applied in a variety of service settings. The dimensions are:

- Script intensity – extent to which a script specifically determines the employee's actions and words. Low intensity will allow ad-libbing, high intensity will not.
- Script complexity – extent to which at some point in the script there is a need and opportunity to abandon the script and go to another one, to simply continue the script or to enter some sub-programme within the existing script.
- Number of scripts – how many must be learned to do the job.
- Percentage of time in scripts – what percentage of time is spent in scripts.
- Percentage of duties in scripts – what percentage of tasks or duties are scripted.

They apply the dimensions to three service settings in which the customer-induced uncertainty (CIU) ranges from low to high (Table 6.5).

Customer-induced uncertainty (CIU) simply reflects the amount and nature of involvement in the service delivery process. It is quite clear that a low CIU almost equates to a standardized format of service delivery where:

Table 6.4 Empirical script norms at three agreement levels

Going to a restaurant	Attending a lecture	Getting up	Grocery shopping	Visiting a doctor
Open door	ENTER ROOM	*Wake up*	ENTER STORE	*Enter office*
Enter	*Look for friends*	Turn off alarm	GET CART	CHECK IN WITH RECEPTIONIST
Give reservation name	FIND SEAT	Lie in bed	Take out list	SIT DOWN
Wait to be seated	SIT DOWN	Stretch	Look at list	Wait
Go to table	Settle belongings	GET UP	Go to first aisle	Look at other people
BE SEATED	TAKE OUT NOTEBOOK	Make bed	*Go up and down aisles*	READ MAGAZINE
Order drinks	*Look at other students*	Go to bathroom	PICK OUT ITEMS	*Name called*
Put napkins on lap	*Talk*	Use toilet	Compare prices	Follow nurse
LOOK AT MENU	Look at professor	*Take shower*	Put items in cart	Enter exam room
Discuss menu	LISTEN TO PROFESSOR	*Wash face*	Get meat	Undress
ORDER MEAL	TAKE NOTES	Shave	Look for items forgotten	*Sit on table*
Talk	CHECK TIME	DRESS	Talk to other shoppers	Talk to nurse
Drink water	Ask questions	Go to kitchen	Go to checkout counters	NURSE TESTS

Eat salad or soup	Change position in seat	Fix breakfast	*Find fastest line*	Wait
Meal arrives	Daydream	EAT BREAKFAST	WAIT IN LINE	Doctor enters
EAT FOOD	Look at other students	BRUSH TEETH	*Put food on belt*	Doctor greets
Finish meal	Take more notes	Read paper	Read magazines	Talk to doctor about problem
Order dessert	*Close notebook*	*Comb hair*	WATCH CASHIER RING UP	Doctor asks questions
Eat dessert	*Gather belongings*	*Get books*	PAY CASHIER	DOCTOR EXAMINES
Ask for bill	Stand up	Look in mirror	*Watch bag boy*	Get dressed
Bill arrives	Talk	Get coat	Cart bags out	Get medicine
PAY BILL	LEAVE	LEAVE HOUSE	Load bags into car	Make another appointment
Leave tip			LEAVE STORE	LEAVE OFFICE
Get coats				
LEAVE				

Items in all capital letters were mentioned by the most subjects, items in italics by fewer subjects, and items in text type by the fewest subjects

Source: Bower, G. H., Black, J. B. and Turner, T. J. (1979)[13]

Table 6.5 A scripting model based on customer-induced uncertainty

	Customer-induced uncertainty		
	Low	Medium	High
Number of scripts in a job	Low	Medium	High
Percentage of job duties scripted	High	Medium	Low
Percentage of work time in scripts	High	Medium	Low
Script complexity	Low	Medium	High
Script intensity	High	Medium	Low

Source: Tansik, D. A., Smith, W. L. (1991)[14]

- Few scripts are used
- Scripts are very precise
- Much of the job is scripted

Fast-food retailing is a typical example.

On the other hand, in a situation of high CIU, scripts:

- Are numerous
- Are complex and allow for variation
- Are not applied in all situations and at all times

This situation is not the exclusive preserve of the professional services as may be thought. For example, the surgeon in theatre must follow a tightly pre-scribed script in the event of a patient having a heart attack, whereas the fast-food employee may find the standard scripts available to be of little value when dealing with an unruly customer.

6.5   The critical incident technique

Organizations need to know what customers expect from the service experi-ence. In particular they need to study what goes on during the encounter with service personnel to see if it lives up to customers' expectations. A method par-ticularly suited to achieving that objective is the critical incident technique which has been described as: a set of procedures for collecting direct observa-tions of human behaviour in such a way as to facilitate their potential useful-ness in solving problems and developing broad psychological principles.[15]

Flanagan[15] described and applied the technique in an industrial setting. By collecting statements from the participants in an encounter it seeks to deter-mine incidents (behaviours, actions) that are especially helpful or inadequate. It is particularly valuable for evaluating employee/customer interactions but can be equally revealing when applied within an organization. For example the fol-lowing questions can reveal effective or ineffective behaviours of a supervisor. Employees, and even management, could be asked to:

- Think of a time when your supervisor did something that you felt should be encouraged as it seemed in your opinion an example of good supervision
- Think of a time when the supervisor did something that you thought was not up to par

What may be interesting is the degree of agreement/disagreement between management and employees as to what constitutes effective and ineffective behaviour by the supervisor.

Applications of the critical incident technique to the service encounter

Communication problems

Having a technically sound operational system is insufficient for delivering service quality and providing customer satisfaction. Positive service encounters require effective oral communication skills on the part of the employees. This is particularly so in the case of high contact service organizations like hotels, airlines, restaurants, colleges etc.

The aim must be to identify, with the aid of the critical incident technique, employee behaviours that are regarded as either effective or ineffective in exchanges with customers. There is an endless amount and variety of customer behaviours that may prove difficult to manage. For example:[16]

- Unreasonable demands
- Demands against company policy
- Unacceptable treatment of employees
- Drunkenness

It may often be the case that customer expectations or demands exceed the organization's and its employees' willingness and/or ability to meet them. In knowing how to handle these demands employees should have a knowledge of customer expectations and how they are formed. Organizations often equip their employees with scripts which specify a range of responses to be used in a given situation. There are inherent dangers with this approach as the customer perceives the organization to be impersonal and inflexible. To overcome this, employees should be encouraged to expand their repertoire of possible responses.

Organizations need to train employees to be competent communicators. There is a large body of research from which communication strategies can be developed. However, there are a number of fundamental principles that every employee should adhere to when confronted with a difficult situation:

- Remain calm – an irate customer can be equated to a pressure cooker so the lid needs to be taken off gently
- Let the customer vent his/her anger – don't interrupt, laugh etc
- Listen with understanding – this diffuses anger and demonstrates concern. Apologise to the customer for being inconvenienced and state that you are there to help. It is vital to show a sincere interest and willingness to help. The customer's first impression of the employee is all important in gaining cooperation

- Restate what the customer is saying, in summary form. This tells the customer that you have listened and understood what has been said
- Don't blame others or make excuses. Instead, take the responsibility and initiative to do whatever you can to solve the problem as quickly as possible
- Find out what the customer wants. If that cannot be met, state why and propose your own solution. The customer may also be asked what he or she would consider a fair alternative
- Once a solution is agreed, act quickly. If agreement cannot be reached, refer the customer to someone else able to resolve the problem.

In all the dealings with the customer it is important to be courteous and considerate and respect the feelings of the customer.

Satisfactory and unsatisfactory encounters

In addition to asking employees for examples of interactions with customers that were difficult and uncomfortable, the views of customers are invaluable for revealing the specific events and employee behaviours that make for a satisfactory or dissatisfactory encounter. Critical incidents (events and behaviour) are uncovered by asking consumers the following:

- Think of a time when, as a customer, you had a particularly satisfying (dissatisfying) interaction with an employee of (service specified)?
- When did the incident happen?
- What specific circumstances led up to this situation?
- Exactly what did the employees say or do?
- What resulted that made you feel the interaction was satisfying (dissatisfying)?

Responses to questions such as these can shed enormous light on the performance of the entire service delivery system. It can reveal specific customer perceptions of how well (or badly) employees responded, failures in the service delivery system and customer needs and requests. It can provide surprises, e.g. excellent service as a consequence of unexpected and unrequested employee behaviour. In addition to individual expressions of satisfaction or dissatisfaction with a particular event or behaviour customers may intimate their overall feelings, for example:[17]

Everything went right – 'a sincere and professional team effort. accommodating, polite but not pushy, warm atmosphere, courteous, efficient and professional, no waiting, best service ever received, everything was perfect'.
Everything went wrong – 'inefficient, unprepared, slow, not accommodating nor attentive, no assistance, unprofessional, bad decor/atmosphere'.

Customer satisfaction or dissatisfaction will depend to a large extent on whether, and how, employees apply their ability, willingness and ingenuity. Implicit in all of this is the recurring theme of how well prepared, motivated and rewarded the employees are. Personality may explain acts of extreme helpfulness. However, employee response must be planned on a much firmer footing. The service organization bears a heavy responsibility for ensuring that employees are well resourced to act in a positive manner.

Encounters of more than human proportions

High contact service organizations are particularly exposed in terms of the number of potential encounter points. A good example is a college library. Given the pressure on staff resources, management could look at ways in which the consumers (students) could play a more prominent role in the production and delivery of the service. To do this questions would need to be asked of existing student experiences. One such study[18] used the critical incident technique for highlighting the problems students encounter when trying to use the library. The results yielded a wide range of problems and comment ranging from use of the catalogue, location of books and library layout. In addition, students expressed feelings of anxiety, a reluctance to ask for help and a lack of information. Some of the comments made by the students indicate the amount of work to be done before the library could be regarded as user friendly:

'The first time I came in the library I hadn't got a clue about anything. You just sort of get in there and it's so big and you just sit there and say "Oh no!".'
'You don't really know what's available . . . it's only if you find out from someone else that it's there, it's not publicized, you haven't got signs.'
'. . . and then the computer kept flashing up at me and I couldn't get rid of it . . . I was getting a bit panicky . . . and in the end I just left it.'

These few examples typify the difficulties/problems that consumers can experience in trying to make full and proper use of a service. The solution is not always to get the consumer to design the system. There may often be procedures and systems that have to be put into practice without any consultation with the consumer. However, it is the responsibility of the service provider to ensure that the potential users are equipped with information skills etc. to use the service effectively.

Another service with similar challenges is hospitals. They have the added problem of serving people (patients and visitors) who may be vulnerable and who are experiencing stress of some kind. The following complaints[19] are clear evidence of unsatisfactory encounters amounting to failure on the part of hospitals to deliver a quality service:

- Waiting for ages in out-patients without any explanation or apology
- Waiting a long time for admission to hospital
- Not understanding what the doctor is saying
- Important test results not being there when they see the consultant
- Not knowing what the options are or who to ask
- Doctors who have no time to listen and ignore what they say
- Being treated like a child and patronized
- Feeling that they are seen as a medical condition, not as a whole person
- Operations being cancelled at the last minute
- Transport home being hours late.

6.6   The importance of body language

Communicating effectively means sending the right signals. For many people, the message they are sending is not necessarily the one that is received. Body language is an area in which things can go wrong. Body language accounts for about 70 per cent of what we communicate, tone of voice about 20 per cent and the actual words about 10 per cent.

Whereas control is often exercised in selecting the words we use, body language is often left to 'fend for itself'. What comes out is the unedited version of what we really feel. Although body language is a study in its own right, the following areas offer a summary of what is involved.

1   **Posture** is concerned with body positions and movement A number of elements are commonly used to express the various positions:

lean:	forwards	arms:	open
	backwards		closed
	sideways		on hips
head:	lowered	legs:	stretched
	raised		open
	tilted sideways		crossed

Combinations of the above are said to indicate a range of attitudes and emotions, e.g. dominance, fear, relaxation, interest, boredom etc. In general it has been said that 'people who feel comfortable with a situation and with themselves raise their head and look openly at you. They may lean back slightly indicating they are relaxed or lean forward to indicate attentiveness. People who are on the attack or who feel aggressive generally adopt a "full frontal" stance with head, shoulders, hips and feet all pointing at you. They will probably raise themselves up and lean forward in a dominating manner. Those who are feeling defensive will probably "close-up" physically, making themselves smaller; hands and arms may protect their mouth or abdomen; legs may be crossed tightly. People feeling superior and arrogant may cross their legs openly (ankle of one leg resting on the knee of the other) and lean back with their hands clasped at the back of their head'.[20]

2   **Gestures** involve bodily actions by the head, hands or other parts of the body. Gestural styles are partly a product of many factors, e.g. culture, occupation, age, sex and so on. They can reflect an emotional state, e.g. anxiety (fidgeting) or a general style of behaviour, e.g. aggression (clenched fist). The hands, in particular, can be used in endless ways to communicate countless messages.

3   **Face** is the most important non-verbal channel. It is particularly important for expressing emotions and attitudes to other people. There is general agreement as to the range of emotional expressions. They are happiness, surprise, fear, sadness, anger, disgust/contempt. These emotions find expression through a communication of eye, eyebrows, lips, and mouth movement. Some emotions are found in certain parts of the face, e.g. raised

eyebrows and an open smile indicating pleasure. Care must be exercised, however, when judging another person's emotional state from his or her face.

4 **Gaze** is important in interpersonal behaviour. Although a non-verbal signal it is essentially a means of perceiving the expression of others. It can be measured in terms of how much time is spent looking at another person or looking at each other. It can be in the form of a brief glance or extended eye contact. It is often referred to as 'staring', looking 'intently', looking 'daggers' or 'looking right through' another person. There are cultural rules about gaze, e.g. 'don't stare' and don't look at certain parts of the body. How much of it there is can be an indication, in certain situations, of attentiveness. Those who indulge it more are said to be better interactors, more persuasive, influential, credible and so on. But again, care must be exercised. It does play an important role in establishing relations between people. For example, a teacher uses the amount of gaze as an indication of whether or not pupils are listening.

5 **Tone of voice** is an important part of communication. It is not only what we say but how we say it, e.g. are the words delivered in a loud or soft manner, quickly or slowly? Is the delivery monotonous or varied? The way a communication is delivered can give rise to a variety of reactions ranging from interest and excitement through to downright boredom.

6 **Proximity** is concerned with spatial behaviour. How close we are to other people will depend on such things as cultural norms (e.g. Arabs tend to stand close) and the type of social situation. In some cases, like a crowded train we have no choice. But in others there are rules of engagement in so far as how far apart we should be. It is generally recognized that there are four main space ranges:

Intimate: 6–18 inches (15–48 cm)
Personal distances: 1.5–4 feet (0.45–1.2 m), closer than which discomfort is often experienced
Social distance: 4–12 feet (1.2–3.5 m), used for formal business purposes
Public distance: over 12 feet (3.5 m) and up to 25 feet (7.6 m) or more. This is the distance kept from important public figures.

To use body language effectively, according to Terry Gillen,[20] we have first, to ensure that it is positive. He groups some aspects of body language into positive and negative, the latter being further subdivided into submissive/inferior and aggressive/superior.

Positive
Smile
Interested expression
Moderate eye contact
Sufficient volume, varied pace and pitch of voice
Open posture
Hands, arms support what is being said

Negative

Submissive/inferior
Wobbly voice
Slow speech
Worried expression
Evasive looks down
Defensive arms/legs
Mouth covered with hand
Excessive distance

Aggressive/superior
Hard voice
Rapid speech
Extremes of expression
Excessive eye contact
Dominant posture
Finger wagging/jabbing
Invasions of person space

Gillen then combines the 'how' of interaction with what is said to illustrate the possibilities (Figure 6.3). The main point about this is that effectiveness in communication stems from actions and words that are in tune with each other.

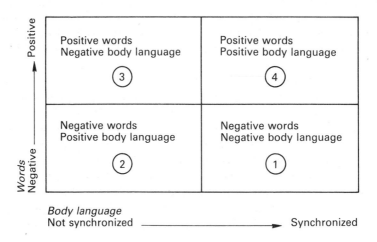

Figure 6.3 *Synchronizing verbal and non-verbal communication. Source: Gillent, T. (1990)[19]*

6.7 Summary

The service encounter can take a variety of forms, ranging from a cursory glance at a sign to a protracted personal interaction. The nature and degree of customer involvement is an important issue in the service encounter.

Of all the types of encounter the interpersonal contact, particularly face-to-face, is the most challenging. The nature of the interaction and the final outcome will be explained by reference to a number of factors.

Encounters are meant to be bound by rules and conventions and participants are expected to abide by them. Performances during the encounter are likened to those witnessed on stage in the theatre. The service provider and customers are, in effect, actors who have been assigned a role with an appropriate script.

Analysis can be undertaken of role behaviour and script generation. The critical incident technique is a valuable tool for determining what the parties to an encounter expect and what constitutes a satisfying or dissatisfying experience. It can assist the organization trying to ensure that the experience, and subsequent memory, is one of satisfaction at the very least. Any encounter represents a moment of truth in which lasting impressions may be created.

Questions

1 Construct a service situation in which a range of behaviours and actions by customers is in evidence and test them against the following:

Does not disrupt the situation ----- Totally disrupts the situation
Easy to deal with ----- Very difficult to deal with
Can be left or dealt with later ----- Needs to be dealt with first
Not annoying ----- Extremely annoying
Acceptable under some conditions ----- Never acceptable

2 Identify types of service encounter where customer power is either reduced or enhanced. Give reasons for your views.

3 Select a service situation and using the instructions detailed in the chapter ask your respondents (sample size 50) to write a script. Display the responses as in Table 6.4. Interpret the findings, e.g. frequency of mention, sequencing etc.

4 Describe three types of situations in which customers can make service employees think negatively, e.g. complaints, unfair accusations, unreasonable requests and then describe the body language that the service employee would exhibit to help defuse the situation.

	Situation	*Body language*
(a)		
(b)		
(c)		

References

1 Shostack, G. L. (1985). Planning the service encounter. In *The Service Encounter*, (Czepiel, J. A., Solomon, M. R., Suprenant, C. F., eds). Lexington Books, D. C. Heath and Company, Lexington, Mass.
2 Langeard, E., Bateson, J. E. G., Lovelock, C. H., Eiglier, (1981). Marketing of services: new insights from consumers and managers. *Marketing Science Institute, Report*, Number 81–104. Cambridge, Mass.
3 Argyle, M., Furnham, A. and Graham, J. A. (1981). *Social Situations*. Cambridge University Press, Cambridge.
4 Elliston, N. (1992). Retail sector. MPhil research, Napier University.
5 Goffman, E. (1972). *The Presentation of Self in Everyday Life*. Penguin, London.
6 Langer, E. (1978). Rethinking the role of thought in social interaction. In *New Directions in Attribution Research* (Harvey, J., Ickes, W. and Kidd, R. eds). Hillsdale, NJ.
7 Goffman, E. (1961). *Encounters: Two Studies in the Sociology of Interaction*. Bobbs-Merrill, Indianapolis.
8 Solomon, M. R., Suprenant, C., Czepiel, J. A. and Gutman, E. G. (1985). A role theory perspective on dyadic interactions: the service encounter. *Journal of Marketing*, **49** Winter, 99–111.
9 Siehl, C. and Bowen, D. E. (1991). The role of rites of integration in service delivery. *International Journal of Service Industry Management*, **2**(1), 15–34.
10 Goodwin, C. (1989). *Using Consumers' Roles to Classify Service Excellence: marketing's impact on performance*. Eighth Annual Services Marketing Conference, American Marketing Association.
11 Mills, P. K. and Morris, J. H. (1986). Clients as 'partial' employees of service organisations: role development in client participation. *Academy of Management Review*, **11**(4), 726–735.
12 Schank, R. C. and Abelson, R. P. (1977). *Scripts, Plans. Goals and Understanding*. Erlbaum Associates, Hillsdale, NJ.
13 Bower, G. H., Black, J. B. and Turner, T. J. (1979). Scripts in memory for text. *Cognitive Psychology*, **11** 177–220.
14 Tansik, D. A. and Smith, W. L. (1991). Dimensions of job scripting in services organisations. *International Journal of Service Industry Management*. **2**(1), 35–49.
15 Flanagan, J. C. (1954). The critical incident technique. *Psychological Bulletin*, **51**(4), July 327–358.
16 Nyquist, J. D., Bitner, M. J. and Booms, B. H. (1985). Identifying communication difficulties in the service encounter: a critical incident approach. *The Service Encounter*, (Czepiel, J. A., Solomon, M. R., Suprenant, C. F., eds). Lexington Books. D. C. Heath and Company, Lexington, Mass.
17 Bitner, M. J., Booms, B. H. and Terteault, M. S. (1990). The service encounter: diagnosing favourable and unfavourable incidents. *Journal of Marketing*, **54** January, 71–84.

18 Andrews, J. (1991). An exploration of students' library use problems. *Library review*, **40**(1), 5–14.
19 *Framework for Action: The National Health Service in Scotland* (1991). HMSO, London.
20 Gillen, T. (1990). *Training Workshops for Customer Care*. Gower Publishing Company, London.

7

Service employees

7.1 Introduction

The person who delivers the service is of key importance to both the customer he serves and the employer he represents. To the customer he is in fact part of the product. His ability and willingness to satisfy, his manner and appearance, all play a part in determining how satisfied the customer is with the service encounter. To the employer, those delivering the service can make or break the organization. On the one hand, they may be the only way that a service brand differentiates itself. On the other hand, they can also be the reason why people do not come back.

In many organizations everything that the frontline employee does is stage managed. He has little discretion or flexibility in the way he offers the service, rather he is restricted to implementing a strict set of rules and procedures. This leaves the job deskilled and the worker demotivated.[1] In other organizations frontline employees can be given too much flexibility and responsibility without the commensurate training or rewards.[2]

Enslavement

Empowerment

7.2 Frontline personnel

Not every frontline employee plays an equally important role in the delivery of service. Lovelock[3] suggests that the two most significant variables in this respect are the degree to which the service offering is customized, and the extent to which customer contact staff exercise judgement in meeting an indi-

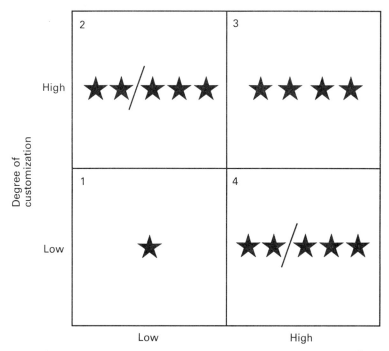

High

Low

Degree of
customization

Low   High

Degree of judgement exercised by customer contact staff

Figure 7.1 *The impact of customization/customer contact on the importance of frontline staff.* ★ *= not very important,* ★★★★ *= very important. Adapted from Lovelock (1991)[3]*

vidual customer's needs (Figure 7.1). In box 1 frontline staff play a relatively minor role in the service experience, e.g. a ticket cashier at the local cinema. Whereas services operating in box 4 rely heavily on frontline staff to satisfy the customer, e.g. marriage guidance councillor. Boxes 2 and 3 will fall somewhere in the middle. The degree of importance attached to frontline employees in these situations will depend on the specific service being offered.

Frontline personnel are not a homogeneous group. The hotel chambermaid and the plastic surgeon are both frontline employees in that they both deal directly with customers. Some of the skills that are required are common to both jobs. These core skills have become common requirements of all frontline staff regardless of the specific service that they provide (Figure 7.2).

In addition to these essentials, most industries also require some supplementary skills. Frontline staff will only provide a quality service if they possess all the qualities required, both core and supplementary. Historically, those who provided services that required a lot of technical ability got away without the core skills. If a doctor was rude, or kept patients waiting, no one complained. No one accused him of providing a poor service. His position allowed him to behave in this manner. Now, though, even those in the professional services are expected to possess core service skills.

Frontline staff act as another element of communication. They help portray the desired image of the company. If the intended image is one of sophistication then do not employ people who chew gum and bite their nails. If it is

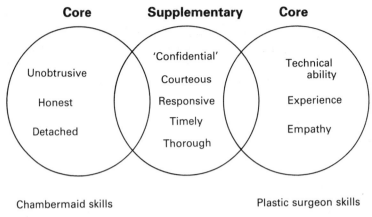

Figure 7.2 *Core/supplementary skills*

important that customers empathize with staff then ensure that service personnel are segmented by their personalities so that they meet the customers'
requirements. In a department store the total pool of shop assistants should be
segmented so that for example, those serving in the children's department are
patient and fun-loving, while those serving in the china department are careful
and light of foot.

7.3   Customer and staff care

'Customer care' is often discussed in the service sector. The concept came to
prominence in the 1980s through the highly publicized customer care campaigns of British Airways and British Telecom. Today, we often hear of companies deploying 'customer care' programmes, but what does it all mean?[4]
     The concept has been defined as 'a fundamental approach to standards of
quality service. It covers every aspect of a company's operations, from the
design of the product or service to how it is packaged, delivered and serviced.
Even the accompanying instructions, so often forgotten by the customer-care
conscious Japanese, are part of the process'.[5] This definition talks of a process
for delivering quality service, and is therefore more substantial and far-reach-
ing in scope, than the smile and charm school approach that has given the concept of customer care a bad name.
     In effect this approach to business is merely a restatement of Levitt's propo-
sition that 'the customer is king'. Taking this analogy a stage further, those
who provide for the king's needs are his 'servants'. Satisfying him is of paramount importance, not only to the selfish king, but also to those who wish to
remain in the kingdom.
     Whether or not the customer regards himself as a king, he has come to
expect 'care' from the service provider. Management have long recognized the
importance of frontline employees in the provision of this care. They are the
key to success during what Jan Carlzon calls the 'moments of truth'.[6]
However, what organizations often fail to recognize is the importance of 'staff
care'. Customers are far more likely to receive good service if the staff deliver-

ing the service are happy in their work. Employers who treat their staff like kings are far more likely to have a motivated and committed workforce who are interested and willing to deliver a quality service. In organizations where the employees have a good opinion of the human resources policy, customers also have a good opinion of the service that they receive.[7] Management cannot expect to deliver customer satisfaction if it has little regard for the satisfaction of its own internal customers – the employees.

7.4   Staff dissatisfaction

One suspects that if you asked service customers the question, 'Are you treated like a king?', that at best you would get some hysterical laughter and at worst you would be physically abused.

For many consumers in this country there is certainly still a long way to go before the transition from 'organization is king' to 'customer is king' is complete.

The dissatisfaction that arises is often laid at the feet of the frontline employees in the service organization. While at times this is unjust, we can probably all recount instances where the blame lies almost entirely with them.

Scratch the surface of most of these situations, and you will find in most cases the employee is also unhappy with the organization. Why should he attempt to make customers happy when he is not happy himself?

In transactional analysis this individual has adopted what Harris,[8] describes as an 'I'm not OK' position. The organization has made him feel 'Not OK', and he takes it out on the customer.

If the service provider is to improve the interaction of these staff with customers, then he has to make them feel, 'I'm OK, the organization's OK, you're OK, and I'd like to help you'.

But before the organization can remove the dissatisfaction it has to be understood. So what makes employees dissatisfied with their jobs?

Many factors have been found to contribute to this problem[9]. These are:

- Role ambiguity
- Role conflict
- Role overload
- Employee/job mismatch
- Performance measured on quantity not quality
- Lack of empowerment
- Lack of a common purpose
- Lack of management commitment

Role ambiguity

Employees do not understand what management or customers expect of them (see Chapter 2). This situation is improved with role clarity; clearly communicate what individuals must do, and tell them how they are doing. However, telling the individual what you want him/her to do is not enough. It is the employer's responsibility to give the employee the ability to perform the job. This can be done by training, leaving him or her a competent and confident performer.

Role conflict

Two or more incompatible sets of pressures impact on the employee's behaviour. This is more likely to arise in situations where the employee is in what Boas Shamir describes as a subordinate service role.[10] In these situations the provider of the service has no more expertise or ability to deliver the service than the ordinary man in the street. The majority of service encounters that take place in fact do so with the employee in this position. Think of the jobs performed by the receptionist in an hotel, the shop assistant, the waiter, and the bus conductor. We all feel that we could do them, and this makes us more critical of the service that is delivered under these circumstances.

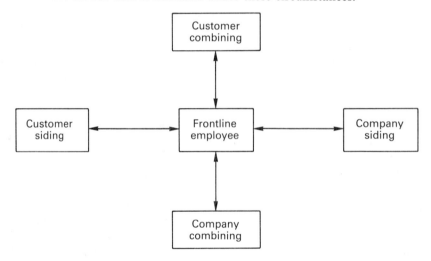

Figure 7.3 *Sources of role conflict*

There are four basic sources of role conflict (Figure 7.3).

- Customer siding conflict: employee wants to do more for the customer than the organization allows (provide a child's portion at a reduced price).
- Company siding conflict: employee takes the side of the organization believing that the customer is acting in an unjustified or selfish manner, i.e. refusing to admit late theatregoers during the performance.
- Company combining conflict: the organization expects him to satisfy demanding customers and do lots of paperwork and administration besides.
- Customer combining conflict: separate groups of customers have different requirements for the service, e.g. some customers may regard the main job of their coach tour guide to be one of information provision. Other members of the party may instead believe that this person is there primarily to keep the tour on time.

So what can the organization do to minimize role conflict?

- Design jobs whose scope is pitched at the abilities of the proficient employee.
- If need be, prioritize the multitude of tasks that the employee is expected to fulfil.
- Define these tasks in terms of customers' expectations.
- Ensure that performance is measured on those tasks which have been given priority. These should be customer-focused tasks.
- Train employees in time management.

Role overload

The name describes the problem! No matter how diligently the individual works he can never do all that is asked of him. He is always behind – causing frustration and dissatisfaction with his performance.

This is most likely to occur where jobs have been badly designed. However, even where the initial job design was excellent, circumstances can change. It may be that the level, or pattern, of demand for the service has changed. If instead of handling equal customer traffic throughout the day, a workforce is faced with periods of relative inactivity followed by periods of intense activity, role overload may result.

Workloads and patterns of demand should be continually monitored and evaluated to reduce the risk of role overload.

Employee/job mismatch

Not every individual performing a frontline service role is an appropriate person for the job. In some cases this is the result of a poor recruitment and selection process. In others, the organization does not really care. It is known that many service companies experiencing high turnover rates among contact staff tend to recruit new staff expediently with little regard for their ability.[11] This is shortsighted, because these individuals probably do not really care much about customer satisfaction. Whatever the job, management should consider the qualities that are necessary to do the job. It should then adopt a selection process that tests for these qualities.

Performance measured on quantity not quality

It can be disheartening for a frontline employee to discover that they work for a company which is more interested in employee efficiency than employee effectiveness. The number of customers that they have dealt with being of more importance than the degree to which these customers were satisfied (see Chapter 10).

Lack of empowerment

Employees who have little flexibility or discretion in the way that they handle customers' demands can find their jobs frustrating. They can be likened to circus animals who slavishly respond to appropriate triggers, with set routines.

Enlightened employers have realized the lack of motivation that normally ensues from such work, and have set about trying to correct this by giving them more responsibility and authority. This is known as *empowerment*.

We would certainly encourage employers to make the individual's job more rewarding through empowerment. However, in giving him this extra responsibility the employer should also be prepared to reward the increased job scope in an appropriate manner e.g. with a higher salary.

Lack of a common purpose

Frequently the individual employee that greets the customer feels quite isolated in that position. He can believe that he carries out his job without the full backing either of the other employees in the back office or indeed of the company's management.

What is needed is for the company to have a common purpose and for everyone employed in it to pull in the same direction with the intention of achieving the common goal.

One way of doing this is to make customer satisfaction the stated goal, and to make everyone in the company treat the other members of staff that they interact with as if they were customers. They should be encouraged to provide a standard of service to these employees that they would wish to receive themselves.

Lack of management commitment

It is one thing for management to develop a common purpose, and to communicate this mission to all its employees, but it cannot expect this alone to motivate the staff. If employees feel that management say one thing to them and then do another themselves, they are likely to become disenfranchised. As Abraham Lincoln said, 'actions speak louder than words'.[12] So, for example, if part of the stated mission is to improve customer satisfaction, then management should not ignore complaints.

Role tension

Any of the dissatisfactions discussed above can lead to role tension in the employee. This tension will affect the level of commitment that the individual is willing to make. For an organization to realize the full potential of its employees, it must attempt to build a committed workforce.

The greater the tension that he feels, the less committed to his employer he becomes. The organization will suffer this lack of commitment, even if it is not to blame for the tension, e.g. discourteous customers can easily make the front-line employee tense.

If such an incident is reported to management, and they take little notice or do not want to get involved, then the level of tension will rise. Management who practise internal marketing are now faced with the conflicting interests of these two groups of customers.

7.5 Staff turnover

One way that a dissatisfied employee can deal with his dissatisfaction is to leave the organization.

There are many companies that accept high rates of turnover as a fact of life in the provision of service. In 1987, counter staff turnover at McDonalds was 150 per cent, and at Burger King was 250 per cent.[13] Unfortunately, the acceptance of this creates a vicious circle (Figure 7.4).

Management think that investing in selection and training is a waste of resource. Since the employee is likely to leave soon, there is little point in developing his skills. After all, this just makes it easier for him to find another job. An employer who thinks in this way fails to see that his lack of investment in selection and training probably contribute to the high rates of turnover in the first place.

Traditional view = training is an overhead and is costly
Enlightened view = training does not cost

Companies should try to avoid high levels of staff turnover for several reasons. In the first place, the management of these companies tends to be less effective. It spends most of its time trying to fire fight the current operation, instead of thinking about the future. For companies listed on the stock market, this can often result in adverse city comment with a consequent fall in the share price, and therefore value of the company. Curtailed expansion will also mean that the good people who have stayed until now, begin to look elsewhere.

Companies with high levels of attrition usually provide poor customer service; because employees providing the service will not have been doing so for long, they will often have little training, or understanding of the company's values or product. Their apparent lack of confidence in what they are doing often results in lower sales.

High staff turnover also results in extra costs for the company. It has to spend more on recruitment, administration, and some basic training. In addition to which there is a cost implication from the productivity losses that are experienced before new staff are up to speed.

However, while high levels of staff turnover should be avoided, the company should not set as its personnel goal, no staff turnover at all. For one thing, an organization that experiences no attrition, goes stale.

Fresh blood can bring new thinking and energy to take a company forward. Without this injection the organization can become complacent, and fixed in its

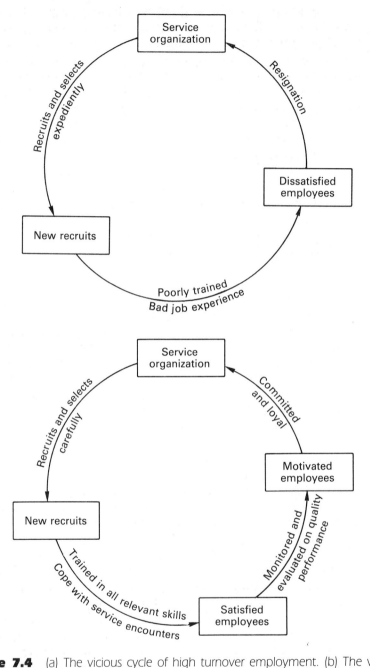

Figure 7.4 (a) The vicious cycle of high turnover employment. (b) The virtuous cycle of low turnover employment

view of how things should be done, resisting the challenge of change. Companies whose management has been in place for some time often resist until it is too late. Consider the dinosaurs and other creatures who once populated this planet, but through a lack of evolution are now extinct.

Another reason why some attrition should be encouraged, is that no matter how expert an organization's selection process is, the odd misfit will manage to slip through the net. In these cases it is always better for the company to let the individual go rather than expend precious resources trying to keep him on board in pursuit of a zero staff turnover rate.

So the benefits to the company of building a workforce with low levels of turnover are increased commitment from staff, which in turn leads to increased productivity and better customer service.[14] Commitment has been shown to be related to personal variables such as gender, and marital status,[15] i.e. personality traits that the company cannot influence. However, it is primarily related to variables that are under the control of the company. For example, the longer an employee has been with an organization, the more committed to it he will be. Conversely, the more that he experiences tension and dissatisfaction with his career progression, the less committed he becomes.

7.6 Building a committed workforce

There are two possible solutions to excess staff turnover. One focuses on the individual employee. The other deals more with the organization's role. These routes are not proposed as either/or options. To secure the benefits of low turnover the company must tackle the issue from both directions. Taken together, the two routes represent what is known as *internal marketing*. The practice of internal marketing means using the traditional tools of marketing-segmentation, NPD, market research, promotion, etc. on potential and current employees (Figure 7.5).

The pre-employment relationship: recruitment

In the same way that customers need to build a relationship with the company before they develop loyalty, the employee needs to form a similar attachment before he becomes committed. This relationship often begins long before the individual becomes an employee.

Many prospective employees will have been exposed to the external communications of the hiring organization even before they consider working for it (see Chapter 10). They may even be a lapsed or current user of the service. This all plays a part in his decision to work for a company.

The company gets another chance to create a favourable impression in its recruitment and selection process. All too often the employer regards this process as a one-sided affair, believing that the onus falls entirely on the applicants to make the company want them. This is a somewhat shortsighted approach.

The company wants the best possible recruits. To ensure that it gets them, the company must be prepared to 'tell and sell'. Recruitment communications should contain the following:

• A clear description of the job specification including job title, reporting structure, and main areas of responsibility

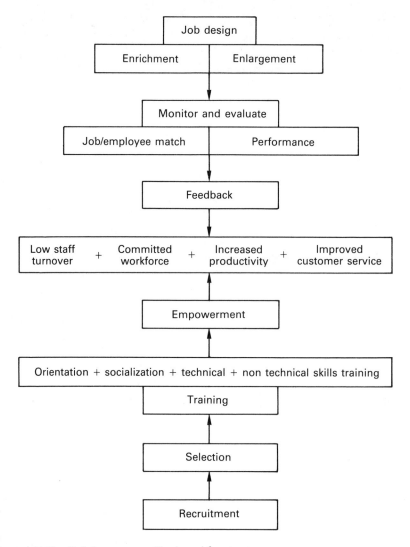

Figure 7.5 *Building a committed workforce*

- A statement of any definite requirements, e.g. academic qualifications, years experience, height (police force).
- Reasons why individuals should consider joining the company.
- A description of the company's culture and mission.

Obviously it is not necessary, or desirable to include all of these in every piece of communication. For example, many of the large accountancy firms produce glossy recruitment brochures that meet the latter two requirements, and neatly perform the telling and selling functions. On the other hand, specific job advertisements placed in the media, may choose instead to focus on the first two requirements. By concentrating on fewer requirements, they may be able to contain advertising costs.

Recruitment communication is most effective when it attracts the right number of the right type of applicants. The company is wasting time if it ends up interviewing applicants who do not meet the company's job specification. Therefore, recruitment communications should seek to tempt appropriate individuals to apply, but at the same time deter unsuitable applicants.

The pre-employment relationship: selection

The importance of selection in the service industry can be summed up in three statements made by Schneider and Schechter.[14]

1 The climate and culture of an organization is a function of the people who are employed there.
2 Most service organizations require interdependent employee behaviour, and therefore everyone operating in the system must be performing well. Individual excellence will not compensate for poor performers.
3 The best predictor of future behaviour is past behaviour.

A cornerstone of the selection process is the face-to-face interview. This again is a two-way process. It enables the company to present a picture of what it stands for, and what the job entails. It should also give the applicant the opportunity to elaborate on his application.

The power in the relationship at this time, tends to lie with the company. It decides on the interview timing, the format, and the techniques and procedures that will be adopted.

To get the best out of this interchange the organization ought to be testing relevant skills. This means that in addition to the obvious technical skill requirements, the organization should have considered what personal qualities are necessary to do the job successfully. Obviously not all service jobs require identical skills. However, William George[16] suggests that interpersonal competence and a service orientation are two basic skills that all service personnel should possess.

In the 1960s and 1970s, role playing scenarios were used to assess these basic skills. However, many applicants found them relatively easy to manipulate, and the assessment of the scenarios was open to wide variations in interpretation.

In an attempt to overcome these weaknesses, quantitatively-based techniques have become fashionable. These are intended to reduce what Woods and McAuley refer to as 'the halo and the devil-horn effect' of the qualitative scenarios.[13] Psychometric testing is one such technique (Table 7.1). In many cases, this test takes a similar form to the traditional IQ tests. The applicant answers a series of multiple choice questions within a tight time frame. Historically, these tests only managed to remove one of the weaknesses of the behaviouralists' approach – the results were not open to the same level of interpretation as before. Individuals are scored using conventional statistical measurement techniques. However, the crudeness of some of the early tests meant that the bright applicants who were aware of the skills that the company was looking for, could see how to answer the questions in such a way that they would achieve high scores on the appropriate skills.

Table 7.1 Psychometric testing variables

Personal attribute	Score	
Persuasive	9	————————-****-
Controlling	6	—————-****————
Independent	7	————————-****—————
Outgoing	8	————————-****———
Affiliative	5	————-****—————
Socially confident	8	————————-****———
Modest	3	—-****————————-
Democratic	5	—————-****—————
Caring	10	————————————-***
Practical	6	—————-****————
Data rational	10	————————————-***
Artistic	9	————————-****-
Behavioural	9	————————-****-
Traditional	5	—————-****—————
Change oriented	9	————————-****-
Conceptual	10	————————————-***
Innovative	9	————————-****-
Forward planning	9	————————-****-
Detail conscious	5	—————-****—————
Conscientious	9	————————-****-
Relaxed	5	—————-****—————
Worrying	7	————————-****—————
Tough minded	3	—-****————————-
Emotional control	6	—————-****—————
Optimistic	7	—————-****—————
Critical	6	—————-****————
Active	8	————————-****———
Competitive	9	————————-****-
Achieving	10	————————————-***
Decisive	7	————————-****———-
Social desirability	7	————————-****———-

This individual displayed the personality suitable
for senior level management

Nowadays, these tests have become much more sophisticated in design. Applicants attempting to manipulate the test become confused and disorientated by the apparent sameness of many of the questions.

Whatever methods are chosen to assess the applicant's suitability, the company must develop a selection system that meets its needs. What it needs are 'winners at the frontline not just warm bodies'.[11]

Employment: the early days

Hopefully, the outcome of the recruitment and selection process will be new recruits who are *willing* to perform the tasks that are required of them. The willingness which they bring to the company may well have to be strengthened and moulded.

While the new recruit to a supermarket checkout operator's position will probably have some image of what it is like to sit at an EPOS (electronic point of sale) checkout desk, the image that he has will be based on his own limited experience as a customer. As a customer, the individual may have had a different perspective of reality. He may have expected it to be quite a sociable job. A former checkout operator describing her job on Channel Four Television said, 'You never see their faces. All you see are their hands. They might just as well be gorillas'.[17]

A company strengthens and moulds the recruit's willingness by training. In addition to shaping his willingness, in many cases the training may also serve the purpose of developing his *ability* to do the job.

Cabin staff recruited to British Airways will not have previous experience of assisting passengers in an emergency landing. They will probably have experience of serving drinks, and should certainly have experience of smiling. The training that they are given will tackle both these 'technical' and 'non-technical' aspects of their job.

Frontline staff are expected to conform to certain role models in the provision of service. This can sometimes mean performing everyday tasks in a slightly different fashion because that it what the company wants. An employee may have to shake hands more vigorously, talk more animatedly, or make more eye contact than he otherwise would, i.e. emotions often have to be 'managed'.[1] Trainers have to work on inhibiting and inducing certain feelings. The overworked nurse is expected to be calm and patient. The swimming pool attendant is not supposed to become irate with the squeals of noisy school children, instead he is supposed to remain detached and vigilant.

Being pleasant to customers is often an intrinsic part of the job. This worked-up warmth is part of many service jobs. The service worker is not encouraged to display his true feelings to the customer. Instead he is expected to do what is known as psychological bowing.[1]

However, employees who are expected to display emotions which they do not feel, will eventually suffer from strain and stress if this situation is an enduring one. Therefore, if displayed emotion is required, then the trainer's job is to change the employee's feelings. The recruit has to learn to 'bow from the heart'.[1]

The recipient of this bowing, the customer, is becoming expert in spotting this 'managed heart', and in many cases he has become cynical of the approach. He is fully aware that individuals doing this type of work will be trained by their company to display the appropriate emotion. How many times have you been instructed to 'have a nice day' by a service worker who mouths it mechanically without a thought or care for what he is saying?

Management are then challenged to think of new ways in which the employee can continue to delight the customer. In addition to this, industries

tarnished by their smile school approach, should certainly aim to hire those individuals who naturally display the kinds of emotions that are required. The less that employees have to be trained to feel these emotions the more spontaneous and therefore convincing they will be to customers.

Of course, different emotions will be relevant to different service industries. Management must consider what the salient emotional expressions are before it begins to train recruits. If the business is debt collection, then frontline employees will be expected to be nasty to debtors. Whereas flight attendants are expected to be pleasant to passengers.[18]

The early days: orientation

Training programmes that seek to orientate and socialize recruits have been shown to be more effective in building commitment and productivity than those which do not. The quicker this happens after the employee joins a company the better.

In addition to providing new members of staff with the necessary tools for their jobs, enlightened employers will seek to use the training forum as an opportunity to get its recruits fully 'on board'. It does this by practising 'rites of passage',[19] otherwise known as orientation and socialization. All companies will not adopt identical approaches to this process. After all, the purpose of the transition is to shape the recruit in such a way that he handles customers effectively. As Rohlen[20] says, 'what is OK to be practised by the US Army, is not quite so relevant for a high street bank'.

Orientation is the process by which the organization helps the new recruit understand the company and its culture. It is particularly important for those service organizations whose frontline employees meet customers at arm's length from any supervision, back up, or control. In these cases it is vital that the employee has been imbued with the company's values. Most orientation programmes ask the recruit to be a receptive, yet passive, audience for this communication. However, since the desired outcome is for recruits to feel enthused about the prospect of working for the company, it is sometimes necessary to work on building his receptivity first.

This often involves the recruit in a more active orientation role. If management anticipate that a recruit may be antagonistic to what they have to say, then it should actively try to squeeze this out. One such technique is the practice of EST (Erhart sensory training). This centres around the belief that it's impossible to overlay emotions and behaviour as they pertain to a particular situation (in this case the delivery of service) on those emotions that are already there. People must be taken apart and then built up again. The recruit must be humbled and displaced, in advance of any orchestrated orientation.

During orientation the organization is then free to blow its own trumpet without fear of a slow hand clap. Senior management involvement in this process usually goes down well. But whatever the chosen route for orientation, the programme should seek to leave recruits with an understanding of the purpose and mission of the company. The organization then has more chance of everyone pulling in the same direction.

In addition to this, any folklore that the company has which demonstrates the culture of the organization should also be communicated. The folklore can be related to a previous employee who made an outstanding contribution to the company's fortunes, or it can be about particular service encounters where the company went to extraordinary lengths to deliver the service.

The contribution that these stories make to orientation is two fold. First of all, people are more likely to remember the values and goals of the company if they are illuminated with actual situations. Second, these myths and heroes create the impression of a private and elite society that the recruit is privileged to join. Remember, in a service organization, orientation should clearly communicate to recruits the central importance of the customer.

The early days: socialization

Now that the recruit understands the culture and workings of the organization, he must be initiated into the workings of its cultural setting. Orientation has told him what to expect in this context, socialization is the process by which he begins to experience it.

Management may build socialization by feeding to recruits the thought that a lot will be expected of them as employees of the company. If the employee does not feel that he is living up to expectations he will begin to feel guilty. In this case the process of socialization has become internalized in the employee, and management no longer has to rely on coercion to ensure motivation.

Another socialization technique is to make recruits publicly acknowledge these rites of passage. In many communist countries public declarations of commitment were often demanded. It then became more difficult to betray the Party.

Some companies socialize their employees by giving them hands-on dirty work experience. They get management to take part in the service encounter, e.g. McDonalds gets all its new managers to serve customers on the shop floor. Indeed, it asks its advertising agency and all other service agencies that it uses to do the same. The purpose of these role adoptive scenarios is to give these employees and those in supporting roles more understanding of the business.

An area of current controversy in the socialization process is the extent to which individuals have to conform to corporate culture. Schein[21] has developed three basic behavioural responses to socialization:

- Rebellion – rejection of all that is expected
- Creative individualism – acceptance of all crucial behavioural norms
- Conformity – acceptance of everything

Of course the response of most employees will fall somewhere between the first and the second category, or the second and the third. The first and third categories are generally regarded as socialization failures. The middle category is most desirable, but it is a difficult position for an employee to maintain.

The degree to which management seeks conformity really depends on their specific industry. If for example, individuality and innovation are important values (as in hairdressing) then the organization should not seek to make these employees conform.

Individuals who are best placed to work in positions that require individuality and innovation, are those who are *intrinsically* motivated.[2] That means that they prefer complexity, novelty, challenge, and the opportunity to master a skill in their employment. Conversely, an individual who is *extrinsically* motivated seeks job simplicity and predictability. He lacks initiative. To perform his job he needs to be told what to do, and then continually supervised while doing it. Jobs of this nature are few and far between. Even jobs that on the surface would appear to suit this type of person, i.e. postman, or a secretary normally benefit from someone who can use their intelligence. The postman who recognizes that a letter is wrongly addressed and delivers it to the correct address is performing a better service for his customers.

Empowerment

An effective training programme will be one which is designed to give recruits the willingness and ability to serve. This, in turn, will certainly help to develop a committed workforce. However, the workforce are likely to be more committed if the frontline employees are also given *authority* to satisfy customers (Figure 7.6).

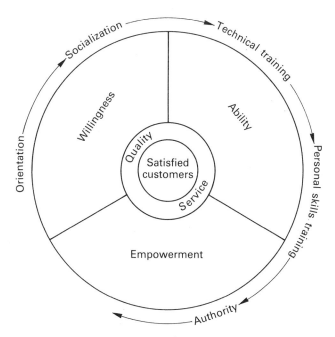

Figure 7.6 *Employee development in the customer satisfaction wheel*

Empowerment of employees is easiest when they have few rules to follow, i.e. the service delivery process is non-standardized. However, many organizations choose to standardize their operation to help control costs and quality levels.

In some organizations it may even be appropriate to standardize the whole operation. For instance McDonald's instructs its counter staff on tray assembly – cold drinks first, then hot, and always put the tray within easy reach of the customer.

However, even in organizations where service delivery is almost entirely standardized the empowerment of frontline employees can help. It can, for instance, provide quicker response times to customer complaints. The employee will not have to find a supervisor who can handle the complaint, and then attempt to explain the cause for the dissatisfaction. Instead he can make his own decision on the spot about the best way to recover the situation (Figure 7.7).

Quick response times to customer complaints are a restrictive use of the concept of empowerment. In this context, it plays no part in service delivery. Instead it is placed in a purely reactive role within the service recovery arena.

In those industries where service delivery is to some extent customized, there are even greater opportunities for empowerment. Here the employee can be given the flexibility and authority to meet the customers' needs. He is placed in a proactive role where he anticipates problems and corrects them during service delivery.

Bowen and Lawler[22] state the main benefits of empowerment as being:

- Quicker response times to customer needs
- Quicker response times to complaints

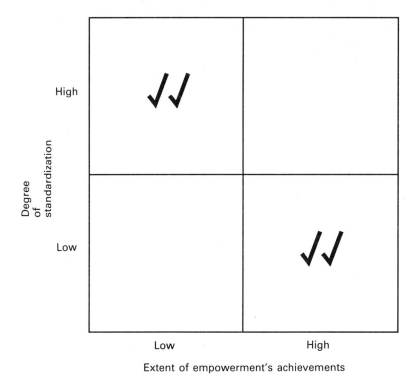

Figure 7.7 *The impact of standardization/customization on the achievements of empowerment*

- Employees feel better about their jobs and themselves
- Employees interact with customers with more warmth and enthusiasm
- Empowered employees can be a great source of service ideas
- Great word of mouth advertising and customer retention

Empowerment is supposed to deliver the dual benefits of enhanced customer satisfaction, and increased employee commitment. However employees are unlikely to be more committed to the organization if they feel that the empowerment is exploiting them. Early attempts at empowerment often failed to consider this factor. The increased responsibility and authority should be rewarded with money (e.g. a pay increase), or in other ways (e.g. faster career advancement).

Even in the cases where management makes concessions to employees in their drive to empower them, not all employees will be happy about the change in the nature of their job. As Bowen and Lawler state, '[they] will respond positively to empowerment only if they have strong needs to grow and to deepen and test their abilities at work'.[22]

Job design

There are two aspects of job design that should be considered in any attempt to empower frontline employees – one is *job enlargement*, the other is *job enrichment*. When people are asked to think of ways that jobs could be enriched they invariably mention things that are really only job enlargements. Enlarging a job means giving the employee more tasks to perform. Herzberg[23] refers to this as 'horizontal job loading', and makes suggestions for ways in which a job may instead be enriched.

However, just as not all employees want to be empowered, they do not all want to be enriched. The chequered history of job enrichment programmes would suggest that the extent to which employees want their jobs to be enriched, depends on the nature of their motivations.

Other aspects of job design that should be considered by those in the organization entrusted with personnel matters are:

- Job specification
- Training and development
- Working conditions
- Appraisal systems
- Promotion prospects
- Salary and benefits

7.7   Maintaining commitment from employees

Encouraging motivation

The previous section examined what the organization should do to help build a committed workforce. To maintain the commitment, the relationship must be carefully nurtured and groomed. Motivation that was built on orientation and socialization programmes during the introductory training may have become quite depleted from everyday bashing at the frontline. So what should the organization do to retain its good staff? And what must it do to keep them committed and motivated?

Organizations can deal with this issue in a variety of ways. Whatever they decide to do, two principles should guide them:

1 Keep the importance of the delivery of quality service and customer satisfaction visible.
2 Top management involvement in the delivery of these goals should also be visible. Not only in terms of what they say, but also in terms of what they do.

A whole variety of techniques designed to foster employee commitment have been proposed.[21] The organization can practise Rites of Renewal which seeks to fine-tune the system using the latest organizational development techniques – quality circles, management by objectives (MBO), team building to name but a few.

However, there is substantial cynicism about their effectiveness. Many regard them as a series of gimmicks designed to make management feel good about the fact that they are doing something. This game will often act as a smokescreen leaving the real issues undisturbed. Hertzberg[23] believes that the only way to motivate employees is to give them challenging work. He lists the following factors as contributing to motivation:

- Achievement
- Recognition for achievement
- The work itself
- Responsibility
- Growth or advancement

All the other techniques are at best offering only short term motivations.

Monitoring and evaluating the employees' contribution

In addition to encouraging motivation the employee's contribution to service delivery should be evaluated in two ways.

1 The employee himself should be given a voice. This is part of the internal marketing concept – if the organization is treating its staff like customers then it must find out their attitudes towards the current organizational practice. Management should seek to gather information on the following issues:

- What are his current satisfactions/dissatisfactions with his job?
- What could be done to reduce the dissatisfactions?
- What things could the organization do for the employee to improve his service offering? (e.g. more training, new uniforms)
- What other improvements could be made to the way that the service is delivered?

2 The customer's evaluation of the service that he received.

Employees should ideally be evaluated and remunerated in terms of their contribution to customer satisfaction (evaluate effectiveness rather than efficiency). This follows the principle of 'what gets measured gets done'. If employees know that they are being evaluated in terms of customer satisfaction, then they are more likely to be motivated to provide this satisfaction.

Feedback

Performance monitoring and evaluation should be concerned with the achievement of customer satisfaction. Employees who help to create this satisfaction must know how they fared. The results of the evaluation should be fed back to employees.

In doing so, the organization hopes to improve their performance, and thereby to satisfy more customers. The appraisal of employees can be carried out on a regular or irregular basis. The appraisals can be tied to a review of pay, but they need not all be. Employees will of course expect to be remunerated for their efforts, and a performance appraisal is a good time for this to be discussed. It will be most appropriate in those circumstances where pay is related to performance. However, the organization would be foolish to encourage employees to believe that their performance will only be discussed when their pay is up for review.

One feedback mechanism that is growing in influence is that which encourages 'service wisdom'.[24] Employees are venerated for successfully handling situations that were not covered in their service manuals or training sessions. The Holiday Inn's 'employee of the month' scheme, or American Express's annual Great Performance Award are examples of this. In exceptional cases, the service encounters that gave rise to the award may become part of the company's folklore.

The feedback process should not be entirely one-way from management to employees. Instead it should be a three-way process between the employee's internal/external customers, his subordinates, and management.[24]

Unfortunately this is still only practised by the most enlightened of companies. Most employers still behave as if the employees belong to them. They feel that the employee owes the organization something for being given the privilege of working there, and do not see that they might owe the employee more than his salary in return for his labour.

7.8 Redefining the roles of employee and customer

So far our discussion has focused on frontline staff since they are most visible in the delivery of quality service. However, for the organization to operate effectively *all* employees must be pulling in the same direction. There is little sense in selecting and developing excellent frontline staff if they are not supported by those in the back office. While the customer does not see these employees it does not mean that they play an insignificant part in the delivery of a quality service.

All employees who are in the back office should treat the other members of the organization that they deal with as internal customers. Whether they provide direct support to frontline staff as in the RAC's command control room

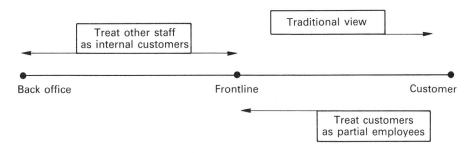

Figure 7.8   Expanding the roles of employee and customer

which feeds information to its recovery vehicles, or direct support to other back office staff, as in the accounts department of an hotel, they should behave towards these individuals in the same way that they would if they were external customers. Everyone in the organization must share the responsibility for delivering customer satisfaction.

The traditional interaction between customer and frontline employee can also be extended (Figure 7.8). Given the inseparability of production and consumption in most service encounters, the customer actually becomes involved in the production of the service. His behaviour (as well as that of employees) affects the outcome. Service organizations would do well to treat their customers as *partial employees*, adopting the same disciplines that we have discussed in this chapter for dealing with employees. The organization should select its customers, and then train them for the service encounter. This training can be given impersonally, e.g. through the company's external communications. They can be used to inform customers of what is expected of them in the service encounter. This tuition can also be given in person, e.g. the health club manager who takes his customers round the club and shows them how to use the facilities.

7.9 Summary

The employees who deliver service are of fundamental importance to both the customer that they serve and the employer for whom they work. In many cases, the source of customer dissatisfaction is in fact, the service employee. He in turn, delivers less than acceptable service because he is dissatisfied with the way that his employer treats him. There are many factors that can contribute to this dissatisfaction – those related to his role, to his lack of empowerment, or to the way that management run the company.

The existence of these problems leads to a lack of motivation and commitment, and often results in a high turnover rate. Management can do several things which should help to reduce the likelihood of these arising. These include recruiting and selecting appropriate employees who match the job specification, training them in both the technical and non-technical skills necessary for the job, developing relevant orientation and socialization programmes, empowering those at the frontline and compensating them in some way for the extra responsibility, and monitoring and evaluating their performance in terms of the quality of service that they provide not the quantity. The results should be fed back to employees to aid their development and thereby improve the service.

Finally, while the focus of this is the frontline employee, the same principles should also be adopted for all service employees. Those who do not have to face the customer themselves should be encouraged to regard other employees as their customers, treating them in the same way that they would expect customers to be treated.

Questions

1 As a service provider, do you think that it is desirable to believe that 'the customer is king'? In some circumstances the customer may be openly abusive towards service employees. How do you think that management should tackle such situations?
2 Think of five further statements to add to this list designed to assess the commitment and motivation that management provides its employees.

- 'This organization is comprised of finger pointers rather than problem-solvers'.
- 'Management does everything to enhance our ability to improve customer service'.
- 'Nobody around here seems willing to take responsibility for making a decision'.
- 'Management is always willing to listen and consider the ideas and comments of employees'.
- 'Overall people in our organization are receptive to change'.

Use these ten statements to ask a number of: 1 employees at different levels within one company or 2 employees in a number of different service industries how much they agree/disagree with the ten statements.
3 Think of a service encounter where you were unhappy with the way that you were treated by the service employee. What was the reason(s) for his poor service? What recommendations would you make to management to help reduce the likelihood of its recurrence?
4 In the chapter, two different types of motivation were described; extrinsic motivation, and intrinsic motivation. For each of the motivations, think of ten service occupations which would be particularly suitable for individuals displaying such characteristics.

References

1 Hockschild, A. R. (1983). *The Managed Heart: Commercialisation of Human Feeling*. University of California Press.
2 Keaveney, S. (1988). Adding value to services through contact personnel. In Add Value to Your Service, (Supernant, C. ed). American Marketing Association.
3 Lovelock, C. (1991). *Services Marketing*. Prentice-Hall, pp. 29–32.
4 Mudie, P. (1987). Internal marketing: cause for concern. *Quarterly Review of Marketing*, Spring/Summer, 21–24.

5   Clutterbuck, D. (1989). Developing customer care training programmes. *Marketing Intelligence and Planning*, 7.

6   Carlzon, J. (1989). *Moments of Truth*, Harper & Row.

7   Firnstahl, T. W. (1989). My employees are my service guarantee. *Harvard Business Review*, July—August, 28–32.

8   Harris, T. (1970). *The Book of Choice*. Jonathan Cape.

9   Parasuraman, A., Zeithaml, V. A. and Berry, L. L. (1990). *Delivering Quality Service*. The Free Press, Macmillan Inc. pp. 89–109.

10 Shamir, B. (1980). Between service and servility: role conflict in subordinate service roles. *Journal of Human Relations*, **33**(10), 741–756.

11 Schlesinger, L. A. and Heskett, J. L. (1991). Breaking the cycle of failure in services management. *Management Review*, Spring, 17–28.

12 Lincoln, A. (1856). Cited in *Oxford Concise Book of Proverbs*, OUP, Oxford.

13 Woods, R. H., and Macauley, J. F. (1989). RX for turnover: retention programmes that work. *Cornell Hotel and Restaurant Administration*, May, 79–90.

14 Schneider, B. and Schechter, D. (1982). Development of a personnel selection system for service jobs.

15 Hall, D. T., Schneider, B. and Nygren, H. T. (1970). Personal factors in organisational identification. *Administrative Science Quarterly*, **15**.

16 George, W. (1990). Internal marketing and organisational behaviour: a partnership in developing customer-conscious employees at every level. *Journal of Business Research*, **20**, 63–70.

17 Supermarket Cashier (1992). Custom-eyes critical eye. Channel Four Television Series.

18 Rafaeli, A. and Sutton, R. I. (1990). Busy stores and demanding customers. *Academy of Management Journal*, **33**(3), 623–637.

19 Van Gennep, A. (1960). *Rites of Passage*. University of Chicago Press, Chicago. (Originally published by Emile Mourry in Paris, 1909).

20 Rohlen, T. P. (1973). 'Spiritual education' in a Japanese bank. *American Anthropologist*, **75**, 1542–1562.

21 Schein, E. H. (1988). Organisational socialisation and the profession of management. *Sloan Management Review*, Fall, 53–65.

22 Bowen, D. E. and Lawler, L. L. (1992). Empowerment: why, what, how, and when. *Sloan Management Review*, Spring, 31–39.

23 Herzberg, F. (1968). One more time: how do you motivate employees? *Harvard Business Review*, January–February, 53–62.

24 Bell, C. R. and Zemke, R. (1988). Do service procedures tie employees hands? *Personnel Journal*, September, 77–83.

8

Managing demand and supply

8.1 Introduction

In service marketing the matching of capacity and demand is particularly difficult because the perishable nature of services means that they cannot be stored.
In addition to this, the customer participates in the creation of the service and
customers in themselves vary. Some customers complete forms quickly, some
slowly, some are brusque, some are chatty. This creates variability in capacity.

Many services are also characterized by quite large demand fluctuations over
short periods. City centre sandwich shops are significantly busier at lunchtimes
than in the late afternoon.

However difficult it may be to match demand and supply, it should be
attempted for two reasons.

First, whenever demand is well below capacity then costs are added to each
unit of sale. Profitability will be eroded and the service may even become
uncompetitive. Many services carry relatively high fixed costs – the customer in
effect rents the facilities. An airline, for instance, has to maintain its aircraft to
a legal standard no matter how few customers are flying.

Secondly, when demand and capacity are out of balance the service itself can
take on a different form. This can be true when a business is running over its
optimal capacity – ask a customer desperately trying to catch a waiter's eye in
a packed restaurant how he feels about the service! Or it can occur where the
business runs under capacity – what's the point of sitting all night alone in a
singles bar? There is a difference between the *optimum* capacity and the *maximum* capacity. As Heskett, Sasser, and Hart[1] note, the optimum capacity for
an airline ranges from 65 per cent to 75 per cent. Above 75 per cent the service
deteriorates as rushed cabin staff deal abruptly with customers. They reckon
that below about 40 per cent capacity the service will also deteriorate. While
for most services the optimum capacity level is below the maximum level, in
some cases the optimum lies above the maximum. Consider the pop concert or
football cup final. No matter where the two capacity levels lie, the service
provider has to strike a balance between profitability and customer satisfaction.

8.2 Financial as well as volume measures

Many service businesses use volume measures to describe their efficiency in
matching demand and capacity. Hotels talk about 'occupancy rates', airlines
have measures of 'seat utilization' . . .

Volume measures, used on their own, can be misleading. An aircraft that is

90 per cent full of passengers can still be operating at a loss if all the passengers are flying on 'standby' tickets costing £100 rather than full fare tickets at £250.

As Lovelock[2] contends however, 'what is needed . . . is a measure of the extent to which the organization's assets are achieving their full revenue generating potential'. He has developed an index of Asset Revenue Generating Efficiency (ARGE) to measure this. In essence one should measure actual revenue achieved in any time period against potential maximum revenue. This overcomes the problem of taking straight volume measures. In the example above the ARGE would be 36 per cent (90 per cent @ £100/£250). It is really a matter of multiplying operational efficiency (per cent capacity level), with the price efficiency (actual price as a per cent of maximum price).

The advantage of ARGE is that the service marketer's mind is focused on opportunity costs, i.e. which market segments/customer types should be selected, and which should be encouraged. What price should they be charged and how much capacity should they be allocated? e.g. how many passengers would have flown at full fare if the standby fare were to be withdrawn? etc.

All businesses need to undertake some kind of long-term planning of demand so that they can ensure adequate capacity. If a bank's customer base is growing by 10 per cent each year, then they will presumably be planning to recruit more tellers and open more branches as the years progress. However we are concerned here with the problem of matching demand and supply over the shorter term.

There are three possible approaches to tackling this problem. First, one can attempt to *predict* the fluctuations in demand, thus allowing capacity planning. Second, one can operate with a relative level capacity and *tailor demand* to fit. Third, one can *tailor capacity* to fit demand at any point. This last has been described by Sasser, Olsen and Wyckoff[3] as the 'chase' strategy.

These approaches are not mutually exclusive – the service marketer often needs to combine elements of all three.

8.3 Predicting demand

Service marketers should begin by trying to understand the reasons for fluctuations in demand. This depends, of course, on a thorough understanding of the customer and the segment(s) that are being targeted.

There are three principle sources of information which can help to explain consumer behaviour leading to demand fluctuation. These are:

- *Historical sales data*. These can be a rich source of data in many service companies. Insurance companies, for instance, collect much detailed information on their clients before registering a sale.
- *Desk research* can reveal much – a lot of useful information is published. It is surprising how much competitors sometimes reveal about their strategy and performance!
- *Customer surveys* can be used to collect information.

In examining data it is often helpful to ask whether demand changes cyclically. These cycles can be hourly (telephone calls for a time check), daily (morning rush hour use of roads), weekly (weekend demand for babysitting services), monthly, yearly (tax advisors) or even longer (election advisors).

It will often be necessary to disaggregate data by customer type to make sense of demand patterns. A grocery supermarket chain may discover that mid-week evening demand peaks are caused by homeward bound workers. These customers may well have markedly different needs from daytime shoppers. They may, for instance, be buying for their evening meal rather than for the household for a week. An evening '5 items or less' priority checkout makes sense.

The service marketer should aim to explain as much of the demand fluctuation as possible. If a predictive demand model can be built then many problems can be overcome. Much explainable variation in demand may, however, be unpredictable, e.g. the demand for skiing holidays may depend on snow reports.

If the majority of demand fluctuation can be explained then two short-term capacity matching strategies are possible.

1   *Customer choice.* The process of customer choice can have large effects on the stability and predictability of demand.

    First, some customers act in a more unpredictable way than others. Decisions can be taken to discard customers exhibiting high degrees of randomness and to replace them by more 'predictable' customers. A hospital might decide to close its casualty ward and concentrate on gynaecology.

    Second, it may be easier to predict the overall demand of a large number of small customers than a few large ones. A law practice may find it particularly difficult to service three corporate clients all demanding simultaneous instant attention.

    Third, whatever their size, one might be able to balance a portfolio of customers so that growth in demand from one is matched by decline in demand from another, e.g. insurance companies sell policies to cover funeral expenses and private health care.

2   *Short-term capacity elasticity.* An underground train may carry 60 passengers standing comfortably – this might be the optimal capacity. However, for short periods during rush hour this might rise to 200 standing passengers. Similarly staff may cope well with excess demand for short periods by working harder than normal or by postponing paperwork etc. It may pay to examine work practices during these busy periods simply to discover ways to improve efficiency during peak demand. It may also be possible to postpone the delivery of augmented quality during peak demand periods. A stockbroker may pride himself on his personal touch in dealing with his customers. This personal contact is an augmented quality. If he is busy, the specific enquiry may be dealt with effectively by an assistant. The stockbroker can still deliver the augmented service by calling the client back the next day.

    Again some short-term capacity stretch can result from involving the customer to a greater extent during peak demand periods. A bank teller may personally complete the deposit slip for a customer when there are no other customers around. However, when the bank is busy the teller should concentrate on those elements of service that cannot be undertaken by the customer. He should leave the customer to do his own form filling.

This overall approach to coping with short-term demand fluctuations can be summarized as 'predict and stretch'. Predict as much demand variation as possible and incorporate an element of short-term capacity stretch to cope with the rest.

8.4   Tailor demand to fit capacity

This approach is describe by Sasser[4] as the 'level' (capacity) strategy. Demand can be left to find its own level, or it can be managed in two ways. The organization can attempt either to shape demand or to inventory it.

Shaping demand

The management strategy is to influence demand through changing the:

Product (service)
Place (or time)
Promotion (communication)
Price

Demand can be shaped either by reducing the peaks or increasing the troughs. The same measure can often simultaneously achieve both. An airline offering discounts on selected off peak flights seeks not only to fill up these seats but also to transfer passengers away from busy flights.

Service

Is the service always appropriate at all times? There are some classic product led approaches to filling up troughs: the college which markets its facilities as a conference centre out of term time; the hotel that is the haunt of businessmen during the week which then offers specialist weekend breaks, e.g. 'Murder Mystery' and 'Musical' weekends; MacDonalds burger bars offering breakfast menus, and conversely coffee shops offering dinner menus.

Service changes fall into two categories: radically altering the service (as in the case of the college/conference centre); and adding value during trough periods – free cocktails in a restaurant, free tennis lessons at a hotel.

Place

One can change the location and timing of service delivery. Dry cleaning companies might, for instance, offer to pick up and deliver in the evenings. Car rental companies sometimes open temporary offices in tourist locations during the summer. Many retail services are delivered from mobile units – these range from library services and banks through to grocers.

Promotion (communication)

Communication can be used to manage the peaks and troughs. Theatres that advertise availability by informing customers of 'sold out' performances may encourage customers to book matinees instead. The demand that an organization is expecting to receive is often communicated to customers. These messages can be explicit – 'Mail early for Christmas' – or implicit. Pricing, for instance, often carries a message about pressures on service capacity. Airlines often have structured price lists where cheaper fares are excluded from certain peak flights. British Rail off peak fares give discounts. Part of the effectiveness of this is that it signals busy periods.

Price

Price can, of course, be an effective way to influence demand. However, in influencing demand there can be other implications. Price itself carries a message. Lower prices in off peak periods may stimulate demand at that time but put off other customers. It is often assumed that price rises are always negatively correlated to demand (Figure 8.1).

This is not always true. A large part of the service product is intangible. Moreover the customer delivers part of the product. As Shapiro[5] says, 'Price can connote quality'. Reducing the price can cheapen the product – and put off customers. This can happen for a number of reasons:

1 Changing prices can lead to uncertainty. Customers can decide not to buy because they believe that by holding off, the price might get cheaper.
2 Lower prices can change the type of purchaser. This can be important in high contact, shared services like restaurants and theatres. Here the other customers are a significant part of the product mix. If a restaurant lowers price and attracts students then it might put off its regular business clientele (or vice versa!).
3 Price itself can be important because it carries snob appeal. It may be important to some consumers to be able to signal that they paid a lot for a service.
4 The consumer can be part of the product. Reducing the price can sometimes be felt therefore to be cheapening the value of the consumer.

If these factors are borne in mind then pricing can be an extremely effective tool with which to alter demand. Moreover, in many services the principle of discounting unused capacity is an accepted norm, particularly if discounts are accompanied by restrictions in the service. A 'standby' airline passenger has paid less for his ticket, but has taken the risk of not catching the flight.

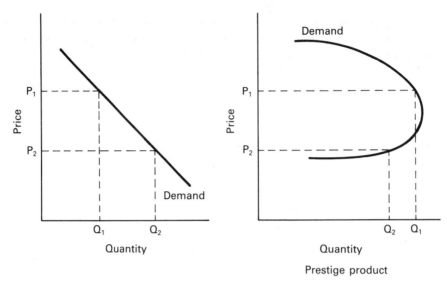

Figure 8.1 *Normal shaped and backward bending demand curves*

Inventory demand

Pricing can be used as an incentive to customers to prebook capacity for a service. This effectively inventories demand. Any booking system has this effect – the customer ringing up to reserve a table in his favourite restaurant, the passenger booking an airline ticket a month in advance to claim an APEX fare, an account holder ringing to make an appointment with his bank manager.

If customers can be channelled into an inventory system then there is a further potential benefit. Demand might possibly be deflected from the peak period. A customer ringing a central reservation system for a hotel chain might be persuaded to take a room in an hotel in an adjacent town.

The problem with inventoried demand is with 'no shows'. Many service companies overcome this by overbooking. This, in turn, can create problems. A system that encourages advance booking and *then* cannot deliver is one that will certainly lead to customer dissatisfaction.

Another way to inventory demand is to adopt a management system for queueing. Time that customers spend waiting can be made productive and enjoyable. Restaurants may ask customers to wait in a bar. This might in turn be an important revenue source. While waiting in the bar the customers might be able to choose their food, thus cutting down waiting time at the table. All of this enhances the productivity of the scarce resource – table space.

8.5   Tailor capacity to follow demand

Capacity can 'chase' variations in demand. If this is the chosen strategy then it is particularly important for the company to understand the components of capacity. One should answer the question – what limits capacity? In a restaurant capacity might be limited by the number of tables. If tables were then laid out in the foyer then capacity might be limited by the numbers of waiting staff. If more waiters were recruited then space might be limited by kitchen space.

Armistead[6] has summarized the different approaches to varying capacity to meet short-term demand fluctuations as:

- Changing the number and hours of personnel
- Customer participation
- Resource transfer
- Subcontracting
- Share capacity

In addition there is the possibility of:

- Scheduling downtime.

Changing the number and hours of personnel

Service products are often highly labour intensive. As a result capacity is often limited by personnel. One common approach to overcoming this problem is to use part-time staff. They can be brought in as demand appears. Pools of casual labour are often used, such as school children in holidays, mothers whose children are at school, moonlighters. In future we expect that pensioners will increasingly be used in this capacity.

These temporary staff can be scheduled so that they provide labour as required. This approach can only be used where the service is standardized and little skill is required, e.g. a supermarket checkout operator. However, there are problems associated with using part-timers, they are not usually committed to the organization which results in high levels of staff turnover, errors and supervision costs. These in turn lead to a diminution in customer satisfaction.

Another way to solve the problem is to employ full time staff but to build flexibility into their hours so that they work more hours when necessary. This approach can, however, result in high labour costs through overtime payments.

Customer participation

Wherever the customer participates directly in the creation of the service then some of the strain on capacity is removed. In effect that part of the capacity becomes variable rather than fixed. This applies in many self-service situations – from supermarkets to restaurants, petrol stations and automatic bank teller machines.

Resource transfer

If staff can perform more than one task in the service operation then labour can be moved to overcome capacity problems. This requires investment in costs to ensure multiskilling – supermarket shelf fillers who can also work at the checkout.

Subcontracting

This approach, in common with customer participation, effectively turns fixed capacity into variable capacity. A common area for subcontracting is haulage because of the high costs associated with running a company fleet. There are often many general haulage contractors who can be used. Therefore the risk of hitting subcontractor capacity constraints are low.

Share capacity

Where capacity is expensive and not too specialized then it can be shared. A concert hall's capacity may be shared between rock bands, comedians and classical concert orchestras. Airlines may share baggage handling facilities. Emergency services share the capacity of the 999 switchboard.

Schedule downtime

Periods of low demand may actually be necessary in many service operations. These times can be used by staff for training, or to catch up on paperwork. In fact if adequate time for these activities is built in to the schedule, and these activities are timed to coincide with periods of low demand, then in effect capacity has been reduced to match demand.

One of the problems associated with an energetic pursuit of demand to fill up troughs is that downtime activities can be forgotten. Eventually this leads to inadequately trained staff with a mountain of half-completed paperwork.

8.6   Queueing: an overview

Queueing or 'waiting in line' is a phenomenon of everyday life for many people. We wait at the bank, on the phone, at the post office, on congested roads, for the lift, and so on. Although reservation systems are in operation, the 'queueing problem' is a fact of life that confronts many service organizations and customers.

However, queueing does have its lighthearted moments by evoking a sense of humour, often perverse, cynical etc, amongst the participants. The following illustrate the kind of comments 'overheard in the queue':

German comes up to a queue at Heathrow airport and asks 'Why are your queueing?'; answer 'We're British'.

Woman at the front of a bus queue asks the driver of a bus that has just arrived, 'How long will the next bus be?'; reply from the driver, 'Same length as this one, 26 feet'; woman retorts, 'And will it have a monkey like you driving it?'

Customs officer at airport is immersed in a large book. One person leaves the queue and goes up to the customs officer. On returning he is asked, 'What is he reading?'; answer 'War and Peace'.

For consumers, time can be bought, saved, spent and wasted. It is time wasted that is perceived as the major characteristic of queueing. Cultures and groups within any one culture differ in respect of their perception of time.[7] Within the specific area of consumer shopping behaviour there is clear evidence of variations between actual (objective) and perceived (subjective) time.[8] People, when asked, tend to overestimate waiting time. This is particularly so where it is simply a question of waiting. On the other hand, where the passage of time is active (people are involved in or distracted by some activity) there is a tendency to underestimate time duration. There is a clear message here for service organizations if their customers are to avoid a very negative and frustrating experience. The words of a time essayist have a depressing ring about them:[9]

Waiting is a form of imprisonment. One is doing time – but why? One is being punished not for an offence of one's own but for the inefficiencies of those who impose the wait. Hence the peculiar rage that waits engender, the sense of injustice. Aside from boredom and physical discomfort, the subtler misery of waiting is the knowledge that one's most precious resource, time, a fraction of one's life, is being stolen away, irrecoverably lost.

. . . Waiting can seem an interval of non-being, the black space between events and the outcome of desires. It makes time maddeningly elastic, it has a way of seeming to compact eternity into a few hours.

Attempts have been made to quantify just how much time is taken up waiting. Although speculative, an example from the USA illustrates the kind of figures involved. The writer[10] states that, 'if we estimate that 200 million Americans occupy queues on an average of 30 minutes per day per person, we arrive at roughly 37 billion hours per year spent in standing in line in the United States'. To get some idea of what this actually represents the writer goes on to suggest that, 'since by some estimates the average American watches approximately 4 to 5 hours of television per day, the time spent in queues would appear to be within an order of magnitude of the time spent watching television'. He concludes with the message that, 'as the private sector spends approximately 25 billion dollars a year in television advertising, airing commercials which viewers may choose not to watch, it would seem that 2 to 3 billion dollars spent on marketing products to people in queues would not be inappropriate, considering that these individuals usually have very little in the way of alternatives to divert their attention'. Cleaners of car windscreens at traffic lights and marketers of mobile phones are examples of the exploitation of the 'waiting market'.

Social justice and the disciplines of the queue

Certain queueing situations can promote a fear of social injustice. How often have you experienced a situation in which you have been standing in a queue for some time when suddenly another check-out or processing point is opened.

Those at the back of your queue, having just arrived, dash over to the new queue and get served almost immediately. This is the fear of social injustice being realized.

It has long been accepted by those who have studied and written about queues that first come, first served (FCFS) is the socially just queue discipline and first in, first out (FIFO) the socially just system discipline. The type of queueing system will have a decisive effect on whether or not social justice prevails. There are essentially four types of queueing lines:

- Single line – where one queue forms to be processed through a single server e.g. waitress-free restaurants, cinemas.
- Snake lines – a number of serving points working one line of customers with the first in line approaching the next available server. This is quite common in many service settings, e.g. post office, banks, building societies.
- Express lines – a separate line is made available for those transacting out-of-the-ordinary business, paying by cheque or having a limited number of purchases or items to process.
- Multi-server lines – a number of serving points, each of which serves a separate line. The most obvious example is the supermarket although it is common in many services.

It is this last type, where people jump from one line to another, that promotes feelings of injustice.

Lines are, of course, not necessary under the take-a-number system adopted by some services, e.g. supermarket delicatessen, doctor's surgery, tax office etc. Here we have a situation of waiting in time without waiting in line.

Managing queues and waiting

People naturally want to spend as little of their time as possible standing in queues and waiting. Given that there will always be 'queues and waits', organizations need to make provision for managing them effectively. There are two ways of looking at this: the statistical perspective discussed earlier where management need to know how many will appear, at what times etc. in order that resources can be deployed to achieve an efficient throughput or the service provider can seek to understand people's expectations and perceptions of waiting with a view to making it more bearable, perhaps even enjoyable. This is the behavioural perspective.

8.7 Queueing: a behavioural perspective

A number of behavioural principles or propositions governing queueing and waiting have been proposed.[10,11] They can be summarized as follows:

- Uncertainties – there is nothing worse from a customer's point of view than not knowing how long you will have to wait. People must be given an indication of how long they should expect to wait and it should err on the side of caution. For example, it is obviously better to say 'you will be seen in twenty minutes or the take-off will be delayed by thirty minutes' where the wait is anticipated by the service provider to be less in both instances. Promising a wait of less than its actual duration should be avoided at all costs. The worst thing to say would be 'We'll be with you soon' or 'The delay in departure will not be long'. In these cases the risk of customer dissatisfaction is increased because their expectations have been raised.

The essential characteristic and apparent attractiveness of the appointment system are its complete lack of uncertainty. Unless you arrive early, there is no waiting involved as people expect to be taken at their allotted time. What is not always understood or tolerated is why a service does not adhere to the appointment schedule. A hairdresser will usually keep to the schedule while the local GP may not. The explanation lies in the greater degree of uncertainty and unpredictability surrounding patient needs in the doctor's surgery.

- Explanation – the length of a delay can be given meaning if people are told the reason(s). There are innumerable reasons for delay but the important point is that customers will make a judgement as to whether it is reasonable, acceptable, or justifiable. One might speculate that failure to inform customers is as much to do with avoiding unnecessary ridicule and censure. British Rail's revelation that a particular type of snow or leaves on the line can cause severe disruption was met with incredulity and annoyance that it was seemingly unable to do anything about it. There is nothing more frustrating from the customers' viewpoint than serving points, e.g. in post offices, banks, supermarkets suddenly closing without any explanation, or where service employees are seen to be 'sitting idly by' while the queues get longer. Ideally an explanation of the real cause of the delay should be given, but in the real world organizations may decide to give out either no reasons or ones deemed more acceptable to the customers.

- Anxiety – this feeling can often be the consequence of uncertainty and no explanation. It is the product of thinking, 'I'll never be seen to', which with the advent of appointments and take-a-number systems is less frequent. However, it can be felt when standing far back in a very long queue entering a capacity constrained facility, e.g. a pop concert, a football match. Organizers can eliminate it with the reassurance that 'everyone will get in'.

- Boredom – waiting can be incredibly boring. If organizations can offer some desirable distractions that take customers' minds off the time the response might well be one of 'how time flies'. There has not been a great deal of imagination generated in this area. Successfully filling unoccupied time is a difficult exercise and one in which there is enormous scope for experimentation and development. Quite often customers take it upon themselves to fill in time by befriending each other.

- Pre-process versus in-process – this is partially related to the previous point in that although customers have to wait they want to feel as soon as possible that progress is being made towards the service commencing. The obvious example is being given a menu on sitting down for a restaurant meal. The important point is that customers need to feel they are involved as quickly as possible. Anything the provider can do to fill in the customers' time before the core service begins will achieve that objective.

- Value – in general people value their time so what they are waiting for has to be worth it. What customers define as 'valued' are as numerous as the reasons for delay mentioned earlier. It is not simply a matter of valued being seen as something highly priced. Long waits are endured to obtain an important prescription. People camp out overnight or wait many hours to obtain entry to various forms of entertainment. The wait is very much seen in terms of 'it's worth it'.

- Equity – people correctly feel aggrieved if the FCFS and FIFO systems mentioned earlier are not observed. The take-a-number procedure operated by many services is a good example of FIFO. It works well when all customers transactions require about the same amount of time, but not where markedly different amounts of time are in evidence. There are instances where FIFO and FCFS would seem to be violated, e.g. an emergency arrival at a hospital, but this is an example where customers accept non-observance of the rule.

  Sometimes what seems to be a breaking of the equity rule is understandable. For example a person waiting in a restaurant for a seat sees a party of four entering and being given a table straight away. The single person may feel a sense of injustice but the restaurant owner cannot be expected perfectly to match his fixed capacity of seating arrangements with the unpredictability of customer demand patterns. Equally a customer in a department store may feel frustration when telephone callers receive priority service. An occurrence such as this can be avoided through the adoption of proper procedures.

The way ahead

It is difficult to envisage a time when queueing and waiting will not exist. What is a real possibility is that in the absence of any affirmative action queues and waits will simply get longer. For many service organizations smoothing out demand over a day, week, year etc. can bring rewards in terms of efficient resource utilization and quality service to customers. However, research will inevitably be required. Robert East and his colleagues in the Consumer Research Unit at Kingston Business School are making a significant contribution.[12] Their research, at present, is focused on supermarkets, post offices, banks and building societies. They believe that organizations can do a great deal about managing demand over time.

In one of their research papers, they analyse demand patterns during the course of a day and days of the week in post offices. Using a comprehensive questionnaire, they ask the following:

- Do people dislike congestion and queueing in post offices?
- When do people use post offices?
- Do people have habits about when they use the post office?
- Can they use post offices at different times?
- Do they know when the busy and quiet times are?
- Is there evidence that people avoid peak times if they dislike queueing?

- What factors are associated with dislike of queueing?
- How does the perception of main offices differ from that of sub-offices?

There has been scarcely anything researched or written on this area so the work of East and his colleagues represents a refreshing example of the way ahead.

8.8 Queueing: a quantitative perspective

The basic, underlying reason for studying and then applying queueing theory is economic. The managers of the bridge that spans the Firth of Forth know that at certain times of day only a trickle of vehicles passes through the toll barriers where the fees are collected; at other times the queues literally stretch for miles. The managers have to ensure that the staff collecting the tolls are used optimally so that the toll booths are manned in the most cost-effective way. On a larger scale, those who run Disney World estimate that on a slack day, 15,000 visitors can be expected while on a busy day the figure is likely to be of the order of 65,000 people. With these numbers to contend with it is imperative that there is a smooth throughput of customers with as few bottle necks occurring as possible. In both these examples the study of queueing theory has aided the optimizing of the situation.

In this context two basic questions are usually asked of queues and it is the answers to these questions which help managers organize the facilities available. One question is: 'What is the average length of the queue?' . . . we want to ensure that the queues are neither too long nor too short for, in either case, the cost effectiveness of the system is in jeopardy. The other question is: 'How long do items have to wait in the queue before they are processed?' Again, we do not want the waiting time to be too long or too short.

There are some basic assumptions that have to be made when dealing with a simple (settled) queue. First, the potential population that is available to use the facility is very large (we often refer to this as an infinitely large population). Second, the probability of all of this infinite population using the facility is exceedingly small. This situation allows the Poisson distribution to be used (n is very large, and P the probability of success is very small). Third, we apply the FIFO (first in, first out) concept . . . no baulking (i.e. jumping the queue) is allowed. Fourth, we deal with discrete data and have one queue only, but can have a number of service channels to deal with this queue . . . Figure 8.2 sets out this situation.

At this stage we will differentiate between a queue and the system (Figure 8.3).

No matter how complicated the queueing model becomes, it all starts by obtaining two basic sets of data; the average arrival rate denoted by λ (the Greek letter lambda); and the average service rate denoted by μ (the Greek letter mu). From these two statistics we derive the traffic intensity denoted by ρ (the Greek letter rho). Traffic intensity can best be thought of as the average utilization of the service facility and has the formula:

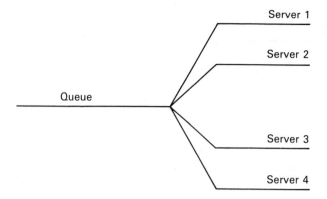

Figure 8.2 *Single queue: multiple servers*

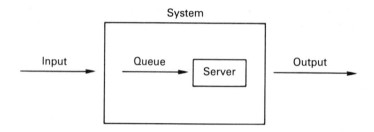

Figure 8.3 *The queuing system*

$\rho = \lambda/\mu$ (note $\lambda < \mu$, otherwise we can end up with an infinite queue).

Asking the question 'how many . . . ?' we have the two formulae:

$M_q = \rho^2/(1 - \rho)$ and $M_s = \rho/(1 - \rho)$

where M_q is the average number of items in the queue and M_s is the average number of items in the system.

Asking the question 'how long to wait . . . ?' requires the following formulae:

$W_q = \rho/(\mu - \lambda)$ and $W_s = 1/(\mu - \lambda)$.

where W_q is the waiting time in the queue and W_s is the waiting time in the system. Another formula that can be useful involves probabilities. Here we ask the question, 'what is the probability that there are n items in the queue?'; this gives us the facility for calculating the 'idle time' of the servers, this formula is

$p_n = \rho^n(1 - \rho)$.

Worked example: Customers in a supermarket join a single queue at an average rate of 30 per hour and are served at an average rate of 35 per hour. Find the average:

1 Number of customers waiting to be served;
2 Number of customers in the system;
3 Time spent queueing;
4 Time spent in the system.

Also find the probability that the server is idle.

Solutions: $\rho = 0.857$.
1 $(0.857)^2 / (1 - 0.857) = 5.14$ i.e. 5 customers
2 $(0.857) / (1 - 0.857) = 5.99$ i.e. 6 customers
3 $(0.857) / (35 - 30) = 0.174$ h, i.e. 10.44 mins
4 $1 / (35 - 30) = 1/5$ h = 12 minutes
5 $P_0 = (0.857)^0 (1 - 0.857) = 0.143$.

It should be self evident that the size of the queue affects the service rate which, in turn, determines the length of time spent in the queue and the system (Figure 8.4).

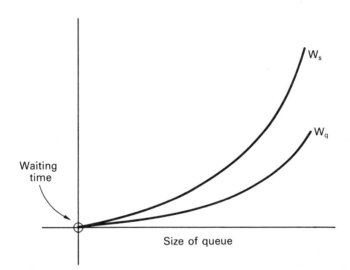

Figure 8.4 *Waiting time in queues. Not drawn to any particular scale – it is designed simply to show the changes in the waiting time relative to the queue size*

Customers of service organizations are sometimes only aware of what goes on 'up-front' in the front office. Queues are joined and then service takes place. There is, however, also the back office where in a sense what happens in the front office is duplicated. An example of this is where customers enter a shop and then decide from a catalogue what they want. They fill in a form join, a queue and then present this form to the cashier, pay for the goods, receive a receipt, join the next queue and then present this receipt to the server. This server puts the receipt in a tray where it now goes to the back office or store-room to join another queue. When its turn comes, the receipt is accessed and the transaction expedited. For the entire operation to work smoothly, and without congestion, it is imperative that both sets of queues (front office and back office) are well researched and workable solutions found (Figure 8.5).

The tendency is to use increasingly more sophisticated queueing models. The drudgery involved in working through screeds of awkward mathematics which took up so much time and mental energy even 15–20 years ago has disappeared; technology now does all the hard work. A great deal of queuing software is available for use with the computer and this has led to much more intricate problems being addressed. The STORM package has a good, user friendly, queueing facility. Queueing theory, based on probability distributions (the Poisson distribution for the arrival patterns and the exponential distribution for the service patterns) lends itself to the simulation process. Here the computer, using random number generation, is able to 'produce within itself' the queueing situation. Using the probabilities associated with different patterns of arrivals and service, it soon discovers where and when potential holdups (congestion) can occur. Because of the speed at which the computer can work it can simulate hundreds of thousands of arrivals to a particular service facility.

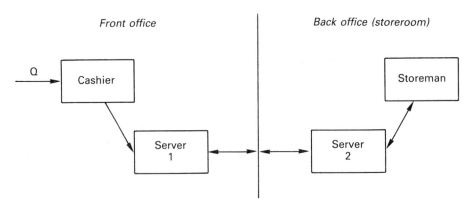

Figure 8.5 Queues can occur in the front and back office

8.9 Summary

Service organizations face a particular problem when it comes to demand management and capacity utilization. Unlike manufacturing, services cannot pile their 'output' in a warehouse and wait for demand to materialize.

Demand for many services can fluctuate in such an unpredictable way that capacity is either unable to cope, or grossly underutilized. Achieving a match between demand and capacity is a difficult goal, but it is an important goal for reasons of cost and customer satisfaction.

It is not simply a matter of aiming for maximum capacity utilization. A delicate balance may have to be struck between profitability and quality of service. This is known as 'optimum capacity utilization'.

A measure has been derived (ARGE) to determine the extent to which an organization's assets are being profitably utilized. It highlights the challenge of achieving the 'right mix of customers' at price levels that will give the service provider an acceptable rate of return.

Demand levels are not totally uncontrollable. The 4Ps can be used either to stimulate demand in times of excess capacity, or reduce it when there is insufficient capacity.

Queueing and waiting are particular features of service. They have a behavioural and a statistical perspective, and both must be understood and managed if customer dissatisfaction is to be avoided.

Questions

1   Why is demand management particularly difficult for service organizations? In what ways can management attempt to tackle this problem?
2   For each proposition/principle of queuing, determine:

(a) Its importance and
(b) The strategies that management should pursue.

Do your strategies vary according to the type of service?
3   Customers arrive at a bank in a random fashion at an average rate of 45/hour joining a single queue. They are served by two tellers who take on average 2 minutes each to serve them. From this information, calculate:

(a) The average number of customers waiting to be served;
(b) How long these customers have to wait to be served;
(c) How many customers will be in the bank;
(d) How long these customers can expect to be in the bank;
(e) The probability that the tellers are idle.

4   Ten men are employed unloading lorries as they arrive at a warehouse. During an 8-hour day 40 lorries arrive and it takes the team 10 minutes to unload each lorry, every team member is paid £6/hour and it costs £20/hour to keep each lorry waiting.

It is decided to increase the team to 14 men which would reduce the loading time to 7 minutes. Prepare a report to management on the viability of increasing the number of workers, basing your findings on the theory of queues.

References

1   Heskett, J. L., Sasser, W. E. and Hart, C. W. L. (1990). *Service Breakthroughs – Changing the Rules of the Game*. Free Press.

2 Lovelock, C. (1991). *Services Marketing*. Prentice-Hall.

3 Sasser, W. E., Olsen, R. P. and Wyckoff, D. D. (1978). *Management of Service Operations*. Allyn & Bacon.

4 Sasser, W. E. (1976). Match supply and demand in service industries. *Harvard Business Review*, November–December, 133–140.

5 Shapiro, B. P. (1968). The psychology of pricing. *Harvard Business Review*, July–August, 14–44.

6 Armistead, C. G. (1988). *Operations Management in Service Industries in the Public Sector*. Wiley.

7 Hall, E. T. (1959). *The Silent Language*. Doubleday, New York.

8 Hornik, J. (1984). Subjective vs objective time measures: a note of the perception of time in consumer behaviour. *Journal of Consumer Research*, **11**, 615–618.

9 Morrow, L. (1984). Waiting as a way of life. *Time*, July 23.

10 Larson, R. C. (1987). Perspectives on queues: social justice and the psychology of queueing. *Operations Research*, **35**(6) November–December, 895–905.

11 Maister, D. H. (1985). The psychology of waiting lines. In *The Service Encounter*, (Czepiel, J. A., Solomon, M. R. and Suprenant, C. F. eds). Lexington Books, D. C. Heath and Company, Lexington Mass.

12 East, R., Lomax, W. Willson, G. and Harris, P. (1991). Demand over time: patterns of use and preference among post office users. *Occasional Paper Series*, Kingston Business School.

9
Service communications

9.1 Introduction

Today's environment is fiercely competitive. It is therefore not enough to develop a service for which there is known demand. It is not enough to say that a good service will sell itself. The service must be communicated to the target market in order to generate and develop a loyal customer base. While communications can be planned before the service is ready for consumption they should certainly not be implemented.

Advertising is one of the most visible ways through which an organization communicates with its customers. In 1991 service organizations in the UK spent some £2000 million on advertising (Table 9.1). This expenditure has grown significantly in recent years – both in absolute terms, and also as a share of total advertising in the economy.

Table 9.1 UK service sector advertising expenditure 1991

Industry	£'000
Retailing	679 548
Financial services	392 281
Holidays and travel	205 961
Entertainment	150 587
Housing and construction	124 831
Transportation	102 769
Communications	87 612
Public sector (central and local government)	76 055
Utilities	59 315
Education	10 752
Miscellaneous	39 058
	1 928 769

Source: Media Register.

9.2 The role for communications

Communication can *add value* to the service in the eyes of the consumer. This is one of its key benefits. In many cases this will enable the provider to charge a premium over that of his competitors. This is important given that the majority of companies have as their principal objective the maximization of profits. Profit is, of course, related to the difference between costs and revenue which, in turn, are influenced by value added.

9.3 Services communication

The key differences between products and services should be taken into account in considering service communication as follows:

- Simultaneous production and consumption. The layout, shop facia, and the appearance and manner of the staff are critical communication variables.
- Intangibility. Service providers should attempt to reduce the risk to the consumer of buying an intangible product by providing tangible clues about the service offering. These clues come from all aspects of corporate communication.
- Heterogeneity. This, too, leads to greater perceived risk. Again communications can help to reduce this factor. It may be appropriate to communicate a service guarantee or promise (Figure 9.1) or to demonstrate how well trained your staff are.
- Perishability. Many promotional tools, e.g. advertising, sales promotion, and direct marketing, have a role to play in shaping demand. This is one of

Figure 9.1   Kwik-Fit advertisement: the communication of a guarantee

the most challenging aspects of service management and arises from the fact that services cannot be inventoried.

Flowing from this there are five key aspects of communication for the service marketer:

- The role of personal selling
- The targeting of employees in external communications
- The management of expectations
- The provision of tangible clues
- Word of mouth communications

9.4   Key communication variables

The role of personal selling

Most service delivery involves human encounter. The way in which that encounter develops can determine whether the customer walks away feeling pleased, satisfied, annoyed, or victimized. Although the customer's expectations help determine levels of satisfaction, the encounter itself will invariably play a significant part in determining satisfaction. The person who delivers the service is often actually part of the service itself. He is not merely facilitating the exchange of a product that is already fully developed and is waiting to be picked from a shelf. Waiting staff in a restaurant deliver not just food but customer satisfaction.

Research conducted by John Bateson for his book *Managing Services Marketing*[1] concluded that personal selling and image-creating strategies were the communications tools most often used by service organizations. He notes that they must choose their contact personnel carefully and train them to interact effectively with customers.

The role of personal selling is not the same for every service organization. The partner in a large accountancy firm will be performing quite a different personal selling role to that of a checkout operator in a supermarket.

In attempting to mould the interpersonal skills of his contact personnel, the service manager should ask himself the following questions:

- Who are the salespeople in the organization?
- What other functions do they fulfil?
- What ought they to be communicating about the service?
- On what dimensions do consumers judge the standard of service delivery?
- What factors shape expectations of each service encounter? Are they related to service complexity? To frequency of use of the service?
- Is it more appropriate for customers to be offered a customized or a standardized response? (Of course service delivery varies not only among people but also within people. We all have our good and bad days. On a good day customization will probably result in an improved service offering, however on a bad day, standardized service has a greater chance of achieving satisfied customers.)

If some thought is given to these factors then the communication function of contact personnel has a greater chance of being effective.

Personal selling is often the most important variable in the development of expectations. No matter what the advertising communicates, or what the consumer's friends say, his expectations will be shaped by any personalized communication that he receives from the company. If your hairdresser tells you that the colourant that he has used will last for eight weeks then that is how long you expect it to last. If a department store says that it will deliver the following day then that is what customers expect. Frontline employees have to be trained to understand that it is important to develop *realistic* expectations in consumers however tempting it may be to overpromise.

Employees as a target of communications

The importance of the employee in the delivery of a quality service means that they should not be ignored when it comes to considering who the relevant communication targets are. The most prolific writer in this field, Leonard Berry[2,3] makes this point.

There are certainly internal pieces of communication that can help improve their job performance. The mission statement is a critical tool in this respect. The employee can also benefit from external corporate communications which appear to be aimed at the consumer. There are several reasons for this.

First, many services are delivered through a geographically dispersed network of branches and outlets. Employees have little contact with head office. In this case external communications can help to maintain their commitment to the organization. It can also help remind them of the corporate culture that was imbued during their induction (Figure 9.2).

It may serve as a reminder or a reassurance of what the organization expects of them, or, as Zeithaml states, 'if [the communications] features employees doing their jobs, it communicates to them that they are important'.[4] However, the proposition that these communications are more effective if they use actual employees rather than professional actors could be refuted. An aspirational role model may be more appropriate and effective.

In the late 1980s a similar theme was researched by London's advertising agencies. There was a view that actresses used to portray women in advertising were so unrealistic that women would not believe the message that the advertiser was trying to communicate. Taking the same scripts but using ordinary women the researchers tested these advertisements to gauge whether they would result in more effective communications. The response was not what was expected. Women did not prefer these advertisements. They actually began to reassess their original responses to the advertising that featured the actresses.[5]

Finally these communications can help to manage customers' expectations and in so doing they can communicate with employees about what to expect from their customers.

When you're only No.2, you try harder. Or else.

Avis can't afford to relax.

Little fish have to keep moving all of the time. The big ones never stop picking on them.

Avis knows all about the problems of little fish.

We're only No.2 in rent a cars. We'd be swallowed up if we didn't try harder.

There's no rest for us.

We're always emptying ashtrays. Making sure gas tanks are full before we rent our cars. Seeing that the batteries are full of life. Checking our windshield wipers.

And the cars we rent out can't be anything less than lively new super-torque Fords.

And since we're not the big fish, you won't feel like a sardine when you come to our counter.

We're not jammed with customers.

Figure 9.2 Avis advertisement communicates management's expectations of employees and shapes customers' expectations of the service

Managing expectations

Communicating with the customer about what to expect of the service is very important. If expectations can be managed so that the customer has more realistic expectations of the service delivery then his expectations are more likely to be met. American Express informs its cardholders that 'Membership has its privileges'. Customers then come to look for their privileges.

Czepiel, Solomon, and Suprenant,[6] note that most problems about customer satisfaction relate to expectations exceeding service delivery. Satisfied customers

171

result from the service experience fulfilling expectations. This is why the management of these expectations is so important. External communication is only one of a number of variables that are influential (Figure 9.3). It is, though, perhaps the most easily controlled.

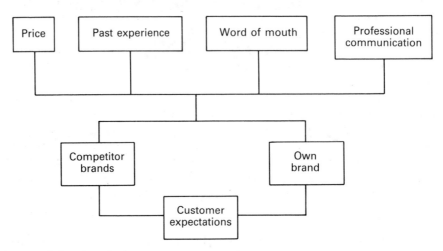

Figure 9.3   *Developing customer expectations*

Raising expectations through communications can increase the risk of customer dissatisfaction. It may be tempting to overpromise in order to get business through the door. However the repercussions often outweigh any initial benefit.

Delta airlines at one time vowed 'we're ready when you are', and Holiday Inn told its customers 'no surprises guaranteed'. Both companies had to revise their communications because they were overpromising. Consumers' expectations were raised and then not fulfilled. They did not expect any delays if they travelled with Delta, nor were they happy when Holiday Inn did indeed produce some surprises.

In the UK, British Rail fell into the same trap by advertising the fact that, 'we're getting there', when it was obvious to the commuting public that British Rail were patently *not* getting there. 'The wonder of Woolies' is yet another example from the same era. This advertising led consumers to re-evaluate their expectations of these services. However, it led them to revise them upwards which in turn led to increased levels of dissatisfaction. Organizations began to realize that while this practice may encourage new business it does not encourage repeat business.

External communications that help develop expectations may involve a 'look behind the scenes' approach. This enables organizations to demonstrate all the effort that they go to in order to provide the service. This has been a popular theme with utilities companies, e.g. British Gas and Scottish Power.

Another approach is to provide customers with a script or scenario of the likely service encounter. Financial services and airline companies have used this approach in the past. Both strategies work well on television. They use this medium to its full potential allowing characters to develop in live action situations.

Most literature on this subject actually suggests that the role of communication is to revise consumers' expectations downwards. This arises from the view that consumers set themselves unrealistically high expectations in the first place.

However a more challenging task for the service marketer is to develop and maintain a quality service that meets or exceeds most consumers' expectations. Product manufacturers that are regarded as being leading-edge companies in terms of delivering quality products such as Motorola and NEC now take as their manufacturing goal six-sigma quality. This is a means of measuring how close production comes to total quality.

Six-sigma quality means that there are only 3.4 defects per million parts produced. Motorola may soon adopt an unheard-of goal 60 defects or less for every billion components it makes. Some Japanese manufacturing companies attempt to go further by manufacturing to zero defects. Toyota have introduced the concept of *poka-yoke* which aims to make the workplace mistake-proof, i.e. to manufacture to total quality.[7] So rather than externally aiming to reduce expectations these organizations instead internally aim to raise quality.

While this is more readily achievable in product marketing, service marketing should not ignore this potential strategy. Indeed, it may be a way of sustaining a competitive advantage. Future developments will certainly see more companies aiming to reduce the gap between expectations and delivery by tackling the issue internally as well as externally.

Tangible clues

The less tangible the generic product, the more powerfully and persistently the judgement of it gets shaped by the packaging. As Levitt states,[8] 'Metaphors and symbols become surrogates for the tangibility that cannot be provided or experienced in advance'.

The consumption of services is often associated with high levels of risk. Much of this risk stems from the intangible nature of services. It is not just the fact that the service cannot be touched in the same way that a product can. It is also that consumers often find it difficult to comprehend what they are being offered. They are more difficult to understand. This risk can be reduced by the provision of tangible clues that relate to the service offering. In a restaurant, the use of starched napery will communicate to customers that it is a quality establishment. Similarly, a bell boy on the steps of an hotel says something of its up-market positioning. These tangible clues make the nature of the service more easily understood.

If any of these signposts are to be used in professional communications then care must be taken to select those that are *relevant* to consumers. The Scottish brand leader in the double glazing market, C. R. Smith chose to focus on their vans in their advertising. In a similar fashion, the retailer John Menzies, features their carrier bag in all frames in the television advertising. In both cases they are tangible clues relating to the service offering, but these signposts are not relevant to consumers. Vans and bags are not *motivators* in the selection of service brands in those markets.

The Caledonian girl in her tartan uniform exemplified advertising that communicated a relevant tangible clue. Relevant because in airline passenger transport the standard of service delivered by the cabin staff will be a key motivator for some consumers in airline selection. It also meets the criterion that Klein and Lewis[9] set; they expect the tangible clues to act as quality surrogates.

Legal and General, the insurance company, have also practised this to good effect with the use of their multi-coloured umbrella. They offer you protection from life's uncertainties, and with this the prospect of a brighter future. The umbrella as a tangible clue communicates this effectively (Figure 9.4).

Figure 9.4 Legal and General logo

The Prudential, a competitor of Legal and General's, has also recently revamped its image. It has adopted a different strategy for its communications. The Prudential is attempting to humanize its image with a two-pronged approach. The advertising conveys the message that the organization is empathetic; it does this by showing all sorts of people in a variety of situations. The inference being that they understand *you*. The second part of the strategy is the logo which communicates the 'face' of the Prudential (Figure 9.5). In the past consumers were somewhat awestruck by these faceless institutions and so the development of a brand personality is entirely appropriate.

Word of mouth communication

Personal recommendation is a powerful communication vehicle in the service sector. The importance that consumers attach to word-of-mouth endorsement by their peer group arises from their need to reduce risk from the intangible and variable nature of services. Service marketers must learn to capitalize on this tool. So how should they do this? The following list presents some of the options:

- Introduce a friend scheme. Encourage current users to inform others of the good service. (American Express offers current card holders a case of wine if they introduce a friend.)

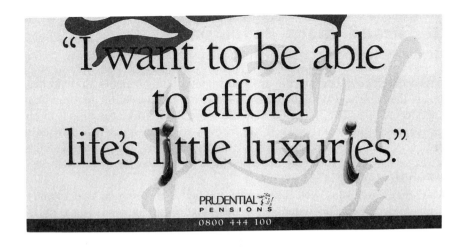

Figure 9.5 Prudential advertisement

- Testimonials. Use satisfied customers' experiences in advertising.
- Persuasion of opinion formers. Use PR to target opinion leaders or early adopters.
- Promotional items. Promotional items can provide tangible clues implying 'club' membership. The Open Golf tournament umbrella, or the Wimbledon sweatshirt are examples of this.
- Feedback. Incorporate it into the communication of a comprehensive complaints procedure. 'If you're happy with what we do tell them (friends etc.), if you're not tell us.'

9.5 Branding services

How are communications developed? In many cases the initial stage of the process is to develop a brand image. Brands have increased in importance in service marketing throughout the 1980s. This trend is expected to continue since:

- There is an increasing proliferation of brands within service sectors. Service markets are becoming more competitive.
- It has been shown to be up to five times cheaper to retain current customers than to attract new ones.[10]
- Product life cycles are becoming shorter. NPD thus assumes a greater importance. The risks of product launches are reduced in the context of umbrella branding.
- The service itself may offer no unique tangible benefit – this can be added by development of brand imagery.

9.6 Brand image development

The process should begin with an assessment of the benefits that accrue to users of the service. Preferably these should be unique. With no branding of the service at this stage, these benefits are more likely to be functional in character, i.e. a car hire firm will get you from A to B, an hotel will provide you with a good night's sleep. However in the development of an augmented service, Lovelock[11] suggests that an assessment of the social and psychological benefits that also accrue is necessary.

Market research may well have to be conducted in order to understand the consumer response. The outcome of this stage is an understanding of what consumers regard as the key attributes of the service, i.e. a social benefit to a businessman of hiring a car may be that he will look more professional, or a big time player to the client that he is meeting if he arrives by hire car rather than by public transport. A psychological benefit may be his enhanced feeling of self importance.

A social benefit derived from staying at a prestigious hotel may well be the company that the guest expects to keep. A psychological benefit could be the pampering/indulgence of the whole experience. It is from an understanding of these benefits that communications are built. They should highlight what it is that motivates people to use the service. By attaching your brand name to the most important motivator(s) you begin to give consumers reasons to prefer your brand over that of your competitors, i.e. you begin to build brand preference (Figure 9.6).

An effective communications package should attempt to take consumers swiftly from the position of brand non-recognition to that of brand preference. There is little advantage in consumers knowing of your service if they do not act on this knowledge.

Brand rejection occurs when your communications message is not motivating. It may not be motivating to those who are not target consumers. That is not a problem. What is more worrying is when the rejectors are in your target. Research must be undertaken to establish who are the rejectors. If it is the latter group then they must be further researched to understand the reasons why?

Consumers who are brand indifferent need more motivation. In many cases this arises because the service has not been experienced. Sales promotion techniques aimed at inducing trial should be considered.

Brand insistence/loyalty is every marketer's dream. How do you get there?

- Encourage repeat purchase using sales promotion. This makes consumers familiar with your service which in turn diminishes risk.
- Keep your current customers satisfied by developing and sustaining a unique service advantage. As Dobree and Page[10] state, branding is one key method of addressing the problem of competitive advantage. Branding is often the best way of sustaining a competitive advantage. A competitive advantage built solely on functional benefits is much easier for competitors to copy.
- Introduce penalties so that the cost of changing brands is high. Financial

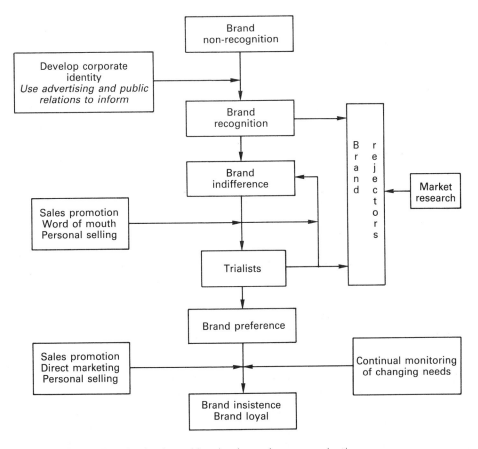

Figure 9.6 *Developing brand loyalty through communications*

institutions, particularly the building societies, practise this to good effect. If you decide to move to a company that offers a higher rate of interest, then the original lending company will charge you a penalty for doing this. This financial penalty will often mean that there is no longer any pecuniary advantage from making the change.

Building customer loyalty will often lead to profit improvement (Figure 9.7). Leading management consultants Bain and Co. have attempted to quantify this gain. They found that loyal customers tend to spend more money, they refer new clients, and they are less costly to do business with.

9.7 Corporate identity

In many cases it is the organization that a service is bought from rather than a specific brand, i.e. Boots may have attempted to segment their service offering into Cook Shops, Sound and Vision and Baby Shops but we expect that most people still see themselves as buying from Boots. For this reason the

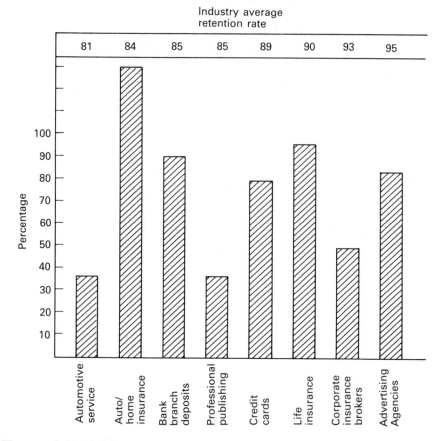

Figure 9.7 *Building customer loyalty boosts profits. Source: Bain & Co 1991. Increase in profits from 5% increase in retention rate*

development of a corporate identity becomes very important. It is also important to develop an image that gives the organization a focus since there are many variables working against the projection of a cohesive image. There are many factors which contribute to the building of corporate image.

Figure 9.8 illustrates the main factors. Some of these are discussed in more depth in Chapter 4, Designing the service environment, and Chapter 7, Service employees. Obviously not all services will use every mechanism; not many solicitors are seen to deploy carrier bags as part of their corporate image, nor will many restaurants run fleet vehicles. Whatever channels are chosen to promote the corporate identity, the task is to create a cohesive image that communicates an appropriate message. To manage this process efficiently and effectively it is important that the identity is carried synergistically across all communications.

In recent research conducted into the management of the UK service sector, companies were asked to describe what it was that captured the image of their companies for consumers. The majority of respondents named something that would be described as corporate identity, e.g. logo, advertising, company uniforms, concorde (no prizes for guessing the service company).

However, another category of respondents described images that were not unique to their company and therefore did not distinguish them from the competition. A final group of companies believed that their customers have no image of them. We anticipated membership of this last group to have been dominated by small companies or those in the public sector – not so (Cottam and Mudie).[12] The responses would suggest that for many services there is still much to be done in the way of corporate communications.

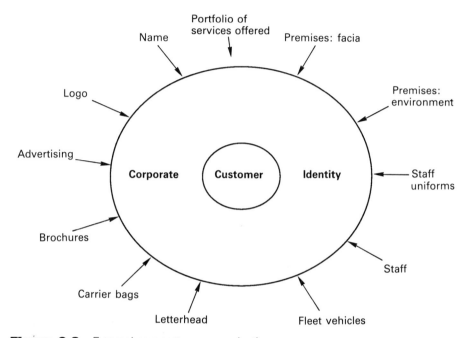

Figure 9.8 External corporate communications

Naming the service

What should a service name communicate? The best names communicate the key benefit that the service offers. Creased Lightening for an ironing service, Typerite for a typing service.

If the marketplace is competitive or the key benefit is different for different groups of consumers then the name should attempt to convey creatively the service that is offered, e.g. Branching Out for a florist, or The Potting Shed for a garden centre.

At a third level, it may be that this cannot be done creatively and so the generic service name is incorporated (often alongside the owner's name) e.g. Martin's Removals, or Fraser's Launderette. The three levels of naming are illustrated for a service that unblocks drains.

Drain Kleer	main benefit communicated
Blockbusters	service creatively communicated
P. N. D. Drainage	service generically communicated

All these approaches are superior to those names that give consumers no hints about the service that is offered. They are easier for consumers to remember because the name itself generates a visual image. These images complement the verbal name and leave the consumer with a more fully developed picture of the company.

The human brain finds it easier to store and retrieve words or names when they also have a visual prompt. This was researched by Lutz and Lutz,[13] whose results confirmed that an interactive image facilitates recall of the company or brand name better than a non-interactive image.

The service name can develop verbal interactive imagery. The interaction is between the company name and the service that is provided. We live in an overcommunicated society. We are producing more information and absorbing less of it. So the easier we make it for consumers to remember the company name the more chance we have of being successful.

Product marketing giants have taken this concept a stage further. They have taken to naming new brands in such a way that the core benefit cannot be missed. Unilver launched a new dairy spread in 1991 called 'I Can't Believe It's Not Butter'. Wall's launched a new range of luxury ice-cream named 'Too Good To Be True'. Does this represent a lack of creativity? Or are these companies trying to make the name itself communicate as much as possible to consumers about the product?

A good example of this approach to brand naming comes from the US toy retailer called 'Toys R Us'. The name itself tells consumers that it is a toy retailer. The 'R' written backwards may be just the way that a child would write it (Figure 9.9).

Figure 9.9   Toys 'R' Us logo

As Berry, Lefkowith, and Clark[14] state, there are four key characteristics that a service name should possess:

- Distinctiveness: identifies supplier and distinguishes from competition
- Relevance: conveys service benefit
- Memorability: understood and recalled with ease
- Flexibility: scope to cover business expansion

Designing the logo

The logo can take this process a stage further. It can help consumers to form a picture of the company by presenting them with visual clues of the service that is on offer (Figure 9.10).

Figure 9.10 Peter Plant cartoon. Source: Marketing Magazine 1992

A good logo helps both the company and its customers. It enables the company to have more impact in its desire to imprint a memorable picture on the consumer's mind. This in turn means that consumers do not have to work as hard to create an image for themselves as they did when only presented with a name.

This is described as pictorial interaction by Lutz, and Lutz.[13] Remembering the picture also means remembering the company name. A colour illustration of the Lucerne logo (Figure 9.11), shows the two upright triangles in silver. The peaks represent the mountains that surround the lake at Lucerne, and the colour symbolizes the wealth of Switzerland. The upside-down triangle in the middle is blue, representing Lake Lucerne. The imagery conjured up is particularly relevant to a multinational sales brokerage that specializes in Swiss products.

Figure 9.11 Lucerne logo

In 1984 British Airways launched a new corporate logo which was intended to reflect the company's new culture. The public image of British Airways in the 70s had been one of a nationalized industry ravaged by strikes and inefficient management practices. The logo that was in place during this period reflected the company image. It was designed at the time of the amalgamation of **BEA** and **BOAC**, and in attempting to incorporate design elements from each of those companies the design solution arrived at was a compromise. The logo projected a solid image, yet it lacked any feeling of movement that might be expected of a travel company.

The revised logo represented a significant step forward. BA's new management working towards privatization wanted to convey a much more dynamic image. The logo was expected to assert BA's superiority to staff, customers, and potential investors. The design certainly captures movement, and helped to project the image of a progressive company, driving forward in the travel business (Figure 9.12).

Figure 9.12   *The old and new face of British Airways*

Yet another way in which a logo can be designed is to take the company name, or the first letters of each word in the company name, and make that the logo. This is referred to as Letter Accentuation. It converts one or more letters in the name to a picture of the service. 'Letter accentuation is not as effective as strict pictorial interaction but does seem to provide a slight improvement over non-interactive presentations.'[13] The Life Association of Scotland is an example of this (Figure 9.13).

THE LIFE
ASSOCIATION
OF SCOTLAND

Figure 9.13   *The Life Association of Scotland logo*

Some recent research conducted by Schechter Group,[15] suggested that consumers showed little recognition of logos, even ones like the American Express Centurion which was only recognized by 21 per cent of US consumers. Perhaps this is because Centurion does not communicate anything that is relevant in the charge card market, or it may be that American Express have suffered from the use of more than one logo. They also use the square pale blue box with the words American Express as a logo. The diffusing of resources and imagery can only serve to weaken the focus of the company logo for consumers.

9.8 The uniform

For many service organizations today, the corporate look is incomplete unless all frontline staff are dressed by the company. This can serve three purposes. First, it helps customers to identify those individuals who are in fact employees of the company. To fulfil this signalling function, the uniform must have 'standout'. There are probably many men owning blue suits and waiting on a railway platform who have been approached by British Rail passengers asking for information about the trains. The uniform of the British Rail employee does not sufficiently distinguish him from the man in the street. A good example of distinctive corporate clothing is that worn by most of the airlines' steward staff.

These uniforms are also usually good at fulfilling the second objective. That of communicating an appropriate corporate image. In the days of restricted air travel, the 'hostess' would be dressed so that the male passengers (and most of them were men!) spent their airborne time fantasizing about the hostess rather than thinking about the dangers of flying. The girls were there to provide reassurance. Nowadays they are there to be efficient and professional and their uniforms reflect this change in approach. Miniskirts are not best suited for efficiency. As Jean Phillips of the Wensum Corporate Company notes, 'When developing a corporate clothing range for an organisation, not only does one take into account clothing design and company identity, but one equally needs to focus on the working environment. Generally speaking, too many companies lose sight of this major requirement'.[16]

And finally the uniform serves the purpose of suppressing individuality.[17] Idiosyncrasies in behaviour and appearance are much less obvious when an individual is in uniform. In effect uniform clothing promotes uniform behaviour. This happens partly because the employee feels a part of the organization and partly because the customer expects the employee act out the image.

9.9 Advertising the service

The advertising of services is often more complicated than for products. In many cases this is due to the intangible nature of the offering. The advertising has to evoke the likely experience of the user, which in turn introduces a second complication. The service can often be unique to each buyer, as is the case for most professional services. The service will be a bundle of attributes that will not all be offered to every buyer at every purchase occasion.

Setting advertising objectives

One approach to the setting of advertising objectives and strategy is to consider the four variables that are used to describe the difference between services and products. In the past, writers have suggested which of the variables they believed to be the most important. Shostack,[18] thought that the provision of tangible clues was advertising's biggest task. Urwin[19] believed that presenting an emotional appeal to consumers was the biggest challenge, and Parasuraman, Zeithaml and Berry[20,21] described reliability as the factor most important for the advertising to communicate.

It is our opinion there is no single correct approach. The advertiser should choose the variable that causes consumers most concern in the purchase of his particular service and attempt to overcome their preconceptions (Table 9.2).

Table 9.2 Setting advertising objectives to address service variables

Service variable	Advertising objective
Intangibility	Provision of tangible clues Reduce risk Provide reassurance
Heterogeneity	Customization Reduce risk Provide reassurance
Inseparability	Staff focus: selection, training etc. Customer empathy
Perishability	Use advertising to manage demand (price offers, selling off the page etc.)

For example, in the film industry, the most important variable is likely to be the perishability of the service. Demand for the service normally declines with the length of time that the film has been on the market. The purchase of financial services on the other hand, is often fraught with uncertainty due to the intangible nature of the service.

Another approach to the setting of objectives is to seek answers to the following questions at the beginning of the development process:

• What is it that motivates consumers to use my service?
• What is it credible to communicate to them in this context?
• Can I deliver what I promise?

In other words, in developing the communication the advertiser has to consider 'What, to Whom, How, When, and Where?'

Setting the advertising objective answers the first of these questions. It determines what the advertising is intended to communicate. This in turn should feed back into the question of consumer motivations. Ideally, the advertising should have as its objective the communication of the key motivator. This motivator will be different for different services. Note, however that the same motivator often applies to more than one service.

This is a simplification of the process. What happens if there is more than one key motivator? Take for example a film processing service. Consumers might say that key motivators are responsiveness and effectiveness (Figure 9.14).

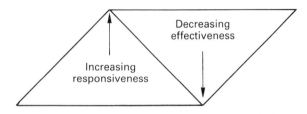

Figure 9.14   *Trade-off between key attributes: film processing*

However there is a trade-off here. Doing things faster usually results in more mistakes. Therefore how does the advertiser select which objective to focus on in the advertising?

He begins by considering to whom he is talking. How important are the various motivators to them? One way of establishing this is to ask consumers to build pyramids for each of the relevant motivators. By insisting that the service under investigation must appear in one of the boxes the researcher gains some understanding of the relative level of importance (Figure 9.15).

However this analysis implies that for any one attribute no two services hold the same levels of importance for consumers. This problem can be overcome by means of multi-attribute analysis (see Chapter 12).

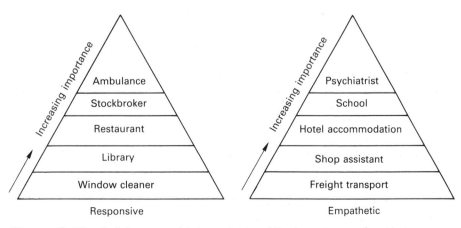

Figure 9.15   *Building pyramids to understand the importance of motivators*

We are assuming here that the service provides every key attribute that the consumer regards as important in their selection of a service brand in that particular market. If it does not, then the company should attempt to develop these if a long-term presence in the market is anticipated.

Setting advertising strategy

The next step is to arrive at an advertising strategy. This determines how the objective will be communicated. Setting the objective will not in itself set the strategy. Quite often there are a number of strategic options open to the advertiser. Consider the case of Reed Employment, a large secretarial employment agency that specialises in temporary assignments.

In the late 80s after a period of relatively little advertising, they decided to launch an aggressive advertising campaign. There appeared to be a number of appropriate strategies that Reed could adopt. These were discussed in research amongst some target consumers (Table 9.3).

Table 9.3 The strategic routes tested by Reed Employment

Strategic routes	Consumer response
The Reed supertemp. A wonderwoman who thrives on every challenge	Stupid/stereotypic
Most office work is a drudge. With Reed temping you get the perfect job.	Not looking for the perfect job
Reed temping gives you better perks – pay, training etc.	Not the main motivation for temping
The Reed 'consultant'. The office heroine who sorts out everything	It may be the reality, but it sounds hard to believe

The secretaries found a weakness in all of them. However the same discussions revealed the main motivator: what it was that made these girls choose to temp. They did so because of the flexibility that it offered them. Work played a relatively unimportant part in the lives of these girls. Other things that they did with their time were more important. Work had to take second place and fit around their other activities. So the flexibility and freedom that temping gave became the strategic route. Although this was a benefit that was not unique to Reed, they made it their property by being the first to brand this generic property (Figure 9.16). The FREEDOM advertisement incorporated the brand name into the single word that said it all for these girls (Figure 9.17). This highly successful advertising campaign made a significant impact on Reed Employment's sales.

It is not possible to be prescriptive in the selection of a strategy. The final choice will depend on several factors (Figure 9.18).

186

Figure 9.16 Reed Employment: Freedom advertisement

Campaign evaluation

The development of advertising is not a one-off job. After the campaign has run some attempt must be made to assess its effectiveness. Part of this process should be an examination of the continuing relevance of the original objective and strategy. While the most efficient use of advertising monies is often to develop a single-minded campaign that can run and run, e.g. Hamlet Cigars, or

Figure 9.17   Reed Employment. Airplane advertisement

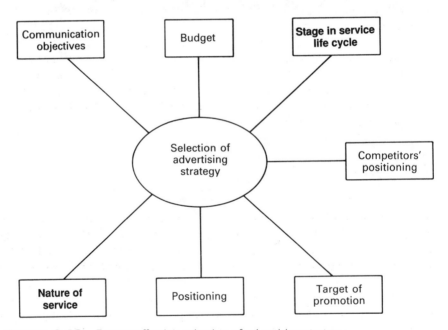

Figure 9.18   Factors affecting selection of advertising strategy

Heineken Lager, the changing nature of the competition and/or consumers can sometimes lead to the need to revise plans. The only way in which this can be determined is by continually monitoring the market.

Advertising professional services

The 1980s witnessed a relaxation in the control and regulation of professional services advertising. It began in 1985 with a test case brought by the opticians.

Research in the USA had shown that the restriction of advertising worked against the interests of consumers because it generally led to higher prices. The absence of advertising left consumers with insufficient information on which to base their brand choice.

The case was decided in the opticians' favour and this led to an Office of Fair Trading Report in 1986 which lifted many of the remaining restrictions on other professional services.

In addition to the methods of promoting services that have already been mentioned, there is another tool that is popular with those in professional services. It is known as a promotional survey.

The organization commissions research into something that it believes will interest their customers. So, for example, an advertising agency might find that its clients would be interested in changing consumer behaviour. The agency will then promote the survey like a new product with headline PR in the trade press, and more detailed coverage in individual presentations. These presentations are then used as soft-selling occasions.

The basic idea is to do something that current and/or potential clients will value. It need not be research. It may just focus on your field of expertise. A law firm could arrange a seminar with prominent legal brains on employment law.

Historically there has been some feeling that the successful professional organization does not need to advertise. To do so reflects adversely on their standing in the industry. This belief may not be as prevalent today as it has been in the past. However, the importance of interpersonal contact and respect means that any form of promotion that brings potential clients face-to-face with the service provider should be encouraged.

9.10 Summary

In the communication of services there are five key variables that are important to marketers. They are personal selling, word of mouth, targeting employees in external communications, managing expectations through communications, and using communications to provide tangible clues about the service. Tangible clues about the service offering can be given in all sorts of ways. Indeed most aspects of corporate identity help to provide tangible clues. The service personnel, their uniform, the company logo, its advertising etc, all contribute to the impression that the customer has of the company, and therefore help to shape his expectations.

For many companies the development of communications begins with the development of a brand image. Because there is often no discernible difference between brands in the market, the image can become the single differentiating factor. By creating an image of the service that is relevant to the market, the company has the potential to develop a loyal customer base. Customer loyalty is a worthwhile goal. For one thing, it usually results in greater profits.

In most cases advertising will be used to communicate the brand image. The advertising of services presents two unique problems. First, the service experience is not identical for every customer. In fact, in many cases each customer receives a service that no one else never experiences. And second, the intangible nature of service leaves the advertising with the job of attempting to evoke the likely experience of the user.

Questions

1 What tangible clues could the following services offer to position themselves as up-market: a driving school, bank, dentist, senior school, sports centre?

2 In 1991 a nurse won compensation for sexual discrimination on the grounds that while she had to wear a hat, her male colleagues did not. Why do you think the hospital wanted her to wear the hat? Can you think of any other examples where employees are asked to wear articles of clothing that would appear to be redundant?

3 Consider the social and psychological benefits that accrue to consumers from the use of the following services: a launderette, safe deposit box, private health insurance, hairdresser.

4 Think of a list of services for whom the following variable is the most important for advertising to address: (a) intangibility, (b) heterogeneity, (c) inseparability, and (d) perishability.

References

1 Bateson, J. E. G. (1989). *Managing Services Marketing: Text & Readings*. Dryden Press.

2 George, W. R. and Berry, L. (1981). Guidelines for the advertising of services. *Business Horizons*, **24**, 52–56.

3 Berry, L. (1987). Big ideas in services marketing. *The Journal of Services Marketing*, Summer, 5–9.

4 Zeithaml, V. A. (1990). Communicating with customers about service quality. In *Service Management Effectiveness*, (Bowen, D. E., Chase, R. B. and Cummings, eds). Jossey-Bass.

5 *Observer Newspaper* (1990). Fanfare for the common man. 4 November.

6 Czepiel, J. A., Solomon, M. R. and Suprenant, C. F. (1985). *The Service Encounter*. Lexington Books.

7 *International Business Week* (1991). Questing for the best. 2 December, 18–23.

8 Levitt, T. (1981). Marketing products and product intangibles. *Harvard Business Review*, May–June, 94–101.

9 Klein, D. M. and Lewis, R. C. (1987). Personal construct theory: a foundation for delivering tangible surrogates in services marketing. In *Add Value to Your Service* (Suprenant, C. F. ed.). American Marketing Association.

10 Dobree, J. and Page, A. S. (1991). Unleashing the power of service brands in the 1990s. *Management Decision*, **28**(6), 14–28.

11 Lovelock, C. H. (1991). *Services Marketing*. Prentice-Hall, p. 18.

12 Cottam, A. M. and Mudie, P. (1992). Working Paper. Napier University, Edinburgh.

13 Lutz, K. A. and Lutz, T. J. (1978). Eliciting strategies: review and implications of research. In *Advances in Consumer Research* (Hunt, H. K. ed). Association for Consumer Research.

14 Berry, L. L., Lefkowith, E. F. and Clark, T. (1988). In services, what's in a name? *Harvard Business Review*, September–October, 28–30.

15 Bird, D. (1992). Image can be damaged by design. *Marketing Magazine*, 6 February.

16 Telephone conversation with Jean Phillips (1992). Managing Director of the Wensum Corporate Company.

17 Nathan, J. and Nicholas, A. (1972). The uniform: a sociological perspective. *American Journal of Sociology*. **77**, 719–30.

18 Shostack, G. L. (1977). Breaking free from product marketing. *Journal of Marketing*, April, 73–80.

19 Urwin, S. (1975). Customised communications – a concept for service advertising. *Advertising Quarterly*, Summer, 28–30.

20 Parasuraman, A., Zeithaml, V. A. and Berry, L. L. (1988). Servqual: a multiple item scale for measuring consumer perceptions of service quality. *Journal of Retailing*, Spring, 12–40.

21 Parasuraman, A., Berry, L. L. and Zeithaml, A. (1991). Understanding customer expectations of service. *Sloan Management Review*, Spring, 39–48.

Part Three
Controlling Service Delivery

10
Performance measurement

10.1 Introduction

Organizations need to know how well they are performing not only in an absolute sense but relative to:

• Predetermined standards set out in organizational goals and objectives
• Competitors (if there are any)
• Customer expectations
• Resources deployed (capital, labour, materials, energy, information)

Performance appraisal will inevitably mean undertaking some form of measurement.

Questions will be asked about:

• What is being measured?
• How is it to be measured?
• Why is it to be measured?

In recent research conducted into the management of the UK service sector, companies were asked to list, in decreasing order of importance, measurements used to analyse the productivity of service. In terms of the 'how to measure' questionnaires to customers received the highest mention. However, when it came to what is measured, global financial indicators like profit, turnover and market share predominated. What was most worrying was the fifth of respondents who undertook no measurement whatsoever (Cottam and Mudie).[1]

Inevitably the measurement process increases in complexity as the size of organization increases. The word traditionally used in this area is productivity. The practice has been to use numerous partial measures of productivity, e.g. number of customers served per employee.

The real difficulty lies in aggregating all these partial measures into a composite measure for the whole organization. In other words, how is the organization's total output and the value added to be explained by the mix and deployment of resources?

Output is influenced by a host of factors such as the level of automation, the quality of raw materials, scheduling of labour, layout of operations and customer behaviour. The danger of using only one partial measure of productivity in the form of labour input is that poor performance may wrongly be attributed to unproductive workers. The explanation may quite easily be found in poor raw materials, poor layout and awkward customers. Ball, Johnson and Slattery[2] give an example of the range of productivity measures in the hotel industry (Table 10.1).

Table 10.1 Example ratios of hotel productivity

	Physical measures	Physical/financial measures combined	Financial measures
Labour measures	Kitchen meals produced / No. kitchen staff	Restaurant revenue / Hours worked in restaurant	Banqueting revenue / Banqueting payroll
	Housecount / Total employee hours	Total room sales / Total reception employees	Hotel revenue / Total management salaries
	Restaurant covers / Hours worked in restaurant	Total room sales / Chambermaid day	Total added value / Hotel payroll
Energy measures	Total guest rooms / Total kilowatt hours	No. cooked meals / Total cooking costs	Hotel revenue / Total energy cost
Capital measures	Total hotel customers / Square foot of hotel	No. rooms sold / Total capital expenditure	Net profit after tax / Equity capital
Raw material measured	Chips prepared (lb) / Potatoes used (lb)	No. bar customers / Cost of liquor used	Food revenue / Cost of food consumed
Total factor measures	No. satisfied hotel customers / Total no. hotel customers	Housecount / Cost of contributing resources	Net profit after tax / Cost of contributing resources

Source: Ball, S. D., Johnson, K., Slattery, P. (1986)[2]

Nowadays the term 'performance indicator' is often used to describe productivity measures. Given the distinctive characteristics of services, the pursuit of productivity measurement is a challenging one.

10.2   The meaning of productivity

Productivity is a measure of relationships between an input and an output, namely:

$$\text{Productivity} = \frac{\text{output}}{\text{input}}$$

It is a standard measure that has been used by manufacturing industries for a very long time, where for example:

$$\text{Total productivity} = \frac{\text{Total output}}{\text{Sum of all inputs}}$$

As total productivity can be difficult to determine and fail to detect explanations for poor performance, more specific measures are used:

$$P = \frac{\text{Production}}{\text{Machine hours}}$$

$$P = \frac{\text{Production}}{\text{Number of employees}}$$

$$P = \frac{\text{Sales}}{\text{Number of square feet}}$$

$$P = \frac{\text{Passenger miles (railway)}}{\text{Number of guards}}$$

It is a topic that generates a great deal of attention. Exhortations are often made about the need to increase efficiency (as distinct from effectiveness) and invariably this is supposed to be achieved by getting more output from the same input or getting the same output from less input. Inevitably, calls are made for more output from less input!

Labour is a major input in any organization (particularly a service) and the focus of this call for increased productivity has been, and still is, the blue collar worker. His counterpart, the white collar worker, has escaped being subjected to productivity measurement. Increasingly, however, the picture is changing. The performance of white collar workers is being measured, although the term 'performance indicators' seems to take precedence over productivity.

It is generally agreed that it is much easier to measure productivity on an assembly line than a service business where the 'product' is often the customers' intangible experience. Services themselves, will, of course, vary in

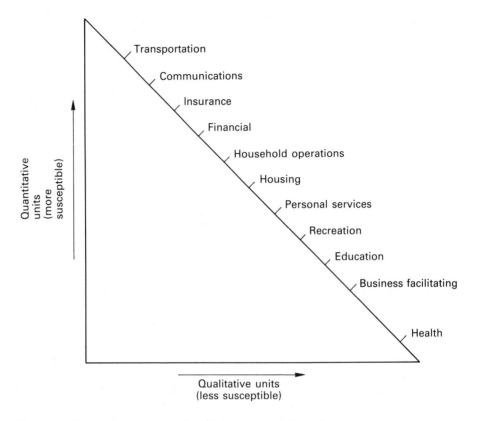

Figure 10.1 *Productivity of services: susceptibility of output to measurement. Source: Rathmell, J. M. (1974)*[3]

terms of how susceptible they are to measurement and the form that measurement will take[3] (Figure 10.1).

Established productivity measures are less easily applied as one moves from the left to the right of Figure 10.1. Measuring productivity in a transportation service poses fewer problems than in a counselling service.

For a transportation service input (e.g. driver hours) and output (e.g. tonne-miles) and the relationship between the two offers a clear measure of productivity. For a counselling service, quantitative input and output measures and the relationship between the two are not so readily available. Counselling involves advice and human relationships, and because of that, understanding the process and impact of such a service is far from straightforward. It is a service where the proper application of knowledge and skills should take precedence over attempts to apply input/output ratios.

10.3   The productivity framework

To develop our understanding of productivity we need to add to the ideas of input and output already mentioned (Figure 10.2).

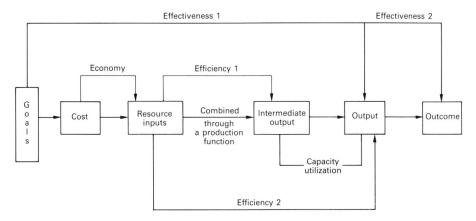

Figure 10.2 The productivity framework

Two words in Figure 10.2 are frequently mentioned in everyday discussion often without clear understanding of their meaning. They are used loosely and often interchangeably. The words are, of course, efficiency and effectiveness. The meanings will become clearer as we look at some examples. However, in general they can be defined as follows:

- *Efficiency* – rate at which inputs are converted into outputs, e.g. calls per sales representative; customers served per catering assistant. The emphasis is often on quantitative measurement and the objective is one of securing the maximum output from the minimum input.
- *Effectiveness* – extent to which purposes/goals are achieved, e.g. the number of productive and profitable calls per sales representative and the nature of customer relationships established and fostered; the number of satisfied customers served per catering assistant. The emphasis is on qualitative measurement and the objective one of meeting customer needs and delivering service quality.

The distinction between efficiency and effectiveness has been defined as 'doing things right' (efficiency) and 'doing right things' (effectiveness).[4] What this amounts to is that efficiency is 'the rate of which inputs are converted into outputs' and effectiveness 'the extent to which purposes are being achieved'.[5]

Figure 10.2 offers a guide to developing an understanding of the various elements and their relationships:

- *Economy*: the cost of selecting and hiring people, materials and equipment and conversion through training and installation into resource inputs capable of providing service. It is not a measure of performance, but can have an impact on the level of performance.
- *Efficiency 1*: the ratio of inputs to intermediate outputs, e.g. the cost per unit of capacity (cost per place in a private nursing home) or cost per anticipated level of demand (cost per meal prepared in a hotel).
- *Production function*: all the resources (staff, buildings, equipment, consumables) are combined to produce intermediate outputs, i.e. the capacity to

produce the relevant service (school places, hospital beds, train seats, restaurant seats).

- *Efficiency 2*: the ratio of inputs to outputs, e.g. the cost per college graduate or cost per number of meals sold in a hotel.
- *Capacity utilization*: the ratio of intermediate output to final output, i.e. how good is management at converting the intermediate output into customer take-up. For example, what percentage of seats will be taken up by customers in a restaurant or what percentage of places will be taken up in a residential home. For services in general, and in particular where advance preparation is involved (meals in a restaurant), accurate demand forecasting will become part of effective marketing management.
- *Effectiveness 1 and 2*: there is no overall agreement as to how effectiveness should be defined. Is it to be in terms of 'output' or 'outcome'?

Output means the service actually delivered to customers. Outcome, on the other hand, is the impact which the service may have on the recipients. It is the quality of the service delivered and its effectiveness in meeting users' needs or achieving its underlying purpose (Audit Commission).[6] For example, a college educates students (output) but has a certain responsibility for graduate employability and destination (outcome). A management consultancy produces a report and advises a client (output) but has a certain responsibility for the impact of the report on the performance of the client company (outcome). In both cases, however, the outcome measure is not completely under the control of the service provider.

For many services, output is defined in a straightforward manner, as in:

- number of commuters transported
- number of home help clients assisted
- number of restaurant meals served
- number of admissions to a leisure centre

What is missing is any reference to the quality of service delivered.

Some services simply have no output or income that can practically be measured in quantitative terms; for example, a counselling service.

If the output of a process appears to defy identification with precision a surrogate measure of output may be used. For example, the true output of the police force could be its contribution to the maintenance of a peaceful, crime free, ordered society, or a public library's true output might be the contribution it makes to expanding the knowledge base of, and to entertaining, the constituent community. As both of these outputs are likely to prove difficult to quantify, proxy measures in the form of 'percentage of reported crime solved' and 'ratio of loans to book stock' are used.[7]

The difficulties surrounding the measurement of output and outcome has led to the development of a different approach which is known as process productivity. It has been argued as being a more realistic and expedient measure.[8] How well the service is delivered is, arguably, a better way for a service like health, where it is difficult to measure changes in health status and where factors other than medical care affect health outcome.

10.4   Improving productivity

Given the standard ratio there are, in theory, five ways to increase productivity:

1 Output increases faster than input
2 Output remains unchanged with fewer inputs
3 Output increases from the same inputs
4 Input decreases more than output
5 Maximum increase in the ratio through an ideal combination of outputs and inputs

Whatever method is selected the true test will be the effect on the quality of service delivered.

Improved productivity must, therefore, take into account effectivenesss as well as efficiency. A number of practical steps can be taken to improve productivity in terms of efficiency and effectiveness:

1 Careful cost control, driven by a management desire to become 'leaner and fitter'.
2 Job design – management and employees in pursuit of productivity improvements, must attempt to answer questions such as:[9]

What work do we do?
How do we do it?
Why do we do it this way?
How can we do it better?

3 Replace human labour with automation
4 Improve employee motivation:

How do employees perceive the organizational culture?
Do they feel part of the organization?
Are rewards commensurate with the tasks done?

5 Select people more predisposed for productivity, for example the predisposition of an air traffic controller is more important than that of a security guard in a low crime area.
6 Isolate, and even extend, the back office so that the benefits of manufacturing technology can be achieved.
7 Schedule resource deployment to match fluctuations in the level of customer demand.
8 Involve customers more in the production and delivery of service.
9 Make sure that highly skilled employees are not doing jobs that could be undertaken by less fully trained staff.

Practical examples: some undesirable consequences

In the drive for greater efficiency, productivity increases may produce an adverse effect.

Example no. 1 – a three-hundred-bedroomed hotel has reduced the number of chambermaids from thirty to twenty as a result of a productivity drive. There are to be no changes in time to do the job and materials/equipment available. The result is a reduction in the cleanliness of rooms, in particular those occupied by families who leave the room very untidy.

Example no. 2 – an insurance company decides to measure the productivity of its employees by client satisfaction. As a result, the claims department rapidly settled claims and nearly bankrupt the company.

Example no. 3 – a hospital increased patient throughput by decreasing the average duration of bed occupancy. Efficiency could be said to have increased. However, to achieve this efficiency, the hospital selected patients offering the likelihood of shorter lengths of stay. Fundamentally, a faster throughput may increase efficiency but at what cost to full and lasting patient recovery (effectiveness). An increase in the number of early deaths would certainly increase efficiency!

What these examples clearly demonstrate is an overriding concentration on increases in quantity and cost reduction. The consequence is an adverse effect on service quality. Greater efficiency is achieved by increasing the numerator (faster turnover of patients) while maintaining the denominator or maintaining the numerator and decreasing the denominator (fewer chambermaids).

There is often a tension between the drive for efficiency and the achievement of effectiveness[10] (Figure 10.3). A service can be efficient but ineffective; alternatively it can be effective but inefficient. This can be illustrated by a hypothetical emergency ambulance service:

One can envisage an ambulance with a highly trained crew that is very efficient and dashes about from accident to accident promptly, treating injured persons with expert skill, placing them in the ambulance and rapidly driving them to the

	Ineffective	Effective
Inefficient	Die quickly	Survive
Efficient	Die slowly	Thrive

Figure 10.3 The contrast between efficiency and effectiveness. Source: Brown, R. (1987)[10]

nearest hospital, then racing off to service yet another emergency. The unit would be extraordinarily efficient if it handled two such emergencies in an hour or about sixteen in an eight hour shift. However, it would be utterly ineffective if the actual number of emergencies in the area averaged twenty per shift. This would be an example of a highly efficient service that is utterly ineffective; more ambulances are needed. Alternatively, one can conceive of a very effective ambulance service where no-one has to wait more than five minutes to receive expert medical attention, ambulances are promptly dispatched, and many lives are saved. However such a service may be extremely inefficient, if in fact it is staffed with so many ambulances and crews that most of them sit around doing nothing for hours on end because there is little demand for their services.[11]

10.5 Consumer participation and productivity

As the consumer is the central character in the provision of service the question arises, 'What contribution can the consumer make to the delivery of an efficient and effective service?'

To test the impact of the consumer's contribution to service productivity, consider the four real-life service scenarios:[12]

Scene 1: a major hotel
Guest A called the desk right after check-in to report a burned-out light bulb in an absence of hot water; both were fixed in an hour.

Guest A also slept better, as the hotel assigned him a quiet room when he identified himself as a light sleeper.

Guest B did not communicate to management until check-out time, when he complained that there was no hot water and he had to read in the dark; he was overheard by new guests checking in, who asked if the hotel was undergoing a disaster.

Scene 2: an airline flight from New York to Los Angeles
Passenger A arrives for the flight with a portable tape player and tape, with a large supply of reading material, and wearing warm clothes.

Passenger A also booked a special meal ahead of time.

Passenger B, who arrives empty handed, becomes annoyed when the crew runs out of blankets and magazines, complains about the lunch and starts fidgeting after the movie.

Scene 3: office of a professional tax preparer
Client A has organized the necessary information into categories that will help the accountant.

Client B has a shoe box filled with papers, including laundry receipts mixed in with cancelled cheques.

Scene 4: a health club
When a new aerobics instructor includes a routine that seems hard to follow, Member A modifies the steps and adjusts the pace to allow for her individual physical limitations.

Member B complains that the routine is too hard to follow and suggests that the instructor be fired immediately.

Reflecting on the four scenarios, two related questions are worth remembering:

1 How many of the Customer B type are there around?
2 What can a service provider do to encourage more of the Customer A type?

In trying to turn the service consumer into a valued participant in the service delivery process, the service provider must recognize the following factors and how they could be managed:

- Consumer predisposition, e.g. personality, attitudes, values – may be difficult to change.
- Consumer potential commitment/willingness to become involved – low to high.
- Consumer knowledge and skills – how easily can they be developed if need be?

In addition to the degree of consumer involvement, the service provider must consider the nature of consumer involvement, i.e. when, where and how in the service delivery process will customer involvement occur.

From self-service at a restaurant or petrol station through to interactions with a doctor, teacher or accountant, the potential for exploiting improvements in productivity can be substantial. Whatever changes in service delivery are proposed, the consumer must be the major beneficiary.

10.6   White collar productivity

The working day for a blue collar worker is often prescribed down to the finest detail (tasks to be done and time taken to do them). For the white collar worker, what they do and how much time they spend doing it, is often left to their own judgement. The blue collar worker can be defined as one category in which the tasks are largely standardized and repetitive, e.g. railway porter, catering assistant, bus driver, street sweeper. The white collar category, on the other hand, includes a diversity of jobs, with differing sets of authority, responsibility and duties. Ruch sought to clear up the problem of the white collar category by isolating two relevant dimensions:[13]

   1 The amount of discretion involved – not the amount of skill, but the degree to which there is a specified procedure to follow in the performance of the job. For example, the hotel receptionist's job is not highly skilled but judgement may be required in handling the different customer enquiries and complaints. On the other hand, the dentist's job is a highly skilled procedure in contrast to the procedure for handling complaints. It would be easier to measure, therefore, the productivity of the dentist (number of fillings, extractions per dentist) than the hotel receptionist's performance in handling customer enquiries and complaints. The general rule is that the less discretion there is in the job, the easier it is to measure. The dentist's job, in productivity terms, is, therefore, more akin to the blue collar worker.
   2 The degree to which there is a physical product involved in the process. For

the McDonald's cook or the dentist there is a tangible output that can be counted and checked for quality (the hamburger and the filling). The hotel receptionist's job has to be experienced, as once it is performed, the evidence disappears. There is no output left to count or check for quality. The general rule is that the more there is a tangible output, the easier it is to measure.

There are problems then in measuring white collar productivity:[13]

- Difficulties in determining the output or contribution
- Tendency to measure activities rather than the results, e.g. number of reports created says nothing about the quality of these reports.
- The input may not show up in output until some time later. There is a lagged effect
- Quality of output is even more difficult to determine than quantity.
- Distinction is often not made between efficiency and effectiveness. The white collar worker may be efficient at developing reports but ineffective by not having enough to do, attending unproductive meetings, or assigned work outside the area of expertise.
- White collar workers are not accustomed to being measured.

Although there are difficulties, effort should be made to measure white collar productivity. The inputs may be relatively straightforward, e.g. number of hours worked, number of hours paid, resources used. It is the process and the output that pose the difficulties. The following issues are worthy of consideration:

- How creative are the white collar employees in the sense of developing and implementing new ideas.
- How efficient and effective is the utilization of the working day – this is an over-riding factor upon which everything else depends.
- How satisfied are the customers – care needs to be exercised since no matter what the white collar worker does, the customer may remain dissatisfied, e.g. lecturer and student, doctor and patient.
- Ability to handle non-standard situations, i.e. crisis management.
- Communication skills and success in keeping people properly informed.

The above list is by no means exhaustive but simply indicates the kind of analysis that needs to be undertaken.

The single greatest challenge facing managers, according to Drucker[14] is to raise the productivity of knowledge and service workers. He stresses that for all their diversity in knowledge, skill, responsibility, social status and pay, knowledge and service workers are remarkably alike in terms of:

What does and does not work in raising their productivity.

The first lesson that came as a rude shock, according to Drucker, is that the replacement of labour with technology does not, by itself, raise productivity. The key to raising productivity is working smarter rather than harder or longer. Drucker believes that fundamental questions need to be asked if the productivity of knowledge and service workers is to be raised. For example:

- What is the task?
- What are we trying to accomplish?
- Why do it at all?

Drucker bemoans the fact that in many professional service jobs, e.g. nursing, teaching, a great deal of effort and time is taken up with paperwork and meetings, much of which contributes little if any value and has little if anything to do with what these professionals are qualified and paid for. The result is job impoverishment rather than enrichment and a reduction in motivation and morale.

Drucker recognizes that for a good many service jobs, e.g. making hospital beds, handling insurance claims, performance is defined on a quantity basis, very much like production jobs. The application of industrial engineering techniques will determine how long it should take, for example, to make up a hospital bed properly. For other service jobs, e.g. knowledge based, raising productivity, in Drucker's view, requires asking, 'What works?' plus analysing the process step by step and operation by operation.

Process is the subject of a new approach that could achieve for office productivity what just-in-time techniques did for manufacturing practice. Business process redesign (BPR) looks at procedures and the way things are organized. BPR is attracting the interest of large service organizations looking for new ways of raising productivity and cutting costs. By simplifying the workflow and reducing the number of stages involved in a procedure, BPR can speed up customer service and involve fewer staff.

The development of schemes relating pay to individual performance has grown dramatically in recent years. According to a recent survey,[15] 47 per cent of private sector companies have performance related pay (PRP) schemes for all non-manual grades and a further 21 per cent were using it for some non-manuals. There was no significant difference between manufacturing and service industries, but there was a difference between the public and private sectors. In the public sector 37 per cent of organizations in the survey were operating PRP schemes for some of their non-manual grades, but only 6 per cent covered all non-manuals. Non-management grades in the public sector were significantly less likely to be covered by PRP than in the private sector, and those employed in senior management. Management and professional occupations were nearly twice as likely to be eligible for PRP in the private sector as those in the public sector.

The supporters of PRP put forward a number of reasons for introducing it, e.g. it's a motivator, it improves quality and productivity and it's fair. The evidence in support of these claims is inconclusive. Instead it can be argued that the actual assessment of performance is open to charges of unfairness. Questions are raised about who does the assessment and how it is done. Furthermore is PRP appropriate to all organizational cultures? Even if it is appropriate, how far can PRP help to promote changes in organizational culture? Can it make organizations more customer performance oriented through improved productivity and service quality?

The challenge of implementing PRP is arguably greater for service organizations than their manufacturing counterparts. There is more uncertainty in terms of process and output and factors outside their employees' control may figure prominently in service situations, e.g. infinite variety of possible break-downs in the service delivery system, difficulties in managing customers.

Some jobs or tasks may not easily lend themselves to concrete performance measures. It is easier to evaluate if hard quantifiable, technical measures can be set. However, softer measures, e.g. related to communication skills should also be encouraged.

It is argued that PRP is a distinct improvement on previous incentive schemes. According to Kessler and Purcell,[16] 'the link between pay and performance remains as obscure as ever and further research is necessary to throw some light on this vexed issue'.

Of course, the most radical question of all in any discussion of white collar productivity would be, 'Why not give the workers a say?'

Giving subordinates a 'voice' in formal performance evaluation of their bosses can prove invaluable as a source of feedback for everyone concerned.[17] Employees can be asked their view of how effective the bosses are in, for example:

- Providing feedback on performance
- Looking for ways to improve existing systems
- Taking action on urgent requests
- Keeping people well informed
- Handling a disruptive employee

Care must be exercised over what to appraise and how to do it. Some might question the accuracy of subordinate appraisals. To some extent this misses the point. Their true value is in offering a view of management performance from those directly affected by it. That view can then be compared with management's view of itself. One study[18] found that managers who perceived themselves to be effective at 'providing clear instruction and explanation to employees when giving assignments', were not perceived as such by those persons supposedly on the receiving end of the instructions!

Involving employees in management appraisal can influence their own productivity as well. What they believe and say about management's expectations of them may hold the key to explaining levels of productivity. The 'Pygmalion in Management' view suggests that most managers unintentionally treat their subordinates in a way that leads to lower performance than they are capable of achieving.[19]

The way subordinates are treated is very much influenced by management expectations of them. The result is that high expectations lead to high productivity and low expectations lead to low productivity. However expectations must, in the view of the subordinate, be realistic and achievable.

A concluding comment about white collar productivity – it is not so readily observable and measurable as blue collar productivity, e.g. the bricklayer is both easily observed and measured – number of bricks laid per hour; whereas a nurse comforting a patient after a major operation may not be viewed as productive activity in the conventional wisdom.

10.7 Service productivity as a relationship between input and output

Efficiency and effectiveness in a service organization are measured in terms of inputs and outputs. But unlike manufacturing or extractive industries, service is a process with customer involvement. Understanding the process is fundamental to explaining the relationship of inputs to outputs. This process, and the inputs and outputs, can be portrayed as approximating to a triangle. The base could be a point (making it truly a triangle) or as wide as the top (making it a square) (Figure 10.4).

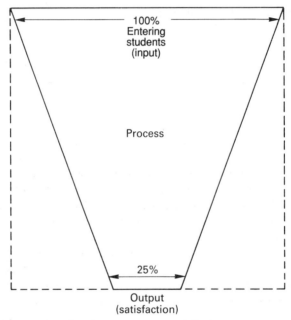

100%
Entering
students
(input)

Process

25%

Output
(satisfaction)

Figure 10.4 *The service triangle: percentage satisfied*

An example will serve to illustrate. Colleges take in students who have expectations. After a period of time one output will be student satisfaction. The width of the base will indicate that of those who have entered, what percentage at the finish were satisfied with what they received. In this case (Figure 10.4) the percentage satisfied would be of the order of twenty five per cent. The dotted line would represent a situation where all the customers who used the service were satisfied. Of course, in addition to determining how many customers were satisfied, consideration would have to be given to how satisfied they were. Notwithstanding dropouts and failures, the percentage satisfied will serve as a measure of how effective the process they have gone through has been. This kind of analysis could apply to many services, e.g. hotels, package holidays, rail commuters.

Equally, the triangle could be portrayed another way (Figure 10.5). This time the emphasis is on the value added by the process. Students enter with

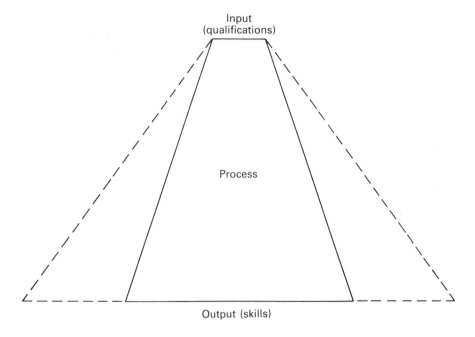

Figure 10.5 *The service triangle: value added*

qualifications, e.g. A-levels and finish with a qualification. But how effective has the process been in developing skills and abilities valuable for entering the world of work? The wider the base (dotted line) the more effective the process has been. Unlike the percentage satisfied measure, the value added approach is more difficult to determine.

Heaton[20] suggested that the productivity of service organizations could be calculated as the product of four operating functions: input, processing, output or follow-up and timing and coordination. He applied this to the unusual example of a mental hospital:

Input: 30 per cent of those admitted do not require hospitalization – gross rating then of 70 per cent.

Processing: only 50 per cent of those needing help receive it due to overcrowding, under staffing and a general lack of skills, understanding and care – gross productivity measurement is then 35 per cent ($50\% \times 70\%$).

Output or follow-up: on release, only 20 per cent is offered appropriate follow-up and assistance due to limited outpatient services – gross productivity measurement is now 7 per cent ($50\% \times 70\% \times 20\%$).

Timing and coordination: there is a time and place for everything. Too little too late is as wasteful as too much too soon. Of the 7 per cent only 50 per cent were admitted, treated and released at the proper time and helped by the proper agencies – gross productivity measurement is now 3.5 per cent ($70\% \times 50\% \times 20\% \times 50\%$).

Therefore out of an initial one hundred patients only three to four were effectively helped. It is hardly the mark of an effective service organization.

Analysis similar to Heaton's is a must for service organizations as it focuses on the process and facilitates understanding of the progress from the input to the output stage. As with the college example mentioned earlier, there will be a number of variables that require investigation. Some of these will be under the control of the service organization and others may be more difficult to control. The nature and deployment of employee skills, materials and equipment are far more controllable than the customers' behaviour and demand levels.

10.8 Technology and productivity

Given the characteristics of services it is difficult to measure productivity with the same precision as exists in the manufacturing sector. To what extent can the adoption of technology improve productivity? A distinction must be drawn between hard technology and soft technology. Hard technology means the computers and other equipment e.g. ATMs, automatic car washes, airport X-ray surveillance equipment. The soft technology involves the systems and processes in operation, e.g. fast food outlets, pre-packaged tours.

Quinn and Paquette[21] suggest that service technologies can deliver lowest cost outputs and maximum personalization and customization for customers.

Production, efficiency and customer customization are achieved, according to them, by 'seeking the smallest possible core unit at which production can be replicated and repeated; then developing micro-measures to manage processes and functions at this level, and finally mixing these micro units in a variety of combinations to match localised individual customers' needs'. This smallest replicable unit will vary by industry but they quote the example of American Express's credit card and travel service operation. 'It can capture in the most disaggregated form details that its various traveller, shopper, retailer and transportation company customers put through its credit card system. American Express can then mix and match the patterns and capabilities of each group to add value for them. It can identify life style change or match forthcoming travel plans with customers' specific buying habits to notify them of special promotions, product offerings or services'. This example illustrates the impact of service technologies on both efficiency and effectiveness. Technology enables such a process to be possible. Precision, speed and accuracy are the hallmarks of the process.

It has been suggested that 'technology gives the quality to service organisations to handle larger volumes of service, to offer a wider range of services, to provide quicker and more accurate services and to permit more efficient management'.[22]

In addition to achieving cost effectiveness and customer satisfaction, the front-line employee becomes more efficient by working faster and smarter. The employee is also empowered to be much more capable of meeting customer needs, and according to Quinn and Paquette, 'it allows relatively inexperienced people to perform very sophisticated tasks quickly, increasing the value-added per employee'.[21] The front-line employee, in effect, has access to information which can be accessed and customized to meet the needs of particular customers. Information is of course the key for effective management and marketing of many service organizations.

Technology in services

The following examples (selected from the *Financial Times*) illustrate applications of technology in service organizations, with particular focus given to the impact on productivity.

Bank

Trials are under way into a new generation of automatic teller machines which carry out functions previously performed by bank staff. Barclays new system will allow customers access to the following services:

- Personalized information on mortgages or insurance with on-the-spot quotations.
- Information on standing orders and direct debits
- Travellers' cheques and foreign currency
- Travel insurance[23]

This is a good example of the customer being empowered, giving him a personalized convenient service which may be regarded as superior to the original encounter with the bank teller.

Retailing

Electronic point-of-sale (EPOS) scanning systems installed in many supermarkets shorten the time spent at check-outs and provide detailed information on which products are selling best and how fast. The next generation of EPOS equipment, electronic data interchange (EDI) systems will replace laborious paperwork by transferring orders and invoices between computers in the retailers' depots and those in their suppliers' warehouses at the press of a button. Replenishment orders will thus be transmitted automatically.[24]

This is an interesting example of the superior access to information, which the retailers' technology has given them, giving power to one party over another. The risks and costs of stock control will now be passed to the supplier.

Insurance

Direct Line, owned by the Royal Bank of Scotland, has changed the face of the insurance industry. Underwriting decisions are incorporated in the computer software used by the telesales personnel when they sell the policy. A caller is simply asked for his or her details (how old they are, where they live, what car they drive) and this is keyed into the software programme which automatically produces a quotation.

The main benefit of computerization in this case is that it gives a very rapid response to customer enquiries, a good quality service and a greater degree of control than in a typical insurance company[25].

Hotels

The Savoy Hotel in London panders to the personal idiosyncrasies of its guests with the help of a computer which it uses to store the personal likes and dislikes of 80,000 guests. Technology will provide many opportunities for hotels to improve efficiency and reduce costs according to management consultants Howarth and Howarth. The Howarth report says it will be more important for hotel managers to be computer literate than good at caring for guests. But there may be a limit to the number of traditions that can be swept away by technology. A balance must be struck between hi-tech and hi-touch. Who would like to stay at a hotel where checking in and checking out would be possible without reference to any staff?[26]

In fact Britain's first automatic hotel opened on 2 March 1992. The 80-bedroom Formule 1 has credit card check-in and out, self cleaning showers and toilets and costs just £17 a night for up to three people. The French-owned hotel in Peterborough, which took just 12 weeks to build, is the first of around 200 proposed for Britain. Despite sleeping up to 240 guests every night, it is staffed by just two managers and five part-time cleaners.

Railways

British Rail have steamed to world leadership in the development of the electronic signalbox which brings the benefits of computer-based automation to train management. The automatic route setting relieves the signalman of much routine work.[27]

Nursing

Nursing shortages in USA hospitals are being eased by a child-sized robot called Helpmate. It frees nurses from fetching and carrying so that they can spend more time with patients. It memorizes the layout and location of every department in the hospital so that it can travel around without cables or tracks. It delivers meals and summons lifts and when the item has been delivered the recipient presses a return button and the machine goes back to its department.[28]

Post Office

All UK post offices will hold on to their rubber stamps but in addition 5500 clerks will be provided with computer terminals to cope with the majority of transactions. It is cheaper, evidently, for UK post offices to process such things as pensions and other state benefits using semi-manual methods rather than to introduce full automation.[29]

10.9   Summary

Productivity is an issue that has been around for some time. It is concerned with the efficiency of converting inputs into outputs. For service organizations, unlike manufacturing, productivity management is more difficult. This is because the input, process and output are not always susceptible to objective definition and measurement.

A number of steps can be taken to improve productivity but care must be exercised when devising an efficiency programme because effectiveness may diminish as a result.

Consumers play a pivotal role in services. Strategies must therefore be devised for developing consumer participation in the drive for increased productivity. In doing so, recognition must be given to the difficulties involved in obtaining this participation.

Productivity measures have usually been applied to the blue collar employee but the white collar employee performance and the impact of technology are becoming more important in the pursuit of efficiency and effectiveness.

Appendix 10.1   A sample of indicators from selected service organizations

1   British Rail

Passenger business

(a)   *Inter City*
- PROFIT/(LOSS) as a percentage of receipts   %
- Receipts per train mile   £
- Receipts per passenger mile   pence
- Passenger miles per loaded train mile (average train load)   passengers
- Total operating expenses per train mile   £
- Percentage of trains arriving within ten minutes of booked time   %
- Percentage of trains cancelled   %

Similar indicators for other aspects of the business
Source: British Railways Board Annual Report and Accounts 1990/1991

2   Museums

(a)   Education

- Number of courses/workshops arranged and their take-up
- Number of school visits
- Percentage of schools in the target areas reached

(b) Enquiries

- Number of enquiries dealt with each year
- Percentage of total enquiries successfully dealt with
- Average time/cost per specific enquiry

(c) Access

- Length of stay
- Number and type of visitors
- Return visitors
- Percentage from a given catchment area
- Relative performance with competition
- Measurement of visitor satisfaction

Other indicators for other aspects of the service.
Source: Museums Year Book 1991–1992, Museums Association, published by Rhinegold Publishing Ltd, London.

3. Further education

(a) Student success ratio

$$\frac{\text{Number of students obtaining a qualification}}{\text{Number of enrolled students}}$$

(b) Post-course success ratio

$$\frac{\text{Number of successful students who gain employment or progress to more advanced education or training}}{\text{Number of successful students}}$$

(c) Client satisfaction

$$\frac{\text{Number of clients expressing satisfaction}}{\text{Number of clients responding to requests for opinions}}$$

(d) Utilization of teaching accommodation

$$\text{Room utilization factor} = \frac{\text{Room-hours used} \times 100}{\text{Room-hours available}}$$

That is, the percentage use of available rooms

$$\text{Seat utilization factor} = \frac{\text{Seat-hours used} \times 100}{\text{Seat-hours available}}$$

That is, the percentage use of available seats.

Source: Measuring Up: Performance Indicators in Further Education, A report by HM Inspectors of Schools, Scottish Education Department, HMSO, London, 1990.

4 Hospitals

Acute Health Services

(a) *Activity indicators*
- Average length of stay
- Average number of patients per bed per year
- Admission waiting lists in relation to the population served
- Turnover interval: average length of time a bed lies empty between admissions
- Urgent, immediate or emergency in-patient admissions in relation to the population served

(b) *Financial indicators*
- Cost per day and cost per case by hospital and district
- Actual and percentage component cost by hospital
- In-patient catering costs per in-patient day by hospital
- Domestic and cleaning cost per cubic metre by district

(c) *Manpower indicators*
- Percentage breakdown of registered, enrolled, learners, auxiliary nursing and midwifery staff for all acute and mainly or partly acute hospitals
- Ratio of acute sector nursing staff to:

   (i) number of day cases and in-patient cases
   (ii) number of day cases and in-patients days

- Ratio of nursing auxiliaries/assistants to domestic staff in acute and mainly or partly acute hospitals

Similar indicators for other aspects of the service.

Source: Clinical Performance Indicators: A Background to Their Use, Northwest Thames Regional Health Authority, December, 1984.

Questions

1 (a) A local community is considering two transit systems both of which will involve a free bus service (i.e. subsidies will be the only source of revenues).

System A will require a £20,000 subsidy and will attract 16,000 passengers

System B will require a £10,000 subsidy but will attract only 10,000 passengers

Which system should be chosen and why?

(b) Two bus systems have equivalent passenger-moving capacity and each system generates 100,000 vehicle hours. The costs for systems A and B are £2m and £1.5m respectively. System A carries 3 million passengers and system B carries 1.5 million passengers.

Which system is more efficient and why?

(c) In a particular hospital 10 nurses and one doctor using 10 beds are able to do 20 minor operations. Another hospital performed 40 operations with the same number of staff.
Which hospital is more efficient/effective?

2 Is there a danger that increases in productivity may lead to reductions in quality? If there is, are there any particular services that are most at risk?

3 Describe the input-process-output relationships found in the following types of services:

(a)   university
(b)   prison
(c)   bank branch
(d)   restaurant

4 How would you assess the productivity of a

(a)   college lecturer
(b)   general practitioner
(c)   member of parliament
(d)   trading standards officer?

References

1 Cottam, A. M. and Mudie, P. M. (1992). Working paper. Napier University, Edinburgh.
2 Ball, S. D., Johnson, K. and Slattery, P. (1986). Labour productivity in hotels: an empirical analysis. *International Journal of Hospitality Management.* **5**(3), 141–147.
3 Rathmell, J. M. (1974). *Marketing in the Service Sector.* Winthrop, Cambridge, Mass.
4 Drucker, P. (1973). *Management: Tasks, Responsibilities, Practices.* Harper and Row.

5 Butt, H. and Palmer, B. (1985). *Value for Money in the Public Sector*. Blackwell, Oxford.

6 Audit Commission (1989). Managing services effectively. *Performance Review*. **5** December.

7 Whynes, D. K. (1987). On assessing efficiency in the provision of local authority services. *Local Government Studies*. January–February, 53–68.

8 Mersha, T. (1989). Output and performance measurement in outpatient care. *Omega*, **17**(2), 159–161.

9 Heskett, J. L., Sasser, W. E. and Hart, C. W. L.(1990). *Service Breakthroughs*. The Free Press, Macmillan Inc.

10 Brown, R. (1987). Marketing – a function and a philosophy. *Quarterly Review of Marketing*, **12**(3 and 4), 25–30.

11 Savas, E. S. (1978). On equity in providing public services. *Management Science*, **24**(8), April, 800–808.

12 Goodwin, C. (1988). 'I can do it myself': training the service consumer to contribute to service productivity. *Journal of Service Marketing*, **2**(4), 71–78.

13 Ruch, W. A. (1982). The measurement of white-collar productivity. *National Productivity Review* (Autumn), 416–426.

14 Drucker, P. F. (1991). The new productivity challenge. *Harvard Business Review*, (November–December), 69–79.

15 Cannell, M. and Wood, S. (1992). *Incentive Pay: Impact and Evolution*. National Economic Development Office and Institute of Personnel Management.

16 Kessler, I. and Purcell, J. (1992). Performance related pay: objectives and application. *Human Resource Management Journal*, **2**(3), 16–33.

17 Bernadin, H. J. and Beatty, R. W. (1987). Can subordinate appraisals enhance managerial productivity? *Sloan Management Review*, (Summer), 63–73.

18 Mount, M. K. (1984). Supervisors, self and subordinate ratings of performance and satisfaction with supervision. *Journal of Management*, **10**, 121–130.

19 Livingston, J. S. (1988). Pygmalion in management. *Harvard Business Review*, (September–October), 121–130.

20 Heaton, H. (1977). *Productivity in Service Organisations*. McGraw-Hill.

21 Quinn, J. B. and Paquette, P. C. (1990). Technology in services: creating organisational revolutions. *Sloan Management Review*, (Winter), 67–87.

22 Cowell, D. (1984). *The Marketing of Services*. Heinemann, Oxford.

23 Barchard, D. (1992). Services grow on branches. *Financial Times*, February 18.

24 de Jonquieres, G. (1991). Retailers plan for last minute rush. *Financial Times*, December 24.

25 Lapper, R. (1992). Fire eaters and contortionists. *Financial Times*, January 6.

26 McLain, L. (1990). Hotels nibble away at the fruits of automation. *Financial Times*, January 17.

27 Lane, A. (1990). Train management switches to the screen. *Financial Times*, January 12.

28 (1990). A little help for nurses. *Financial Times*, January 11.

29 Knight, P. (1991). Putting a stamp on progress. *Financial Times*, October 17.

11

Satisfaction guaranteed (providing guarantees and handling complaints)

11.1 Introduction

Getting things right first time, all the time, for every customer, may be the stated goal of many companies. Forte's company philosophy states that it intends 'To give complete customer satisfaction, by efficient and courteous service, with value for money'.[1] Complete or total customer satisfaction is a goal that more and more service organizations are striving to achieve. Even the public sector now refers to its users as customers, and their views are taken into account in the design and monitoring of the service. This is done in the belief that higher levels of satisfaction will be built in this way. The Audit Commission, whose job it is to control local authorities, recently said that, 'services need to be provided *for* the public, rather than simply *to* it'.[2]

However the totally satisfied customer is becoming an increasingly elusive creature. As Sir James McKinnon, director-general of OFGAS (the gas industry regulator) says, 'customers are increasingly aware of their rights and are more confident about seeking redress'.[3]

Increasing confidence levels is only partly responsible for declining levels of satisfaction. Many would argue that the increasing expectations that consumers hold is at the root of this problem. Therefore, it is simply unrealistic to expect that there will be no dissatisfied customers. Of course companies should attempt to minimize levels of dissatisfaction by providing a better service. However, at the same time they should also consider what to do for those who are dissatisfied. Analysing dissatisfied customers, designing efficient systems for handling complaints, and the provision of guarantees are ways in which management can build levels of satisfaction.

11.2 Dissatisfied customers

What do they do?

Customers who are unhappy with a service are less likely to complain about the situation than they are when they are unhappy with a product. So what happens when a customer is dissatisfied with the service he receives (Table 11.1)?

Table 11.1 Extent to which dissatisfied customers took action: services and products

	Total	*Goods*	*Services*
Bases: complaints	4111	1610	2501
	%	%	%
Complaints for which:			
Respondents took action	67	76	61
Had unsatisfactory outcome	29	25	31

Source: Consumers Association Annual Consumer Complaints Survey (1989)

Most of them do not complain to the company. These dissatisfied customers simply do not buy the service again. In doing so they appear to be causing the least damage to the service organization.

However, the dissatisfied customer is not likely to keep the bad news to himself. At the same time as deciding not to buy the service again he is probably spreading the bad news. Dobree and Page[4] reckon that dissatisfied customers tell an average of nine or ten others about their problem.

Instead of keeping quiet about his dissatisfaction, he could complain. This action is actually helpful to the organization for several reasons. First, it gives the organization a second chance to 'delight' its original customer. It also diminishes the risk of bad publicity, either from personal word of mouth communication, or in more damaging leaks through the press to the general public, and it provides information that should be useful for development of the service.

Historically companies have shied away from the whole issue of customer complaints preferring instead to devote resources to generating business. Retaining business through service recovery is still not widespread.

11.3 Who complains?

Research has shown that those consumers who do complain about the service they receive, tend to be the loyal users of the service. In terms of numbers, they represent only a tiny fraction of the total number of dissatisfied customers. Bell and Zemke[5] estimate that 4 per cent complain, with the remaining 96 per cent going on to tell nine or ten others of their dissatisfaction. This statistic has been corroborated by other work.[4]

A great deal of research has been carried out to establish the characteristics of those who complain. Hustad and Pessemier,[6] and Warland, Hermann and Willits,[7] found them to be predominantly young women, who were intellectually, socially, and economically upmarket. Perhaps they complain more because they are less daunted by confrontation. Perhaps it is because their expectations are higher than for many other groups of consumers. There is certainly evidence to support this latter view. Studies have found that these consumers are the ones most likely to be unhappy about the performance of the services that they purchase.[8,9]

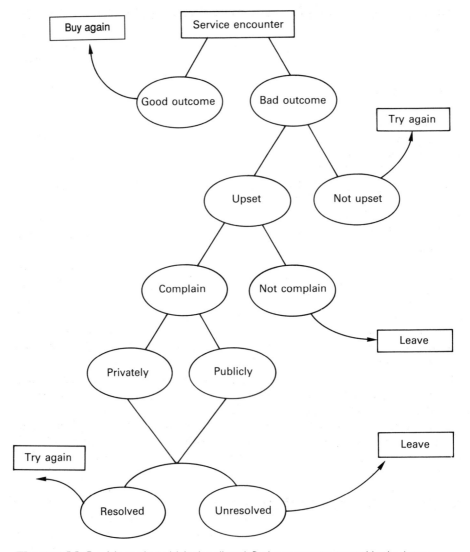

Figure 11.1 *Means by which the dissatisfied consumer can tackle the issue*

Of the three possible outcomes of poor service delivery (illustrated in Figure 11.1) not upset, upset/complain, and upset/no complaint, it has been found that the two groups that were furthest apart demographically were the upset/complain, and the upset/no complaint. Those that were not upset tended to be the older, more conservative members of society[7].

To whom do they complain?

Channels for making a complaint

Complain to the service provider
There are a number of options open to the customer who decides to complain (Table 11.2). He can go back to the company and complain to them. This is in

Table 11.2 Courses of action taken by dissatisfied customers

	All respondents
Weighted base	2043
Unweighted base	2061
	%
Action taken:	
Complained to seller	30
Wrote or phoned manufacturer	8
Wrote or phoned the head office	14
Wrote or phoned trade association	1
Contacted TSO	2
Consulted CAB	4
Consulted a solicitor	3
Wrote or phoned OFT	2
Took other action	2
Took none of these actions	44
Can't remember	11

(Some respondents took more than one course of action so percentages add to more than 100)

Source: Consumers Association Annual Consumers Complaints Survey (1989)

fact, the most likely first course of action. Best and Andreasen[9] found that on the whole, sellers have a virtual monopoly on complaints handling. The company imposes their own standards, sets the resolutions and decides on any level of compensation.

The unhappy customer can complain in private, e.g. by writing a letter of complaint, or in public, e.g. by creating a scene on the premises.[10] The public complaint is most feared by those companies that do not provide a good service in the first place, or do not have a good complaints handling procedure. Customers sometimes choose to air their grievances publicly in the belief that they are more likely to have them satisfactorily resolved by behaving in this manner in front of other customers.

Successful resolution of complaints by the company also reduces the risk of attracting the attention of the legislature or even the voluntary consumer watchdog. The vociferously negative comments of the *London Evening Standard*'s commuter watchdog no doubt played a part in the establishment of the Passenger's Charter. Had there been no cause for complaint there would have been no watchdog. Had there been no watchdog there would have been less incentive to change.

Complain to a consumer watchdog
So instead of approaching the offending company, the consumer can take his complaint to an organization that has been set up to protect or promote consumers' interests. Some of these organizations deal with all kinds of problems and enquiries, e.g. the Citizen's Advice Bureau, which receives public funding,

and the Consumers' Association which has no grants or subsidies from government or industry.

There are also industry-specific bodies, e.g. OFGAS for the gas industry, OFFER for the electricity industry, or Greenpeace for the environment. The first two were set up when these industries were privatized. They were given statutory powers to protect consumers' interests. The smaller ones rely on voluntary help and fund-raising for their existence. If these organizations cannot resolve the complaint by conciliation then, in some cases, the aggrieved customer can seek redress through arbitration.

Take legal action

If the dissatisfied consumer finds no joy through any of the above channels he must then resort to the final method of redress and take the matter to court. He can raise an action of damages for breach of contract. In so doing, he can seek compensation for any loss which occurs as a result of the failure, or he can seek reimbursement for the cost of having the fault put right. This course of action is open to the consumer regardless of whether the original contract was written or merely spoken.

The scope of the law of contract has been modified by various statutes specifically related to the purchase of services by consumers. Statutory changes in recent times have reflected the growth in consumer movement. The Consumers' Association believes that it was as a result of their campaigning that the Unfair Contract Terms Act was passed by Parliament in 1977.[11] Some of the more significant pieces of legislation in this area are, the Consumer Credit Act (1974), the Unfair Contract Terms Act (1977), the Sale of Goods Act (1979), and the Supply of Goods and Services Act (1982).

At common law people are free to agree between themselves whatever they choose. This is fair practice where both parties have equal power. However, in many exchanges this power is not equally distributed, and it tends to be the relatively uninformed consumer that is in the weaker position. Thus the Consumer Credit Act 1974, among other things, introduced a system of licensing of consumer credit business; the Unfair Contract Terms Act 1977, curtails the extent to which a supplier can introduce exclusion or restriction from liability clauses into their contracts with individual consumers; the Sale of Goods and Services Act 1982, entitles consumers to a 'reasonable standard of service'. In very extreme cases for example where the supplier has made absolutely no attempt to carry out the service, it may be open to the customer to report the matter to the police as a case of fraud. While this course of action is unlikely to provide the customer with any recompense, the threat of it may act as a powerful bargaining tool.

11.4 Why do they complain?

Consumers complain because they are dissatisfied. They are dissatisfied because their expectations are not met, and obviously the higher their prepurchase expectations, the more likely they are to be dissatisfied. This is why a key role for communications in service marketing is the management of expectations. To understand more fully why they complain, we have to examine expectations and satisfaction more closely.

Expectations and satisfaction

What does 'satisfaction' mean? The concept itself is an abstract one. The achievement of satisfaction can be a complex and precarious process. The roles played in the service encounter by individual personalities contribute to this.

In the same way that totally satisfied customers are hard to find, the totally dissatisfied customer is also an elusive creature. Most consumers are satisfied to some extent and there are various research techniques that attempt to measure this (see Chapter 12). While one should understand the extent of customer satisfaction, it is perhaps more important to understand the underlying cause of this satisfaction.

Not only are customers more likely to be dissatisfied with services than they are with products, they also complain less[12]. One reason why they do not complain as much comes from the active part that they play in specifying the service. If a trip to the hairdresser results in a bad haircut, who is to say that it is because the hairdresser is lousy. It may be that the client did not communicate clearly enough what he wanted.

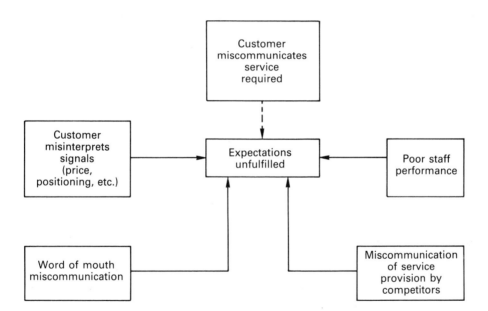

Figure 11.2   *Major causes of unfulfilled expectations*

Miscommunication on the customer's part is only one reason why his expectations may not be fulfilled (Figure 11.2). Some of these factors are within the control of the service provider, some are not. It is certainly up to the provider to reduce the likelihood of miscommunication or misinterpretation by making the service clearly understood. It is also the responsibility of the company to ensure both that it clearly understands a client's instructions, and that the client clearly understands what will be delivered. Service providers should take the lead in designing initiatives to reduce these problems.

Prior to using a service, the consumer will often have in his mind four different scenarios of the service that he might experience. They are:

- The ideal
- The anticipated
- The deserved
- The minimum tolerable

The consumer can expect any of these (Figure 11.3). As we have seen before expectations shape satisfaction. If the 'minimum tolerable' is expected then this, or anything better may lead to satisfaction. Equally anyone expecting the 'ideal' will be dissatisfied with anything less.

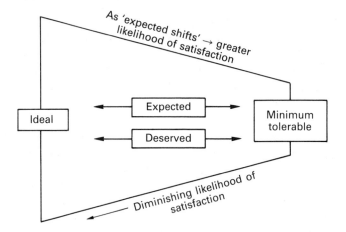

(1) The closer 'expected' expectations are to the 'minimum tolerable' the greater the likelihood of satisfaction.
(2) Satisfied customers can appear anywhere on the spectrum. What determines their position is the position of 'expected' outcome.

Figure 11.3   *Impact of expectations on satisfaction*

Sometimes customers have a view about what they 'deserve', even if these are set at a low level. For instance the patient may believe that at the very least he 'deserves' to return from surgery alive. (This may also be the minimum tolerable!)

If the customer has a strong idea of what he deserves, perhaps formed from a guarantee, or previous usage, then his expectations will be set at that level. His expectations will be more firmly held and will probably result in greater levels of dissatisfaction if the service fails to deliver. This is one reason why British Rail have set themselves easily achievable performance standards in their Passenger's Charter.

The 'deserved' outcome can also modify expectations downwards, e.g. if a builder is instructed to build a house that must be finished in two months, then the level of workmanship that his customer receives is likely to suffer from corner-cutting as he struggles to meet the deadline. If the customer realizes the constraints that he has forced the builder to work to, then his 'deserved' outcome should be set at a low level.

What the customer believes he deserves, may however, still be lower than his 'anticipated' or expected outcome. If this arises then the customer will be dissatisfied. He may have chosen not to believe what the builder told him at the outset about the most likely consequences of the tight schedule, choosing instead to expect the outcome to be better than the picture painted.

Parasuraman, Zeithaml and Berry[13] define a narrower band for expectations. They describe a 'zone of tolerance' between adequate service provision and the desired service provision (Figure 11.4). This zone expands and contracts. It can also remain unchanged in magnitude, while moving up or down the spectrum. It varies according to the service and to the individual customer.

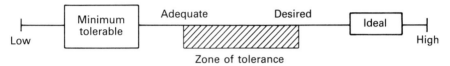

Figure 11.4 *Levels of expectations. Based on Parasuraman, A., Zeithaml, V. A. and Berry, L. L. (1990)*[13]

However, it is not only prepurchase expectations that condition whether or not a complaint is made. It is also the expectation of the likely outcome from complaining. If consumers expect to achieve something by complaining then they are much more likely to complain. Some psychologists would go even further, by suggesting that even if there is no possibility of rectifying the situation, it is still best to express anger, in order to accept the dissatisfaction[14].

The average consumer would probably not take this advice too seriously no matter how beneficial it may be to him psychologically. He is much more likely to weigh up all the costs and benefits associated with complaining. His emotional well-being will be only one factor. If he perceives the benefits to outweigh the costs then he will complain. Table 11.3 lists the factors that help fashion the costs and benefits of complaining.

Table 11.3 The costs and benefits of complaining

C o s t s	Inconvenience	Special trip to complain. Form-filling, letter writing. Forego service during complaint process
	Uncertainty	Difficulty finding correct complaint procedure. No indication of the action that will be taken
	Unpleasant	Treated rudely, have to hassle. Feel guilty, embarrassed
B e n e f i t s	Emotional	Chance to assert rights, chance to vent anger, receive an apology
	Functional	Refund, replacement, repair
	Altruistic	Other customers prevented from experiencing dissatisfaction. Would feel guilty about not complaining
	Product improvement	Organization would improve its offering

Based on Richins, M.[15]

11.5   What do they complain about?

As we have stated, there is a lower incidence of complaining in the service sector than there is for manufacturing. Of the complaints that are made a lower
proportion of these are resolved, and the ones that are, take longer to clear up
(Table 11.4).

Table 11.4 Actions taken by dissatisfied customers and the results of these
actions

	All complaints	Goods	Services
Unweighted bases	2 886	1 641	1 245
Weighted bases	26 098	14 664	11 434
	%	%	%
Took action and had a successful outcome	51	68	29
Took action, had unsuccessful outcome and pursued further	20	16	24
Took action, had unsuccessful outcome did nothing further	29	16	47
Total	100	100	100
Had successful outcome after further action	4	4	4
Total remaining dissatisfied (after first action or second (if taken))	33	20	50

Source: Consumers Association Dissatisfaction Survey (1985)

One of the main reasons for this is that nearly all problems that occur with
products can be openly demonstrated and discussed. If a car does not start, it
does not start. If a vacuum cleaner fails to clean carpets then this too can be
demonstrated. Whereas, who is actually to blame for problems that arise in the
consumption of services is often open to judgement and debate. Even where
the complaint is justified, the service provider may still feel that his own position is also quite defensible. This is often to do with verbal and non-verbal signals from the consumer that the service provider attempts to interpret.
Communication is a transactional process.

Imagine a company rings a courier in a panic. It desperately needs to get a
document to Paris the following day. The courier goes to extraordinary lengths
to see that it gets there, and this results in some extra costs. When the company receives the invoice it is outraged by the price. The service provider mis-
interpreted the signals about urgency from the company.

A large party in a restaurant spends a long time deciding what they want to
eat, apparently preferring to chat with fellow diners. They do not appear to be
in any hurry, or to want an attentive waiting staff. When the bill arrives they

leave no tip, saying that they were disappointed with the time that they spent waiting for their food.

These are two examples of service scenarios where the service provider would feel that the complaint was unjustified. However, the customer would feel that the service provider was to blame. After all, he misjudged the customer's requirement.

Customers complain about different problems in different industries (Table 11.5). In banking, account errors are the biggest source of complaints, whereas in air travel, cancellations and flight delays generate the most complaints. Even within an industry, there will be varying weaknesses from different service companies. Each operator should have an understanding of his own weaknesses, and those of his main competitors.

Table 11.5 Major sources of complaint

Reason	Total	Auto repair	Bank	Insurance	Government	Hospitals	Airline
Not done right	**	***	*	*	*		
Too slow	**	*	**	**	**	**	
Too expensive	**	**		*		**	
Indifferent personnel	**		*	*	**	**	*
Unqualified personnel	*		*	*		*	*
Lack of courtesy	*		*			*	
Lack of personnel						*	
Poor scheduling							**
Reservations							*
Poor food							
Music	*				*		
Unspecified	*		*				

Source: American Society for Quality Control. Gallup Survey (Autumn 1985)

<10%	–
10–20%	*
20–60%	**
60%+	***

The value of the purchase that consumers complain about in services is also different. The cheaper the service, the more likely there are to be complaints. Quite the reverse is true for products. This has much to do with the intangible nature of services. Higher cost services tend to be more complex, which tends to lead to greater intangibility, and therefore more ambiguity about the exact nature of the service provision.

Expensive services probably also attract less complaint because they are offered by experts or professional people.[9] This leaves the service provider in a position of authority and power. The consumer feels more intimidated by this apparent superiority and is less likely to make a complaint. Most people no longer feel intimidated about complaining in a restaurant. Many more would think twice about complaining to their lawyer.

The organization's role in minimizing dissatisfaction

Total customer satisfaction is unlikely to be achieved even on a temporary basis. However, improvements in the level of satisfaction can often be achieved through the development of an augmented service. The core service can be augmented by providing a guarantee, or by providing good after-sales service. Today's increasingly competitive environment means that it is foolish to hold on to the old adage 'customers come and customers go'. As *Serving Them Right*[16] notes, this is foolish not only because it is expensive to recruit new customers, but also because they are harder to find. Part of a good after-sales service policy should be the provision of an efficient and effective means for handling complaints.

Even just allowing the customer to let off steam can help. Perceptions of satisfaction and fairness will be enhanced if this is then acknowledged with an apology which provides even a small 'tangible token of restitution'.[17]

11.6   Service recovery

Successful complaints handling is known today as service recovery.[18] This is where the organization treats dissatisfied customers in such a way that it manages to hang on to their loyalty. Service recovery takes place where the service provider operates a comprehensive guarantee. It also occurs where the organization that is not working to any specified guarantee, meets or exceeds the expectations of the complaining customer in the way in which they handle complaints.

Dissatisfaction with the service can become more intense if the complainant does not feel that the complaint is being handled appropriately. This individual is already in an irritable frame of mind and therefore staff need to be trained to handle the situation sensitively. Ideally these employees should be empowered to take decisions about the best course of action. However, many companies find this an uncomfortable suggestion believing that the employee will always err on the side of the customer, and perhaps be over-generous with any compensation. Other companies take a more progressive view, as Jan Carlzon CEO of SAS said, 'What's the danger of giving away too much? Are you worried about an oversatisfied customer? That's not much of a worry. You can forget about an oversatisfied customer, but an unsatisfied customer is one of the most expensive problems you can have . . . the danger is not that employees will give away too much. It's that they won't give away anything because they don't dare'.[19]

If the empowerment of these frontline employees is not possible, then senior management themselves must be prepared to play an active part in the resolution of complaints. Top management involvement usually goes down well with customers, because customers like to deal with those who have the power and confidence to act on their behalf. They should be called in at the slightest hint that the customer might be dissatisfied with the way his complaint is being handled.

11.7 Effective complaint-handling procedures

Companies that take a pragmatic view will accept that they can make mistakes. They will recognize that customers will occasionally have a better idea of the way that the service should be delivered. Indeed a dearth of complaints is more often a danger signal than a cause for celebration. It is to the organization's advantage to encourage customers to air their views, and it must set up a complaint-handling procedure that does just that. As the President of world-wide quality at American Express says, 'the formula that I use is: better complaint handling equals higher customer satisfaction, equals higher brand loyalty, equals higher profitability'.[20]

When designing a complaint handling system, it can often be difficult to strike the right balance between making the system easily accessible, and making it too accessible. The organization wants to encourage users to make justifiable complaints, but it is counterproductive to set up a complaints procedure that creates the impression that the organization is expecting lots of complaints. This usually means that the service provider does not believe that he is offering a good service. Customers will very quickly pick this up, and begin to start looking for problems. It would be much more productive to provide a better service in the first place.

Historically, dealing with customer complaints was considered a second rate occupation for marketing professionals. It was much more stimulating and glamorous to be developing new products and advertising campaigns. Customer complaint-handling was regarded as a maintenance function and a cost centre to the business.

Figure 11.5 *Complaints systems can be too accessible*

Fortunately nowadays, many companies take a more enlightened view. They incorporate complaints handling into their strategic mix, and call it Customer Service or Customer Care. Management now recognizes the benefits of letting marketing staff experience first hand the issues and problems of their customers. There is an old management saying, 'If you're going to be a general, you have to remember what its like to be a private'. The organization can benefit in several ways by staffing customer service with these employees. It raises the profile of the department in the company. It makes a statement to all employees about the importance that the company attaches to the resolution of complaints. In doing so, it communicates the significance of providing a quality service, and finally, it generally also leads to improvements in the way that complaints are handled. Employees charged with complaint-handling will often make suggestions about the powers they need to do the job well, and ways in which the department could be run more effectively.

11.8 The benefits of effective complaint handling

Companies that devote resources to an effective complaints procedure benefit in many ways:

- They are given a second chance to make good their relationship with a dissatisfied customer.
- Adverse word of mouth publicity is avoided.
- They will understand what would improve their current service.
- They will know where their operations problems lie.
- Employees may be motivated to provide a better quality service.

To make the best use of a customer service department it is not enough to deal expediently with each complaint as it is received. Naturally, this is all that the aggrieved customer is interested in. Initially, it should also be what interests the company most.

There are many examples of companies who have gone to extraordinary lengths to try to please a dissatisfied customer. Most of them are American. As a nation they seem to be more clued up to the benefits of dealing with complaints effectively. They are less reticent about going 'over the top' in an overt attempt to keep a customer.

However, in addition to dealing with complaints, the company should also attempt to learn from its mistakes. It does this by putting in place management information systems that enables customer service staff to record every complaint that is made and then to report these complaints (Figure 11.6). Management must be able to identify the cause of complaints if they are to aid the development of the service.

For example it has been estimated that British banks spend more than twice what they ought to in order to operate their service.[21] This is because their procedures are so error-prone that they keep losing documents and waste precious time and money tracking them down, or regenerating them. This prob-

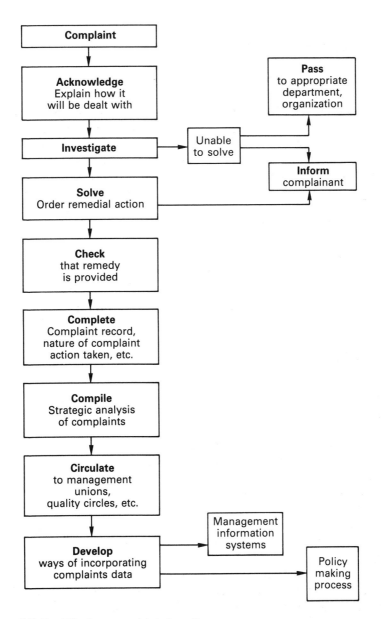

Figure 11.6 *Effective complaints handling process*

lem has come to light because customer complaints were monitored. They now know the source of the problem so all they need to do is deal with it. As Einstein said, 'The formulation of a problem is far more essential than a solution'.[22]

While complaint monitoring will give some indication of the levels of satisfaction that the service is achieving it must be supplemented with other measures. Remember, not every dissatisfied consumer complains. Market research should be used to assess overtly the satisfaction of both current and lapsed user (see Chapter 12).

11.9   The provision of guarantees

In addition to handling complaints effectively, the service provider may also decide to offer consumers a guarantee. To invoke a guarantee, a customer generally has to begin by making a complaint, and so all the principles of efficient complaint handling still apply.

The function of the guarantee is that it reduces risk to consumers both before and after purchase. Pizzaland guarantees its customers their pizzas in five minutes or they get their money back (and the late pizza besides!). In this situation, customers know that once they have placed their order the delivery of their food is imminent. They also know what to expect if it does not appear.

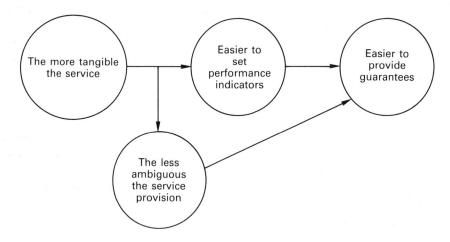

Figure 11.7 *Tangibility and the provision of guarantees*

In reducing risk, the guarantee often diminishes much of the ambiguity often associated with service provision. However, ambiguity often arises from the intangible nature of the service, and the more intangible the service, the more difficult it is to provide guarantees (Figure 11.7).

For example, it is easy for a cobbler to guarantee to repair shoes in 24 hours or to provide his service free of charge. The smart cobbler should rarely find himself working for nothing. If he expects to turn round all shoes in a 24 hour period, then once he has taken on all that he can manage in this time, he can just refuse to accept any more under the conditions of the guarantee.

It is more difficult for a tutor to guarantee the results of his students. There are many intangible aspects of such a service, and not all of these are under the control of the tutor. This is not to say that those responsible for providing services with some intangibility should not provide guarantees. Too often those who provide the more intangible services shelter behind the shield of difficulty when it comes to the provision of guarantees. These companies will often regard a sincere apology as sufficient acknowledgement of a complaint.

However, is an apology enough for the consumer who goes to all the trouble of complaining? Even those offering intangible services can offer something a bit more tangible than an apology when it comes to compensating the aggrieved customer. This also applies when the situation giving cause for complaint cannot be retracted or rectified at a later date, e.g. if a retailer refuses to accept payment by credit card because the credit card company has mistakenly refused to authorize the customer's use of the card, the customer will be embarrassed. No matter what the credit card company now does it cannot retract that situation. Sending the customer a bunch of flowers will probably be greeted with more enthusiasm than a wordy apology, and may stand a greater chance of effecting service recovery.

Many companies operating in such industries, particularly where the market is competitive, use guarantees as a positioning tool. They use it as a means of differentiating themselves from the competition, e.g. when Thomson Holidays first offered 'No surcharges guaranteed' it was the first tour operator to do this. However, the uniqueness of this benefit was short-lived. Like so many service developments, it was easily copied. Note also that this particular guarantee only applied to one aspect of the service.

Sometimes companies adopt a more all-embracing approach. Instead of providing a specific guarantee, they guarantee total customer satisfaction. We can probably all think of services that provide 'satisfaction guaranteed'. Whether or not we believe them is another matter. Many such companies attach no meaning to these statements. Using them merely as a form of words intended to convey a quality service.

Other more reputable companies that provide this sort of guarantee, probably suffer as a result. They genuinely mean that they will do everything in their power to make customers satisfied. The principle is part of the company's philosophy, and employees are aware of the importance that is attached to satisfying the customer. The customer however, may well remain sceptical.

11.10 Designing a guarantee

The all-embracing guarantee of the sort just described, is in fact, not the best type of guarantee that a company can offer. The best guarantees meet the criteria set out in Table 11.6.[23]

Table 11.6 Qualities of the ideal guarantee

Guarantees should be:
Easy to understand
Easy to invoke
Unconditional
Credible
Focused on customer needs
Meaningful (significant penalty or payout)
Provide clear performance standards

Easy to understand

The guarantee should be as short and simple as possible. It should be written in clear, plain English to help prevent any ambiguity from creeping in. The ideal is to think of an advertising endline; normally only one sentence in length, and with the intention of being highly memorable.

Easy to invoke

Companies are often fearful of making guarantees easy to invoke because they are frightened of the potential cost. They can see the benefits of offering guarantees to consumers, but cannot see what benefits are to be gained by making them easy to invoke.

Most builders that install damp proof courses provide guarantees. However, they are so difficult to invoke that they are of little benefit to the customer. In order to invoke his guarantee, the dissatisfied customer must first pay for a site inspection. The company who carried out defective work insist that their company carries out this inspection. Their opinion is hardly likely to be unbiased. To save costs, they generally find some explanation for the damp that exempts them from liability. Therefore to invoke his guarantee, the customer has to go to further expense. He will expect the process to take some time, and will expect to have to wrangle in order to achieve any sort of satisfactory outcome. It is not an easy guarantee to invoke.

Unconditional

For the same reasons that it is important to make it easy for dissatisfied customers to complain, it is best to make the guarantee as unconditional as possible. This type of guarantee communicates to staff and customers that the service provider believes in the quality of their offering. Naturally, it is only sensible to offer such a guarantee if the service is a quality one.

Credible

To provide a guarantee that customers regard as incredible casts doubt on everything that the company does. Driving schools that guarantee learner drivers will pass first time are making unbelievable promises. The learner will know that there are many factors affecting whether or not they pass the driving test that are outside the control of the instructor, e.g. the nerves of the learner, or the mood of the test instructor. A table of pass rates relative to other driving schools would probably prove more credible, and would serve the main purpose of providing a guaranteed risk reduction.

Focused on customer needs

A guarantee should be guaranteeing aspects of service that are important to customers. It should not be focusing on what the company regards as important, or on what the company thinks customers regard as important.

The enlightened service provider should have identified those aspects of his service that are critically important to customers, not only to aid the design of a guarantee, but also to enable him to design a quality service.

Meaningful (with significant penalties or payouts)

The guarantee is not meaningful if the penalties that accrue to the provider, or the levels of compensation paid to the customer are insignificant. In both these cases there is little incentive for the company to improve its service offering. Most dissatisfied customers will not take the trouble to complain. Even if they did, the company would not suffer high payout costs and so is less likely to work on service improvements.

British Rail have come in for a lot of criticism in this respect, over the low targets that they have set themselves in the Passenger's Charter. The Consumers' Association called it 'little more than a glossy public relations con'.[24] Many factors affect what customers regard as significant levels of

Figure 11.8 Austin, The Guardian, March 5 1992

compensation. These include the cost of the service, the seriousness of the failure, and customers' perception of what is fair (deserved) for that service.[25]

Provide clear performance standards

Employees should know the targets they are trying to meet. The achievement of these standards generally denotes the provision of a good service. The Pizzaland guarantee already mentioned states what the company regards as the maximum time that a customer should have to wait for a pizza. This guarantee has given kitchen and waiting staff clear performance standards.

11.11 Recent market developments

Privatized industries

The present government places more emphasis on customer satisfaction than any previous government has done. This trend began in the mid-1980s with concern over the government's privatization programme. Many felt that customers would suffer in the rush to transfer ownership of public utilities from the state to the private sector. They believed that private industry is driven more by profit motivation than by customer satisfaction.

However, historically customers were, in fact, more likely to enjoy quality service from the private sector. In a competitive marketplace satisfying customers is likely to bring profit improvement. It is under conditions of monopoly power, that satisfying customers is not necessary in order to survive. The dissatisfied customer has no option but to continue buying from the monopoly supplier.

The government attempted to address the issue of customer satisfaction as they legislated for the powers needed to divest of these assets. The legislation that they passed made provision for other companies to enter the market, e.g. Mercury in the telecommunications industry, thus eroding the monopoly power.

It also made provision for the voice of the consumer in the privatization legislation; watchdog bodies were set up to monitor their activities, e.g. the Gas Consumers Council (GCC) was set up under the Gas Act 1986, with statutory powers to protect customers' interests. In 1992 the GCC actually forced British Gas to lower their proposed price increase. This is the sort of protection that the consumer enjoys.

Although it was the Thatcher government that really pushed the principles of the free market and competition throughout British industry, the previous Labour government had introduced performance indicators for some public services as far back as 1978. Some of these included quality of service targets.[26] The industries that have been privatized have taken these performance standards and built them into guarantees.

British Gas was the first to take this step (Figure 11.9). It spent heavily promoting the new scheme, obviously believing that its 'commitment to customers' pledge, would help shape an empathetic image of the company.

Another case in point is that of British Telecom. The rapidly increasing

Figure 11.9   British Gas advertisement: Banishing gripes

number of complaints that OFTEL (the telecommunications watchdog) was receiving about the quality of BT's service, led them to apply pressure on BT to introduce a compensation scheme in 1989. Since then research has been conducted by the Consumers' Association to discover what improvements customers would like to see in the service they receive from BT. Compensation for poor service ranked second only to itemized bills.[27] So it would appear that the introduction of a compensation scheme may go some way to reducing the level of dissatisfaction with the service.

Public services

But what of the services that remain under the government's control? They play a significant part in the UK economy, currently accounting for 40 per cent of GDP. This sector has not escaped the current drive for satisfied customers. The prime minister believes that his Citizen's Charter is the only available catalyst that will reform these services to the benefit of consumers. As he said, 'the main thrust of the Charter is to empower the individual'.[28]

Consumers should benefit because publicly provided services are to be run more efficiently. It is intended to separate the roles of purchaser and provider, as is already the case in grant maintained schools, hospitals with trust status, and the Training and Enterprise Councils.

The government, whether central or local, then becomes primarily a setter of standards. It raises taxes to pay for services which are provided by either private or public bodies. The Audit Commission, the local authority watchdog, is currently devising ways of measuring the effectiveness of these locally provided services, regardless of who actually provides them. Within its new powers and duties it is required to specify performance indicators, and produce league tables of good and bad performers. There will certainly be difficulties in comparing different levels of effectiveness. How does one compare an area that provides a few high quality places in nurseries, with an area that provides for every child but does so with reduced quality?

The Charter mark

In order to provide impetus for the Citizen's Charter the government has launched the Charter Mark. This is an award given to a maximum of 50 orga-

Figure 11.10 Charter Mark logo

nizations a year that can demonstrate excellence in the delivery of their public service. The award is open to all public services who serve the public direct, and to the privatized utilities. September 1992 saw the first awards being made.

For a policy that was at one time regarded as the Prime Minister's greatest contribution to government policy, the award ceremony received little publicity. Perhaps this was due to the confusion over the selection criteria. Some companies that did not receive an award complained that their demonstration of excellence was greater than other award-winning companies. An examination of those companies that received an award would show that in many cases their contribution to excellence was fairly insignificant.

11.12   Potential future developments

Private sector charter mark

In the private sector, there are industry-specific endorsements of quality service, e.g. Les Routiers and Egon Ronay for restaurants, and FIMBRA for financial services. However, to date there is no all round seal of approval like the Kitemark from the British Design Council, or the Vegetarian Society's tick.

The current TQM (total quality management) certifcations of BS5750 in the UK and IS9000 for the European Community, focus more on the back office and ways in which the company could be run to provide a better quality service. They do not look at customer satisfaction, and therefore from a marketing viewpoint, are insufficient indicators of quality service.

The European Foundation for Quality Management perhaps comes closest, with its European Quality Award. This is designed along the lines of the Baldrige and Denning awards, but it is not specific to services.

However, this award will probably be too elitist to make much of an impact throughout the service sector. What is needed is an award that the general public will recognize, and one that can be achieved by small and large organizations alike. A private sector charter mark would be a step in the right direction.

11.13   Summary

As consumers' expectations continue to rise, levels of dissatisfaction rise too. Companies with a long-term future are those that attempt to minimize dissatisfaction. Given that it may not always be possible to get it right first time, this means dealing with complaints effectively.

Dealing with complaints effectively has several benefits. It reduces the possibility of adverse word-of-mouth publicity. It also gives the organization a better chance of recovering the future loyalty of the aggrieved customer. Remember that loyal customers are more likely to complain. Finally, it provides management with information that will help them design an improved service offering.

The process of service recovery may be aided by the provision of a guarantee. The main purpose of which is to reduce risk both before and after consumption. Guarantees should aim to be: easy to understand; easy to invoke; unconditional; credible; focused on consumers' needs; meaningful (in terms of payout or penalty); and provide clear performance standards.

Questions

1 Why should a company encourage its dissatisfied customers to complain? Why do you think that many companies do not like to receive complaints?

2 (a) Think of organizations that you have found easy to complain to, or those that you imagine would react well to complaints. What is it about these organizations that make them easy to complain to?

(b) Think of some others where complaining is not a pleasant process. What is it that characterizes these companies?

3 Why do you think that more companies do not offer guarantees to cover the service that they provide?

4 The following two scenarios describe less than satisfactory service encounters.

Employment agency

A young secretary in her late 20s climbs the dirty, unlit stairs. At the top is a closed door with an entry phone. She pushes the buzzer. No reply. She tries again. Still nothing. She turns to leave. As she does so she hears a scratchy voice through the entry phone, 'just hang on a minute, luv, I'll be with you in a jiffy'.

A couple of minutes later she finds herself in a smoky cramped office. She is sitting opposite a recruitment consultant. He has his back to her and is laughing and chatting with his colleagues. Eventually he turns round finishing a cup of coffee. Without even a word of introduction he launches into the paper work. The girl has been given no chance to explain why she is there or what she is looking for.

The form filling takes about half an hour. It is designed to give the employment agency (and therefore prospective employers) details of the girl's experience, qualifications etc. There is no privacy for the girl during this encounter. Anyone in the office can hear what she is saying. At the conclusion of the interview, and without warning, the consultant asks her to follow him . . .

He leads her to a small room. Hands her some paper, looks at his watch and tells her she has 10 minutes to complete the typing test. The equipment is quite old and despite being unfamiliar with the system she completes the test satisfactorily.

She returns to the consultant's desk. He is on the telephone to his girlfriend and makes no acknowledgement of her presence. When (eventually) he does return to the girl he suggests that he has two positions on his books which would be ideal for her. She tries to explain that he does not really know what she is looking for, but he is not listening. He is on the telephone trying to arrange interviews. Luckily the relevant people at both companies are not available.

The consultant appears to sense that the girl is impatient. As he pulls another file out from his desk he concludes the interview telling the girl he will be in touch some time next week.

The girl has spent an hour and a half in the employment agency.

Car rental

Our customer wants to hire a car for the weekend. He wants to collect it from Heathrow which is where his shuttle lands. He telephones the local branch of a national car hire company – but they cannot help him. He must ring the Heathrow office direct and no, sorry they do not have the telephone number handy, could be ring Directory Enquiries.

He finds the number and rings the Heathrow Office. The telephone is answered reasonably quickly, but he is asked to 'hold the line for a minute'. He can hear the receptionist asking for a cup of tea from a colleague. Her conversation lasts for 3 minutes – while his 'phone bill mounts. Eventually the assistant does return to him. It takes some time to go through the booking process. Many of the questions appear to be irrelevant. At the end of the call our customer explains that he will be in a hurry when he arrives so could they make sure everything will be ready for him.

The following day our customer is contacted by a telephone salesperson, 'As an old and valued customer of Fast Drive you have the opportunity to take part in a special promotion. Upgrade your Ford Fiesta to a Granada and you will be entered in our prize draw with the chance to win a fortnight's holiday for two in the Bahamas'. He is not tempted.

Two days later he arrives at Heathrow to collect his Fiesta. His car is not ready. In fact they have no record of his booking. They do not think they have any spare cars. They will check with head office.

After fifteen minutes the assistant returns. They have found a car that he can have. She hands him a completed Visa slip to sign. It is almost twice the price he was quoted on the telephone. The assistant checks their rate card to see if she can match the price he was given to any of their special deals. During this process he realizes that there are other even better prices than he was originally offered. He feels somewhat disgruntled.

His car is parked at the far end of a large car park. He stumbles across in the dark to find a dirty car that does not look as if it has been washed for some months. The inside is full of crisp wrappers and cigarette ends. Weary from his journey our customers decides to ignore this and get to his destination as soon as possible.

Seventy miles down the motorway the car breaks down. There is nothing in the car to explain what to do. Luckily a police car passes some moments later. They radio for motorway assistance – who arrive within 10 minutes and want £50 to tow him away. They do telephone the hire company who send another car. This arrives 2 hours later.

For each of these scenarios:
(a) Why do you think the customer does not complain?
(b) Design a guarantee for each of these services that would reduce the likelihood of similar situations arising in the future.
(c) What performance standards did you set in your guarantees?

References

1 Trusthouse Forte (1991). The company philosophy as stated in Annual Report and Accounts.
2 The Audit Commission for Local Authorities in England and Wales (1988). *The Competitive Council*. HMSO, London.
3 McKinnon, Sir J. (1992). Article in *Financial Times*, February 12.
4 Dobree, J. and Page, A. S. (1991). Unleashing the power of service brands in the 1990s. *Management Decisions*, **28**, 6.
5 Bell, C. R. and Zemke, R. (1988). Do service procedures tie employees' hands? *Personnel Journal*, (September) 76–83.
6 Hustad, T. P. and Pessemier, E. A. (1973). Will the real consumer activist please stand up: an examination of consumer's opinions about marketing practices. *Journal of Marketing Research*, **10**.
7 Warland, R. H., Hermann, R. O. and Willits, J. (1975). Dissatisfied customers: who gets upset and who takes action. *Journal of Consumer Affairs*, **9**.
8 Miller, J. (1977). Studying satisfaction: modifying models, eliciting expectations, posing problems and making meaningful measurement. *Conceptualisation and Measurement of Customer Satisfaction and Dissatisfaction*, (Hunt, K. ed). MSI.
9 Best, A. and Andreasen, (1977). Consumer response to unsatisfactory purchases: a survey of perceiving defects, voicing complaints and obtaining redress. *Law and Society Review*, (November), 701–742.
10 Dayand, R. L. and Landon, E. L. (1977). Towards a theory of complaining behaviour. *Consumer and Industrial Buying Behaviour*,
11 Holmes, A. (1992). Quote in a letter from Ashley Holmes of the Consumers' Association.
12 Consumers' Association (1989). Annual Consumer Complaints Survey.
13 Parasuraman, A., Zeithaml, V. A. and Berry, L. L. (1990). *Delivering Quality Service*. Free Press.
14 Kubler-Ross, E. (1969). *On Death and Dying*. Macmillan.
15 Richins, M. (1990). Consumer perceptions of costs and benefits associated with complaining. In *Refining Concepts and Measures of Consumer Satisfaction and Complaining Behaviour* (Hunt and Day eds).

16 Liswood, L. A. (1989). *Serving Them Right*. Harper and Row.

17 Goodwin, C. and Ross, I. (1992). Consumer responses to service failures: influence of procedural and interactional fairness perceptions. *Journal of Business Research*, **25**, 149–163.

18 Hart, G., Heskett, J. and Sasser, W. E. (1990). The profitable art of service recovery. *Harvard Business Review*, July–August, 148–156.

19 Carlzon, J. (1989). *Moments of Truth*. Harper and Row.

20 Rasmussen, M. (1988). How to handle customers' gripes. *Fortune*, 24 October.

21 Top Consumer Complaint Account Errors (1988). *American Banker*, (November).

22 Einstein, A. (1954). *Ideas and Options*. Crown.

23 Heskett, J. L., Sasser, W. E. and Hart, C. W. L. (1989). *Service Breakthroughs – Changing the Rules of the Game*. Free Press.

24 Consumers' Association (1992). Quoted in *The Times*, March 5, Times Newspapers, London.

25 Hart, C. W. L. (1988). The power of unconditional guarantees. *Harvard Business Review*, July–August, 54–62.

26 The Nationalized Industries (1978). *CMND 7131*. HMSO, London.

27 Consumers' Association (1990). On the right lines. *Which Magazine*,

28 Major, J. (1992). Tories boost people power. Times Newspapers, January 28, London.

12
Monitoring and evaluating the service

12.1   Introduction

Most markets are too competitive nowadays to leave anything to chance. They are usually populated by a growing number of service companies all attempting to build their own market niche. Thus it becomes more important to try to get it right first time. Putting aside luck and good fortune, the best chance a company has of achieving this is by incorporating market research into the development and evaluation processes. This means listening to the customers. The company should give them a voice even before it has anything to sell to them. By listening to what they want in the first place, the company is more likely to launch something that meets their expectations.

Giving the customer a voice and then listening to what they say is an integral part of a service marketing system. It is also an ongoing process. When the service becomes available, the company should begin to monitor and evaluate its performance with the help of its customers. An holistic approach to this evaluation means treating as customers, not only those who purchase the service, but also those who deliver it. This evaluation will often lead to improvements in the service being made. And so the whole process begins again.

In all of this it should be remembered that while market research can help to

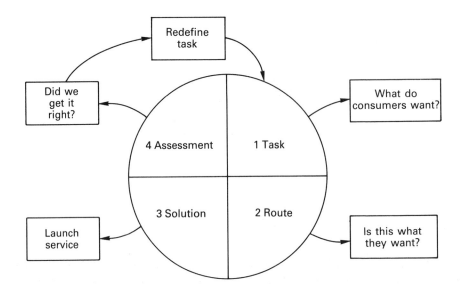

Figure 12.1   *Market research and the service development cycle*

reduce risk, it does not eliminate it. Market research findings should be used as an aid to decision-making. They should not be used to make the decision.

Information   + Judgement = Decision
Better information   + Judgement = Better decision

12.2   The market research process

Market research is really just a means of gathering information. The Market Research Society of Great Britain defines it as: 'the means used by those who provide goods and services to keep themselves in touch with the needs and wants of those who buy and use those goods and services'.[1] In product markets, the manufacturer rarely comes face to face with his customers. He is generally separated by the distribution channel. At least in the provision of services, the customer is often present, and therefore feedback often more direct.

However, services cannot rely on the existence of this direct contact to provide them with all the information they need about their consumers. For one thing, the company is restricted to talking to its current customers. It has no means of finding out why people switched to another service or have never considered using their service in the first place. A more systematic approach to gathering the information is required (Figure 12.2).

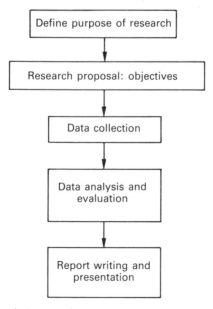

Figure 12.2   *The market research process*

The company must begin by defining its research objectives. What information does it want to discover?, e.g. does it want to know what expectations customers have of the service, or what variables contribute to customer satisfaction?

It then has to go out and collect the data which can be analysed to provide information for presentation to the interested parties.

12.3   Data collection

In some cases, the information that is required is already available. This is known as desk research or secondary data (Figure 12.3). The company's own information systems can be a good source of data, e.g. supposing that a doctor wanted to know the average length of time that patients had been with his practice, or that he wanted to know what were the three commonest reasons for a patient visiting the surgery, then the best way of finding this out would be to look at his own records.

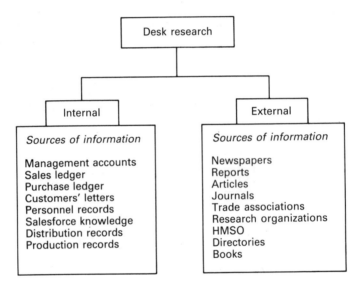

Figure 12.3 Sources of desk research data

The information can also be available because people have been asked the specific question in the past by another research company, i.e. the Central Statistical Office gathers all sorts of data on the nation's education for its *Social Trends* publication.

Technology has made a significant impact in the back office. Not only in terms of assisting service delivery, but also in helping to develop management information systems of a power not even dreamt of a decade ago. Management are now much more aware of the potential of information. They understand the benefits to be gained from gathering and structuring the information that they process, e.g. fifteen years ago the accounts department of a mail order company would no doubt have been able to tell you the age pattern of their debtors, and maybe even the average spend of a customer. Without manually going through order forms however, it is highly unlikely that there would have been any data on all the items that each customer had ever bought from the company. It would, thus, have been difficult to uncover patterns in their spending behaviour. Nowadays, management will often have these facts available at the touch of a button.

However, there are many management questions which cannot be answered by an exhaustive search of all desk sources. The company must then resort to what is known as field research or primary data. In most instances this will mean commissioning a market research company to conduct the fieldwork. These data are gathered in one of two ways. It can be collected by observation or by interview.

Observing respondents

Behaviour can be observed where the respondent is aware that he is being studied. A recent article which appeared in *Marketing Magazine* read as follows, 'I stepped into the Supermarket Simulator, and gasped in amazement. In front of me was a bar-shaped handle, and as I took hold of it the rest of the trolley materialised, together with aisles of goods, fellow customers and even assistants stocking shelves. I pressed on the bar and apparently moved forward. Then suddenly the handle recoiled and struck me painfully in the upper midriff. The trolley wheel had jammed, the illusion was complete. It was the year 2000 and I was a respondent entering the Consumer Research Applications Shopping Simulator (CRASS) in order that my entire shopping behaviour should be observed and recorded'.[2]

Observation can also be used where the subjects under investigation have little or no awareness of their participation in the project. One application is known as 'Mystery Shopper' or 'Mystery Customer' research. The researcher attempts to experience the customers' contact with the service. He approaches the service encounter posing as a customer and reports back on the treatment that he receives.

This technique can be used to analyse the customers' experience in almost any service setting, e.g. TV rental shops, cosmetic counters, night clubs, car hire companies. However, it need not be restricted to those services where the customer is physically present. It can be used to evaluate the way in which telephone calls are handled by an organization. Are they answered promptly, politely, effectively etc?

Business Efficiency Monitoring (BEM), a company specializing in this type of research, believes that the most effective mystery customer surveys have four essential qualities:[3]

- Independence: results are treated with more trust if a third party has compiled them.
- Objectivity: the best surveys are those where the researcher is looking for things that require a 'yes' or a 'no' response. 'Were you greeted when you entered the restaurant?', 'Was the telephone answered before it had rung five times?' This means that there is then no ambiguity in the assessment.
- Consistency: comparisons are usually made across a number of locations. Therefore consistency of approach is essential.
- Qualification: surveys whose results can be quantified provide management

with more usable information. These results can be tracked over time to gauge whether or not the quality of the service is improving.

Interviewing respondents

Interviews can be conducted with respondents face-to-face, by telephone, by post and most recently by computer. Since the purpose of conducting quantitative research is to be able to provide an accurate picture of the market, all respondents must be asked an identical set of questions. To ensure that this takes place the data are collected by means of a questionnaire. The results of individual questionnaires can then be combined so that an overall assessment can be made.

12.4 Questionnaire design

The designing of questionnaires is a skilled craft which is very underrated. Most people expect to be able to write questionnaires with little difficulty because they ask questions in their everyday life. If the research is being conducted by a professional research organization then they will design the questionnaire. If the research is being conducted 'in-house' then someone within the company will have to attempt it. While it is not the intention of this chapter to turn readers into questionnaire design experts some basic points of principle can usefully be made. Good questions should be:

- Clear and unambiguous
- Easy and quick to understand
- Simple to respond to
- Relevant to the respondent

Putting this another way:

- The respondent must first of all understand the question.
- Having understood it, he must then be willing to answer it.
- And not only must he understand it, and be willing to answer it, he must also be able to answer it.

Questions can be open-ended:

'What sort of service were you expecting before you arrived here today?'
'Can you tell me why you chose to fly with x airline?'
'How would you describe the quality of the tuition that you have experienced?'

The open-ended question allows the respondent to say exactly what he thinks. He is not forced into giving a certain response and this reduces the possibility of bias. However this type of question makes the questionnaire more difficult for the interviewer to complete, without being a shorthand secretary. In many cases it also makes it more difficult for the respondent to answer. He has to think about his response, not just tick a box. It also makes the analysis a more arduous task since the responses cannot be precoded. The questionnaires cannot immediately be data processed upon returning from the field.

Or questions can be closed:

'Can you tell me what was the most important reason in your decision to fly *x* airline?' Tick one from the following list:

Reliability
Price
Pleasant staff
Recommended by colleague
National carrier
Good in-flight entertainment
Only direct flight to destination
Used them before

'Which word best describes the quality of tuition that you have experienced?' Tick one from the following list.

Excellent
Good
Average
Poor
Extremely poor

The closed question on the other hand is far easier for both the interviewer and respondent to complete. It also speeds up the analysis. So why do researchers ever use open-ended questions?

For one thing, the researcher may not have enough information to compile a list like the one illustrated above in the airline question. Or it may be that he knows they can introduce bias. It can do so by presenting the respondent with alternatives that he had never thought of himself. Or it can 'force' him to choose from a list of unsuitable alternatives.

Scaling techniques

The list of alternative responses can be presented in a variety of ways.

1 **Ordinal scale:** (see airline question list). The respondent is asked to rank the attributes in order of importance. When the responses are summed for the whole sample it will show a ranking of the attributes in terms of importance. Values are then attached to these positions. In this case 8 = most important, 1 = least important. What it does not show is any measure of the difference between them, i.e. all the attributes may be of roughly equal importance to a respondent or they may have very different levels. This scaling technique provides no way of differentiating these positions.

2 **Verbal rating scale**: (see tuition question list). The scales can be balanced. That is with an equal number of positive and negative statements. Or they can be unbalanced:

Essential
Very important
Fairly important
Not at all important
Undesirable

Unless the researcher has good reason to adopt an unbalanced scale, a balanced one should be chosen, i.e. qualitative research conducted amongst the Strangeways prison rioters would probably find that they had little in the way of positive feelings towards the prison service. In which case a scale that was predominantly negative would be the most appropriate.

Scales can have any number of points. The normal range is three to eleven, although five is probably the optimum. More than this makes the process laborious. Less than five does not give the researcher or respondent much chance to differentiate responses. Researchers have suggested that a problem with five point rating scales (or any odd numbered scale) is that the neutral mid-point is a haven for those who cannot be bothered to think about their reply. An even number of alternatives forces the respondent to come down on one side of the fence. However he may genuinely feel ambivalent to the attribute/issue.[4]

3 **Numerical rating scale**: the positions on the scale are given a number and only the ends of the scale are labelled.

Very courteous	5
	4
	3
	2
	1
Not courteous at all	0

These are often easier and therefore faster for the respondent to complete.

4 **Diagrammatic rating scale**: Here the alternatives are represented by a drawing or a diagram, e.g. different sizes of boxes, or ticks.

All of the above scales give an overall measure or rating of the variable under discussion, i.e. importance, satisfaction, intention to purchase.

5 **Semantic differential**: This is a relatively new measurement technique,[5] and is widely used in practice (Figure 12.4). As the name suggests it measures

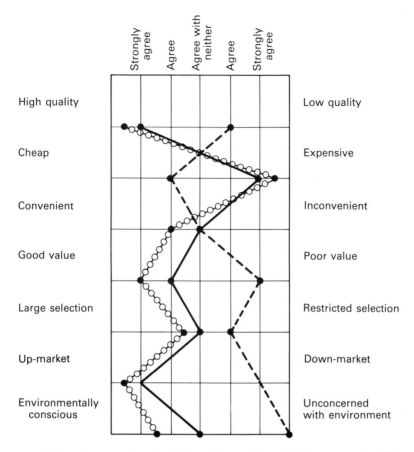

Figure 12.4 *Supermarket brand profiling using bipolar semantic differential scales.*——*Supermarket A;* --- *supermarket B;* o—o—o *supermarket C*

the difference between words. It uses a list of brands and a numerical or verbal rating scale. It then asks respondents to rate each of the brands on each of the attributes using the chosen scale.

For example in Figure 12.4 respondents were asked to rate three super-markets. They were given a list of attributes, and asked to rate each brand in terms of the degree to which they agreed/disagreed that the brand held the attribute.

This kind of measurement provides far more detail about the service than the overall measure given with the earlier techniques. It is relatively simple to use and is easily adapted for any particular market.

The data gathered in this way can be plotted on two dimensions to give a perceptual map of the brands' positions in the marketplace (Figure 12.5). Any two of the attributes can be chosen, and a whole series of maps can be drawn to cover all the qualities that were analysed.

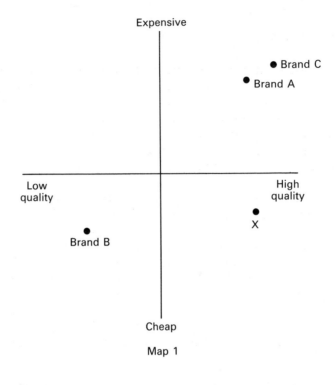

Map 1

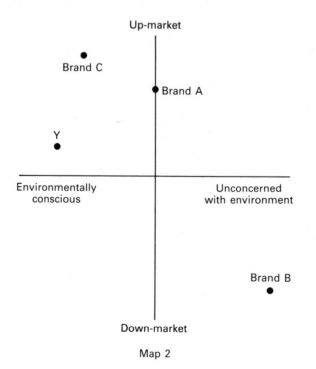

Map 2

Figure 12.5 Perceptual maps of supermarket brands

Multiattribute analysis

The main shortcoming of the previous analysis is that it gives no indication of whether or not it is a good thing for a supermarket to be environmentally conscious or to be in a convenient location. The researcher has no idea of how important/unimportant any of these attributes are. Therefore he does not really understand whether the market positioning is one to be revered or reviled.

To overcome this weakness multiattribute analysis can be conducted. This asks respondents to do two things:

1   To rank each of the attributes in terms of their importance.
2   To rate each brand on each attribute (as in semantic differential questioning).

The respondents' answers to the second question can then be used to plot the 'ideal' position on the map, e.g. position X on map 1 (Figure 12.5) might be consumers' ideal positioning for a supermarket on the price/quality trade-off; quality being more important than price, but cheaper rather than expensive products being preferred. Similarly on map 2 the 'ideal' might be position Y. In both cases there appears to be no brand approaching the ideal positions. The analysis has therefore highlighted gaps that exist in the marketplace.

12.5   Applications of market research

Designing a quality service

There are numerous ways in which research can be used to assist in the design of a quality service. The role that it plays depends on the extent of novelty of the service (Figure 12.6).

Researching a service which lies on the left of the spectrum will tend to be a

Figure 12.6   *The new service development spectrum*

multi-staged process requiring considerable investment in terms of time and money. On the other hand, research into service development which lies at the other end may mean no more than an informal observation study.

The completely new service

The research programme that should be adopted for service development in this area is adapted from the model devised by Booz, Allen, and Hamilton[6] for product marketing (Figure 12.7).

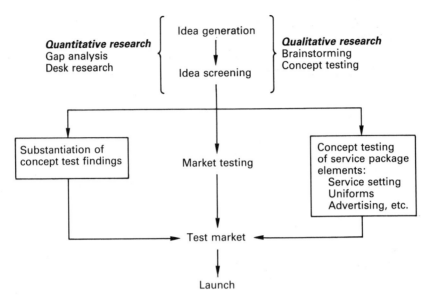

Figure 12.7 *Market research and the new service development process*

Idea generation

The qualitative research that would be conducted at this stage is known as 'brainstorming'. It is run in group discussions and is designed to get respondents to think laterally as opposed to logically about the problem area. The group moderator usually begins with a few 'warm-up' questions to get the creative side of the brain functioning, e.g. 'Can you think of ten uses for a brick?' The research is intended to give the company some idea of what it would take to create the 'ideal' service.

To try to make respondents less inhibited there are some rules. No ideas are laughed at no matter how silly they may appear. Nor are anyone's ideas challenged. The more ideas the better at this stage.

Quantitative research takes the form of 'gap analysis'. This is the process described in the previous section on multiattribute analysis. This research is pivotal in the delivery of a quality service. It highlights the 'ideal' service positioning. To undertake this analysis requires some knowledge of the market since a list of salient attributes is necessary for the questionnaire.

Parasuraman, Zeithaml and Berry[7] have developed a model for evaluating service quality (SERVQUAL). Their research shows that there are five basic dimensions of service quality that should be tested: reliability; responsiveness; assurance; empathy; and tangibles. Unless previous research has shown otherwise, all areas should be investigated in the design of an ideal service.

Screening

The first stage of research may have generated dozens of ideas. So how does the company begin to take this list down to a more manageable size?

Quantitatively, it can analyse any desk research that is available. This might provide information on potential market size, similar services already in place overseas, etc.

The company can also attempt to rank the positions highlighted by the gap analysis. Which ideas are most compatible with the company's:

> strategic goals?
> financial objectives?
> technical know-how?
> legal and environmental constraints?

Qualitatively the ideas can be screened using concept testing research. Ideas generated in the first stage are now evaluated again in the group setting. The following diagnostic questions illustrate the nature of the testing.

- Do they understand the concepts?
- Are they believable?
- What do they perceive its attributes to be?
- What are its perceived advantages/disadvantages over current market offering?
- Which of the concepts is the most interesting?
- Would they use this service?
- Who is the target market?
- Would it cannibalize?
- Could the ideas be improved in any way?

Market testing and test market

This research takes the preferred concept from the previous stage and tests it quantitatively. Until now the financial commitment to any development has been minimal. The results of research at this stage, however, will determine whether or not to proceed to a launch. New services that get the thumbs-up at this stage then require substantial investment. Therefore it is important that this research is sensitive and accurate.

If the testing were for a consumer product, some samples would be mocked up, and consumers would try it. The respondents would be aware that they were taking part in product development research. The purpose of the research would be to estimate market penetration, and repeat purchase levels at various price points.

In many cases, products that test favourably in the market test are taken through one final stage of research – the test market. This is where a limited proportion of the total target market is exposed to the new product, e.g. one TV area. All elements of the marketing mix are in place. Consumers are unaware that they are being researched. They see the promotions, and go out and buy the product through its normal distribution outlet. The test market is monitored by analysing sales using a range of measurement tools.[1]

However, this process is not quite so straightforward for a service. To design a market test environment that closely approximates the finished service requires some creativity. There is still a lack of knowledge about precisely how to proceed at this stage in the development process for a service. There is certainly scope for research to establish some principles.

It may be more appropriate to combine the market test and the test market to conduct an 'open' test market. This would be similar to a test market in that the service would be available in its normal market environment. However, unlike a normal test market where the target consumers have no idea of their complicity in the research, in an open test market the consumers' attitudes and opinions are openly and systematically sought.

For example, a company wishing to set up a chain of nursery schools could develop a service based on the results of its concept testing research. It could launch one establishment and research its success before proceeding to its optimum market penetration.

Running concurrently alongside the market testing other pieces of qualitative concept testing research may be conducted. These would examine the appropriateness of service package elements. Some of these findings may be substantiated with quantitative research, e.g. advertising is an area that companies often test in advance of any launch.[8]

Launching a new brand into an existing market

In many ways the development process is similar to that for a completely new service. It would begin with a qualitative and quantitative assessment of the ideal service. In addition to this, qualitative research would be conducted to examine the relevance and appropriateness of the brand name to the particular service market.

If the results were positive, the company would then complete the process described by Figure 12.7 (see Chapter 9 for a further discussion of brand image development).

Fine-tuning an existing service

Service sector research again differs from that which would be conducted for a product. There are two reasons for this. First, the organization can witness the consumers' experience, i.e. it can observe or interview customers during and after the service encounter. And second, frontline staff will witness the customers' interaction with their company on a daily basis. They then become a good source of development ideas. Both approaches focus on the critical incident. They are examining the areas of both service process and service outcome (Figure 12.8).[9]

The process begins with an evaluation of the current service. This can take the form of a Satisfaction survey, (see Measuring satisfaction below) and/or a mystery customer survey. This research might highlight areas where the service can be improved.

In addition to this, consumers' and employees' opinions can be sought. There are few people more likely to have ideas about the way in which the service could be developed. This information would normally be gathered through group discussions.

Underpinning the process should be informal research. Traditionally this would have meant monitoring customers' letters to pick up on any complaints

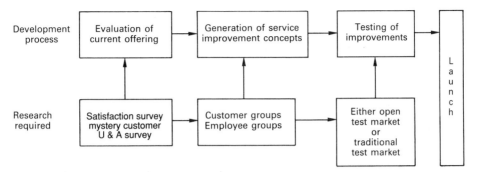

Figure 12.8 *Using research to fine-tune a service*

or suggestions. Nowadays, the use of 0800 telephone lines for the customers' 'voice' is becoming increasingly popular and this would be another source of information. The company should also seek to create a culture that encourages employees to become involved in the development process. Employees should know who to inform of any development ideas that they have. The generation of these ideas should also be integrated into the company's career structure or reward system.

Measuring satisfaction

The company cannot sit back and relax once the service has been launched. Researching the consumer view must continue. The company will want to know how it is performing in the market. It will need to know if its customers are satisfied and if not, what it can do to put right the situation. So how does a company monitor customer satisfaction?

A quantitative satisfaction survey based on multiattribute analysis provides a useful starting point.

Satisfaction survey

Suppose that MBA students as they join a Masters course are asked to describe the factors that influenced their choice of educational establishment. Their list would probably contain the dimensions in left-hand column of Table 12.1.

They are then asked to rank the list of attributes:

Most important   = 5
Least important   = 1

This is shown for a hypothetical student in column 1 Table 12.1.

If the list had contained eight attributes and not five, then the scale would have been: most important = 8, least important = 1.

Finally they are asked to state the degree of importance that each holds for them. Using, for example, the following scale:

Very important			5
Fairly important			4
Neither important or unimportant			3
Fairly unimportant			2
Very unimportant			1

Table 12.1 A multiattribute expectation/satisfaction matrix

Attribute	Pre-consumption expectations			Service experience score			Post-consumption satisfaction		
	(1)	(2)	(3) ((1)×(2))	(4)	(5)	(6) ((4)×(5))	(7)	(8)	(9) ((7)×(8))
Reputation	5	5	25	4	5	20	4	4	16
Standard of lecturing	4	4	16	5	5	25	5	4	20
Quality of materials	3	3	9	2	3	6	2	3	6
Sports facilities	2	2	4	3	4	12	3	3	9
Location	1	2	2	1	2	2	1	3	3
Expectation score			56*			65			
Satisfaction score									54

*Maximum possible score = 75 (where the individual gives each attribute in column 2 a score of 5)

This is column 2 on Table 12.1

The validity of using an importance scale has been called into question because of the ambiguity and somewhat imprecise meaning of the word. Wilkie and Pessemier[10] and Oliver[11] suggest instead, that each attribute should be measured on the semantic differential that suits the word best, e.g. good–bad, attractive–unattractive. This may be true for academic works. However, if different attributes have different scales the questionnaire becomes more complex and difficult to administer. The choice between the two methods should be based on the depth of diagnostic information required from the survey.

In this case the student had an *Expectation score* of 56 out of a possible score of 75. This maximum would occur where the student had given an importance rating of 5 to each of the variables.

The same two questions are asked at the end of the MBA course to give a *Revised expectation score* or a *service experience score* (columns 4, and 5). In situations where the service takes some time to consume, this revised score must be calculated since experience of the service will often change what it takes to make the customer satisfied. In this case the student took up sport during the course and so its importance increased and its ranked position rose. Notice that his expectations have now been revised upwards to 65.

And finally, to compute a *satisfaction score*, the following two questions are asked of the same list of attributes:

Q1   A ranking of the attributes (column 7, Table 12.1):

Most important   = 5
Least important   = 1

Q2   How did the service perform against expectations (column 8, Table 12.1)?

A lot better than expected 5
A little better than expected 4
Just as expected   3
A little worse than expected 2
A lot worse than expected 1

Models have been developed where the respondents have instead been asked to discuss their degree of satisfaction. As in the following scale:

Q3   The degree of satisfaction.

Very satisfied   5
Fairly satisfied   4
Neither satisfied or dissatisfied   3
Fairly dissatisfied 2
Very dissatisfied   1

Many writers prefer the earlier scale. This is because on the one hand, this scale has been shown to be independent of the level of expectations, and at the same time to be highly correlated with satisfaction.[12] However, in many senses it is more important that the service results in satisfaction than that it lives up to expectations. Indeed the earlier scale tends to ignore the possibility of expectations being revised during the service process.

The satisfaction score for this student is 54. He is therefore dissatisfied. To achieve satisfaction the score has to be equal to, or greater than, the expectation score.

The satisfaction survey process is summarized in Figure 12.9.

In the case of an infrequently and/or irregularly purchased service like an MBA, the customer should be asked to complete a satisfaction survey as he leaves the service encounter (a benchmark survey having been undertaken at its commencement).

However, most people like to please. They will often say what they think the company wants to hear. Therefore conducting the research in this way can introduce bias into the findings. Where at all possible the survey should be conducted by a professional research company outside the service environment.

In addition to measuring satisfaction, the research should also attempt to measure future behaviour intentions.

Mystery customer research

Another way in which companies measure satisfaction is with mystery customer research. The company that designed a service which was intended to deliver satisfaction could measure its performance against these standards. Suppose a chain of hotels understood the major variables that contributed to quality to be:

- The cleanliness of the room
- The responsiveness of room service
- The peaceful atmosphere
- The accuracy of their bill

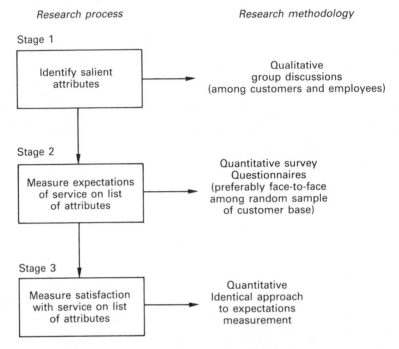

Figure 12.9 *The measurement of expectations/satisfaction*

It designed a service to meet these criteria and in the process set standards for employees to achieve. The hotel could then send round mystery customers to check on performance. Companies are encouraged to inform employees that they are conducting research of this nature. Otherwise they could be accused of 'spying' on them. Researchers are encouraged to report the findings in such a way that individual employees cannot be singled out.[13]

The weakness of this technique for measuring customer satisfaction is that time will have passed since consumers were first asked about the variables that were important for the creation of a quality service. Even if this 'ideal' service had in fact been delivered, the customers' views of what constitutes quality may have changed.

The mystery customer survey can be used as a proxy for a satisfaction survey. It is certainly a useful supplement to such a survey. But perhaps its most important contribution is in the evaluation of employee performance.

Evaluating dissatisfaction

In the case of our MBA student, the customer was dissatisfied. An organization hoping for a long life has to understand the reasons why this has happened? There are several ways that the organization might choose to do this. It could conduct follow up interviews with satisfaction survey respondents whose results showed that they were dissatisfied. The objective of this would be to understand in more detail the reason for their disappointment.

Another source of information about dissatisfaction comes from the complaints that customers make. All complaints that are made to the company should not only be dealt with expediently, they should also be recorded so that management can utilize them strategically.

Frontline employees could be questioned about the complaints that they receive. It is best to do this formally and systematically to ensure that all verbal complaints are recorded. They are more likely to be recorded if the employee receiving the complaint is empowered to act to put it right. Those charged with the achievement of customer satisfaction are more likely to pressure management to enable them to deliver it. However, the empowerment cannot be divided solely between management and the frontline worker. All employees should be empowered. Otherwise it would be all too easy for those at the frontline to blame back office staff, e.g. if a waiter often gets complaints about the temperature of the food that he services, he could point the finger at the kitchens saying that they often forget to tell him when an order is ready. Neither group of employees really cares about the customer. If instead they were driven by a desire to make customers happy (by tying pay to customer satisfaction?) there would be less finger-pointing.

The effective monitoring of complaints is not a sufficient measure of dissatisfaction. Only a tiny proportion of dissatisfied customers actually complain. Most of them do not take the trouble to inform the company of their dissatisfaction, but they often take the trouble to inform their friends. Therefore in addition to analysing complaints, the company should actively attempt to monitor levels of dissatisfaction, and understand in detail the reasons for the dissatisfaction.

One category of dissatisfied customers who should not be forgotten, are those who are so dissatisfied that they reject/leave the service. In all cases where the company can identify such individuals their reasons for leaving should be sought. Knowing what caused their dissatisfaction, and acting on it may prevent another customer leaving in the future.

Monitoring corporate image

For many service companies, projecting the right image is fundamental for securing market success. A company will have adopted a market positioning that it expects has the greatest potential. To realize that potential, the company must project an image that fits this positioning.

Having developed the appropriate image, the company should set up an Image tracking study to check that this is indeed what is being communicated about its service. This research is generally quantitative and employs an identical questionnaire for each successive piece of fieldwork.

The tracking begins with a benchmark study which is conducted before the image is launched. This defines the scope of the task. The company knows where it currently stands, and it knows where it wants to go. It now has to monitor its progress towards this goal. The tracking would normally contain questions in the following areas:

- Awareness of the company (spontaneous and prompted)
- Awareness of any specific communication exercises, i.e. advertising, publicity (spontaneous and prompted)
- Image of the company using a battery of statements that reflect the company's intended image (spontaneous and prompted)
- Buying behaviour (past behaviour and future intentions)
- Reasons that govern choice of brand

This study is repeated at frequent intervals. The timing of the fieldwork should be spaced so that enough time has elapsed between each survey to allow some image shift to take place, but it should not be done so infrequently that those charged with altering the image feel no sense of urgency. In most cases, two surveys a year would probably suffice.

In addition to a quantitative tracking survey, the company might conduct a qualitative image study to flesh out its understanding of consumers' opinion. Projective techniques are often used to unlock this information. For example. the respondents are asked to say what sort of person, animal, flower, car, or chocolate bar best describes the company.

To give a context for the findings of both the qualitative and the quantitative research, the company should be analysed alongside its competitors..

Understanding employees

Most service companies sink or swim on the strength of their employees – particularly those at the frontline. These individuals often provide the only unique benefit that a company offers. Companies therefore need their commitment and motivation in order to deliver quality service. By listening to what they have to say about their jobs, and understanding their needs, the company creates the opportunity to build their loyalty and effectiveness.

The company should seek information from them on two accounts. it should ask them to represent the case of the external customer, e.g. what do they think it is that the customer wants, what do they like/dislike, what problems do they face in their purchase/consumption of the service?

Employee appraisal

The company should also treat employees as their own internal customers. Taking the job that the employee does as the product, the company should seek the same sort of information from them that it would seek from an external customer:

- Are they satisfied with their job?
- What could be done to improve it?
- What could be done that would put them in a position to offer a better service?
- What are their aspirations?
- Do they have skills that are underutilized?

This sort of information should be collected at an individual employee level. It can be gathered in the form of an appraisal. As well as evaluating past performance and achievements, such an appraisal should encourage employees to set their own objectives for the next few years. In their book *In Search of Excellence*, Peters and Waterman[14] note that human beings are more likely to overrate rather than underrate their potential.

Performance appraisal

The employee should also expect to be evaluated in terms of his performance. The employee appraisal often focuses on what the company can do for the employee. The performance appraisal, however, takes the employee as the focus and asks – what is the employee doing for the company?

His performance should be measured in terms of the variables that contribute to customer satisfaction. These are the things that really matter, and they should be measures of effectiveness, not of efficiency. In addition to the methods of measurement discussed in Chapter 10 (Performance measurement), performance can be measured through a customer satisfaction survey or by means of mystery customer research.

Employee group discussions

The views of employees' should also be encouraged at group level. The sort of information that a forum of this nature throws up often never surfaces using more direct methods of questioning. Once the employees relax, the discussion can become more like a Tupperware party than anything work-related. Group discussions like these can be a powerful way of encouraging a team-spirit. If the group is successful in this respect, respondents will feel energized. They will feel a sense of belonging, and so the discussion becomes a socialization mechanism.

12.6   Using the applications of market research

All too often funds are deployed on research without sufficient thought being given beforehand to how useful the findings will be. Such projects produce information that is rarely acted upon. Needless-to-say, none of the research suggested in this chapter is of that nature. Only the bare minimum in terms of research has been described.

So what should the company do with all these findings? Why did it bother to conduct the research? In the first place research was conducted to help design a quality service that matched customers' needs. In doing so, it helped to set performance standards for employees to meet. It then proceeded to monitor the satisfaction that was being achieved, and to evaluate the performance of its staff. This analysis is then used to determine which improvements, if any, are required to maintain the provision of excellent service.

12.7   Summary

This book has focused on the development of principles which help to build excellent service. But what exactly *is* excellent service? And how does a company ever know whether or not it is achieving this goal? Indeed, how does a company design an excellent service in the first place?

In all of these cases the answer lies in asking the consumer. He can describe what he means by 'excellent service'. A service which meets these requirements can then be designed. Performance can be measured against these variables to evaluate service delivery against his expectations.

Customer involvement in the development of excellent service is an ongoing commitment. There should be continuous monitoring of both performance against standards and of the relevance of the standards themselves. These standards often change over time as expectations develop.

The consumers' voice can be listened to in many ways. It can be heard informally, e.g. management chatting to customers, or reading customers' letters of complaint, or, more formally, a variety of market research techniques can be employed.

There are many elements of service design and delivery that should be monitored and evaluated using market research. This chapter is designed to be of practical help in this respect. It aims to provide a basic overview of the market research process. It looks at the techniques involved, and then examines some relevant applications of these techniques.

Questions

1 Choose a service that you have some experience of, and think of either three brands or three different market positionings, i.e. up-market, mid-market, and down-market. Then:

   (a) Write down a list of attributes that are relevant in the particular service market that you have chosen.
   (b) Rate each of the brands/positionings using a five point agree/disagree scale.
   (c) Plot your responses on a bipolar semantic differential table.
   (d) Ask some friends or colleagues for their ratings and see how the responses compare.

2 Are customers always satisfied with an effective service? Think of examples where the customer may not have been satisfied but the service is still deemed to be effective.

3 The following data are taken from a survey conducted by an insurance company. There were two groups of respondents – the company's customers and their frontline employees. The data presented in

the table below summarizes two questions: (1) the importance of the dimensions listed. (2) To what standard they are perceived to be done.

Dimensions	Customers (1)	(2)	Employees (1)	(2)
Customer sensitivity	3.92	2.43	4.21	3.37
Flexibility	3.86	2.41	4.17	3.31
Job knowledge	4.27	3.19	4.50	3.45
Communication	4.05	2.95	4.55	3.64
Initiative	3.67	2.54	4.00	3.13
Integrity	3.97	2.87	4.29	3.64
Responsiveness	4.09	3.68	4.51	3.31
Motivation to serve customers	3.97	2.73	4.27	3.32

(ratings were done using a five-point scale 1 = not important, or never well done, to 5 = very important, or always done well.)

(a) Draft a written report which highlights the main conclusions that can be drawn from these findings.
(b) What action would you recommend the company's management takes to address this situation?

4 The management of one of the UK's leading high street banks is concerned with how customers rate the service, and what they think of the bank's employees. Design a questionnaire that could be sent to the bank's customers to ascertain this information.

References

1 Chisnall, P. (1986). *Marketing Research*. McGraw-Hill.
2 Knight, D. (1992). Shopping in the new millennium. *Marketing Magazine*, 19 March.
3 Joliffe, S. (1992). Quantifying customer service via mystery shopper surveys. *Conference Paper Presented at the Market Research Society Conference*, March 1992. Market Research Society.
4 Kress, G. (1988). *Marketing Research*. Prentice Hall.
5 Osgood, C. E., Suci, G. J. and Tannanbaum, P. H. (1957). *The Measurement of Meaning*. University of Illinois Press, Illinois.
6 Booz, Allen, and Hamilton, (1982). More new products die abourning than in 1968. *Marketing and Media Decisions*, May.
7 Parasuraman, A., Zeithaml, V. L. and Berry, L. L. (1988). SERVQUAL: a multiple item scale for measuring consumer perceptions of service quality. *Journal of Retailing*, **64**(1), 13–37.
8 Cowley, D. (1989). *How to Plan Advertising*. Cassell. Chapter 9.

9   Bateson, J. E. (1989). *Managing Services Marketing: Text and Readings.* Dryden Press.

10 Wilkie, W. L. and Pessemier, E. A. (1973). Issues in marketing's use of multi-attribute attitude models. *Journal of the Market Research Society*, **x**, 428–441.

11 Oliver, R. L. (1980). Product dissatisfaction as a function of prior expectation and subsequent disconfirmation: new evidence. In *New Dimensions of Consumer Satisfaction and Complaining Behaviour.* (Day, R. L. and Hunt, H. k. eds). Bloomington: Indiana University.

12 Oliver, R. L. (1981). Measurement and evaluation of satisfaction processes in retail settings. *Journal of Retailing*, (Fall) 25–48.

13 Market Research Society (1992). Code of conduct. *Market Research Society Yearbook.*

14 Peters, T. and Waterman, R. H. (1983). *In Search of Excellence.* Harper and Row.

Index

Equipment, choice of, 63–4
Equity rule, 160
European Quality Award, 239
Expectation/perception gaps, 80–1
  management of, 171–3

Face (as signal), 118–19
Fast-food restaurant (service setting), 71–2
Feedback, 144–5
Financial services (service setting), 70–1
Front office, 47–8, 52, 65
Fronts (use of equipment), 105
Furniture, use of, 64–5

Gap analysis, 254
GASP (generally accepted service principles), 90
Gaze (as signal), 119
Gestures (as signal), 118
Goods (definition), 3
Guarantees, 232–6
  design of, 233–6

Heterogeneity, 168, 184, see also Variability
Hotels (service setting), 72–3

Importance scale, 257, 258
Impression management, 105–6
Input and output productivity measures, 208–10
Inseparability (of services), 9–10, 184
Intangibility (of services), 7–8, 14, 15, 168, 184
Internal marketing, 133, 145
Interpersonal encounters, 103–5
Interval scale, 249
Interviews:
  recruitment, 135
  research, 248
IS 9000 (quality certification), 239

Job design, 142–3
Job enlargement, 142–3
Job selection, 129

Knowledge workers, 205

Launch preparations, 256
Legal action, complaints, 222
Letter Accentuation, 182
Lighting, choice of, 65–6
Logo, 174, 180–3

Management role, 28, 130
  complaints handling, 228
Market research, 244–5
  applications, 253–63
  data collection, 246–8
  questionnaires, 248–53

Market testing, 255–6
Mass service, 45
'Moments of truth', 27, 79, 126
Motivation:
  consumer, 185
    encouraging, 143–4
  employee, 262
Multiattribute analysis, 253, 254, 257
Mystery customer surveys, 247, 259–60

New brand launch, 256
New service development, 253–6
Norms, 104
Numerical rating scale, 250

Operating systems, 45–7
Opportunity costs, 150
Organization:
  charts, 24–5
    flat, 26–7
    upside down, 25
  future forms, 38
  performance, 79
  variables, 29
Orientation, employee, 138–9
Output measurement, 200
Over/underload, 34

Perception/expectation gaps, 80–1
Perceptual maps, 252, 253
Performance ambiguity, 15
Performance evaluation, 195, 207, 263
  standards, 236
Performance indicators, 197, 213–15, 236
Performance related pay, 206–7
Peripheral services, 16
Perishability (of services), 10, 149, 168–9, 184
Personal recommendations, 174–5
Personal selling, 169–70
Physical evidence, 6, see also Tangible clues, 173–4
Posture (as signal), 118
Power, level of, 107
Pre-employment relationship, 133–6
Price, influence on demand, 153–4
Private sector charter mark, 239
Privatized industries, customer satisfaction, 236–7
Process (definition), 6
Process flow diagrams, 51–5
Production processes, 47
Productivity measures, 197–8
  consumer contribution, 203–4
  framework, 198–200
  improving, 201–3
  input and output, 208–10
  technology for, 210–12
  white collar, 204–7

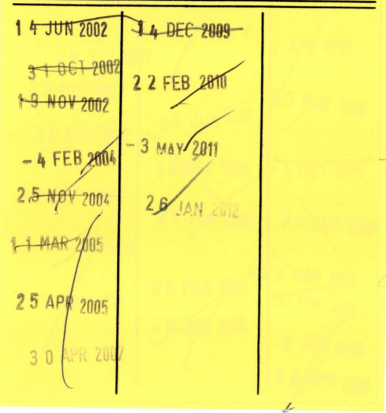